seeking asylum | alone

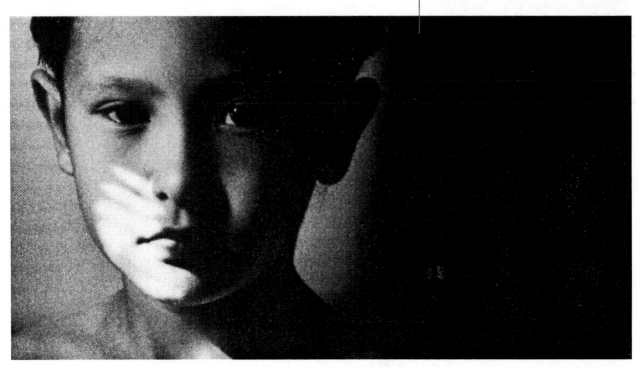

Published in Sydney by:
Themis Press
An imprint of the Federation Press

PO Box 45, Annandale, NSW, Australia 2038
71 John St, Leichhardt, NSW, Australia 2040
Ph 61 2 9552 2200 Fax 61 2 9552 1681
E-mail: info@federationpress.com.au
Website: http://www.federationpress.com.au

National Library of Australia
Cataloguing-in-Publication entry

Bhabha, Jacqueline and Crock, Mary E.
Seeking asylum alone : unaccompanied and separated children
and refugee protection in Australia, the U.K. and the U.S.

Bibliography.
ISBN 9781921113024.

1. Refugee children - Australia. 2. Refugee children - Great Britain.
3. Refugee children - United States. I. Bhabha, Jacqueline.

362.87083

Design: Winge Design Studio
Printing: Ligare Pty Ltd, Sydney, NSW

seeking asylum | alone

a comparative study

A Comparative Study of Laws,
Policy and Practice in Australia,
the U.K. and the U.S.

Jacqueline Bhabha and Mary Crock

In Collaboration with Nadine Finch
and Susan Schmidt

A REPORT FUNDED BY THE JOHN D. AND CATHERINE T. MACARTHUR FOUNDATION, THE AUSTRALIAN RESEARCH COUNCIL & THE MYER FOUNDATION

ABOUT THE AUTHORS

Jacqueline Bhabha has worked on issues relating to migration and refugee protection for 20 years, first as a practitioner in the U.K. and more recently as a researcher, writer and teacher in the U.S. She is the Jeremiah Smith Jr. lecturer in law at Harvard Law School, the executive director of the Harvard University Committee on Human Rights Studies, and an adjunct lecturer on public policy at the Kennedy School of Government. From 1997 to 2001, she directed the Human Rights Program at the University of Chicago. Prior to 1997, she was a practicing human rights lawyer in London, and at the European Court of Human Rights in Strasbourg. She received a first class honors degree and an M.Sc from Oxford University, and a J.D. from the College of Law in London. Her writing on issues of migration and asylum in Europe and the U.S. include a co-authored book, *Women's Movement: Women Under Immigration, Nationality and Refugee Law* (1994), an edited volume, *Asylum Law and Practice in Europe and North America* (1992), and many articles including "Get Back to Where You Once Belonged: Identity, Citizenship and Exclusion in Europe" (1998), "Inconsistent State Intervention and Separated Child Asylum Seekers" (2001), "Internationalist Gatekeepers? The tension between asylum advocacy and human rights" (2002) and "The Citizenship Deficit: On Being a Citizen Child" (2003). She is currently working on issues of transnational child migration, trafficking, adoption, and citizenship. She teaches international human rights and refugee law and serves on the board of the U.S. section of International Social Services and the *Journal of Refugee Studies*.

Mary Crock has worked in the area of immigration and refugee law since 1985. She is an Associate Professor and Associate Dean (Post Graduate Research) in the Faculty of Law, University of Sydney. She is chief examiner in the various Specialist Accreditation programs in immigration law across Australia, and editor of the *Immigration Review* (Butterworths). She has served in executive positions for the Law Council of Australia (International Law Section) and the Refugee Council of Australia; worked as adviser to the Australian Senate (Inquiry into Australia's Refugee and Humanitarian Program, 2000) and as consultant to the Human Rights and Equal Opportunity Commission (on immigration detention). Her books include: *Protection or Punishment: The Detention of Asylum Seekers in Australia* (1993); *Immigration and Refugee Law in Australia* (1998, 2nd edition forthcoming 2006); *Future Seekers: Refugees, Asylum Seekers and the Law in Australia* (2002) (with Ben Saul); and *Future Seekers II: Refugees and Irregular Migration in Australia* (2006) (with Ben Saul and Azadeh Dastyari). She was guest editor and author for the "Refugee Issue" for the *University of New South Wales Law Journal* (2000) and for the "Migration, Human Rights and Mental Health Special Issue" of the *International Journal of Law and Psychiatry* (2004). She has written many articles on immigration and refugee issues, including works on judicial review and "court stripping" (various); immigration detention (2003); interdiction and the *Tampa Affair* (various); and children and refugee status (2004). She teaches migration law, refugee law, and related subjects for both undergraduate and postgraduate law students at the University of Sydney.

Nadine Finch is a barrister who practices at Garden Court Chambers in London. She specializes in immigration, asylum, and human rights law and has a particular interest in representing children and those who have been trafficked to the U.K. She also practices in the family court in cases involving children or parents who are subject to immigration control. She was a contributor to the Fifth and Sixth editions of *Macdonald's Immigration Law and Practice* and one of the co-authors of *Putting Children First: A guide for immigration practitioners*, which was published by LAG, and *Working with children and young people subject to immigration control: Guidelines for best practice* (2004) which was published by the Immigration Law Practitioners Association. She also contributed to *Child first, migrant second: Ensuring that every child matters* (February 2006), another Immigration Law Practitioners Association publication, and wrote a chapter for *The Asylum Seeking Child in Europe* which was published by Goteborg University. She works closely with a number of non governmental organizations in the U.K. on issues related to unaccompanied and separated children and also trafficking and has spoken at a number of national and international conferences on these topics.

Susan Schmidt conducts research, writing, and policy analysis on the special needs of refugee children. She previously worked as the director for children's services with Lutheran Immigration and Refugee Service (LIRS), coordinating foster care and family reunion services for unaccompanied and separated minors. She is author of several reports for the Bridging Refugee Youth and Children's Services project (www.BRYCS.org), including: *Growing Up in a New Country: A Positive Youth Development Toolkit for Refugees and Immigrants*; *Raising Children in a New Country: A Toolkit for Working with Newcomer Parents*; and *Separated Refugee Children in the United States: Challenges and Opportunities*. She was an expert contributor on refugee children for the UNHCR publication, *Refugee Resettlement: An International Handbook to Guide Reception and Integration*, and is co-author of the LIRS publication, *Working with Refugee Children: Issues of Culture, Law and Development*. She holds a Master of Science in Social Work degree from Columbia University.

Acknowledgments

This report was enabled by research grants from the John D. and Catherine T. MacArthur Foundation, the Australian Research Council and the Myer Foundation. Related reports document policies and practices toward children seeking asylum alone in the United States, the United Kingdom and Australia. Overall coordination for the Seeking Asylum Alone project was provided by Professors Jacqueline Bhabha of Harvard University and Mary Crock of The University of Sydney.

Research for this project involved the work of many people across the three countries studied.

United States:

Research interviews in the U.S. were conducted by Katherine Desormeau (Boston, Massachusetts); Celeste Froehlich (Phoenix, Arizona and El Paso, Texas); Lisa Frydman (Los Angeles, California); and Susan Schmidt (Houston, Texas, Miami, Florida, Washington, D.C. and all others.) Joanne Kelsey and Wendy Young of the Women's Commission for Refugee Women and Children conducted the interviews with children in various stages of the U.S. immigration process. Susan Schmidt collected and organized most of the data and wrote the majority of the sections detailing the U.S. circumstances, with the assistance and supervision of Professors Jacqueline Bhabha and Mary Crock; Lisa Frydman wrote about various other legal alternatives for children in the U.S.. Katherine Desormeau, Nicola Brandt, Susan Frick, Eileen Palmunen and Leah Zamore provided helpful editorial assistance. Professors German Pliego and Robert Raymond of the University of St. Thomas (St. Paul, Minnesota) provided statistical computations on U.S. Asylum Office data.

United Kingdom:

In the U.K. research for the project was undertaken by Nadine Finch, Ben Ward, Shu Shin Luh and Ariadne Papagapitos. Assistance was also provided by Louise Arthurs, Syd Bolton, Alex Browne, Laura Brownlees, Melissa Canavan, Jane Coker, Heaven Crawley, Kathryn Cronin, Sarah Cutler, Judith Dennis, Jack Cunliffe, Bill Davies, Samantha Day, Jane Dykins, Liz Farrall, Karen Goodman, Vicky Guedalla, Alison Harvey, Catriona Jarvis, Kate Jessop, Helen Johnson, Douglas Joy, Mike Kaye, Selam Kidane, Ailish King Fisher, Sarah Lerner, Adrian Matthews, Paul Morris, Chris Perkins, Margaret Phelan, Kate Philips, Raj Rayan, Susan Rowlands, Alison Stanley, Jane Sufian, Samar Tasselli, Sally Thompson, Clare Tudor, Heather Violett, Val Watson, and Sarah Young.

Australia:

In Australia, assistance was provided by partners in the Australian project: Eva Sallis of Australians Against Racism Inc; Howard Glenn and Kate Gautier of A Just Australia; and Simon Moran and Alexis Goodstone of the Public Interest Advocacy Centre Inc. Additional funding for the Australian work was also granted by the Sidney Myer Foundation (Melbourne, Australia). Cathy Preston-Thomas, Azadeh Dastyari, Daniela Gavshon and Leah Friedman were the principal researchers for the Australian report. The following people worked on research and/or design of the Australian fieldwork programs: Catherine Chang, Alison Kesby, Jessie Hohmann, Courtney Mead, Louise Pounder, Edward Santow, Carol Elliot, and Riz Wakil. Contributions are also gratefully acknowledged from: Mohammed Al Jabiri, Andrew Bartlett, Kaye Bernard, Deslie Billich, Frank Brennan, Jennifer Burn, John Cameron, Christian Carney, Jim Carty, Anna Copeland, Clyde Cosentino, Georgina Costello, Camilla Cowley, Stephen Cowling, Stephen Churches, Pamela Curr, Marianne Dickie, Stephen Duffield, Keiko Forster, Penny Gerston, Nazir Gul, Alanna Hector, Abby Hamden, Brian Harradine, Parastu Hatami, Libby Hogarth, Graeme Innes, Marg Le Sueur, Marion Lè, Karen Lee, Mary Anne Kenny, Vanessa Lesnie, Nitra Kidson, Souvira Kheuaphim, Marg Le Sueur, John Lynch, David Manne, David Marr, Melissa McAdam, Ron McCallum, Bernadette McMenamin, Kerry Murphy, Louise Newman, Tiong Nguygen, Younis Noori, Natalie O'Brien, Lowijta O'Donohue, Judyth O'Neill, Milivoj Oreb, Sev Ozdowski, Margaret Piper, Beth Powell, Erskine Rodan, Ariane Rummery, Zachary Steel, Frederika Steen, Marg Straffa, Melinda Tankard-Reist, Charlene Thompson, Jack Smit, Michael Walker, Judyth Watkins, Stephen Watkins, and Belinda Wells.

We are indebted to the children who shared their stories with us for this project. We are particularly grateful that they trusted us with their stories despite their frequent negative experiences of adult intervention. We are also grateful to the numerous government employees, legal representatives, immigration advocates, academics and social service providers who gave generously of their time, experience and recommendations to make this report the substantial product that it is. We sensed from the vast majority of those interviewed a desire to improve the current system so that children could be better served and protected by the asylum systems in the three countries studied.

Contents

Executive Summary

"Seeking Asylum Alone" is a two-year comparative study documenting the circumstances and treatment of unaccompanied and separated children who cross borders in search of protection. The study was conducted in three countries—the United States, the United Kingdom, and Australia—where the distinctive problems facing child asylum seekers are significant and unresolved. Jacqueline Bhabha, a lecturer at Harvard Law School and Mary Crock, an associate professor at the University of Sydney Faculty of Law, oversaw the research which was conducted by an international team. Individual country reports describe the research and findings in the U.S., the U.K., and Australia respectively.

This report compares and contrasts policy and practice in the three countries, highlighting points of divergence and examples of good practice as they emerge from the research. It describes the nature and scale of the migration of unaccompanied and separated children, and the reasons why children flee from their homes and travel alone, enduring the trauma of separation from family and the hardships of the journey to seek out a place of safety. The report draws on government data, published and unpublished legal decisions, advocates' accounts, court proceedings, and interviews with many of the key participants in the child migration process, including unaccompanied and separated children themselves. It notes that the arduousness of the children's journeys is often complicated by encounters with untrained or insensitive

state officials, unsuitable policies and procedures, detention practices, and other administrative hurdles which are oppressive and terrifying rather than reassuring and protective. As a result, stories of children in distress, withdrawn into deep depression, or paralyzed by acute anxiety are commonplace.

The report describes a disturbing and systematic protection deficit at the heart of the immigration systems of all three countries studied. This lacuna is a product of the political marginality of children, their lack of bargaining power, and their exclusion from decision-making processes. But the normal exclusion of children as a voiceless group of citizens is compounded in the case of the population studied in this report by two aggravating circumstances— their non-citizen status, and their lack of access to parental or other protective adult involvement. The tension between migration control, law enforcement, and a children's rights perspective inheres in almost

all stages of the asylum-seeking process that children go through in each of the three countries studied. Though international law has addressed both the substantive and procedural aspects of child migration to some extent, generally these international standards have not been translated into binding policies under domestic law. The report demonstrates that both substantive legal and procedural issues regarding children who travel without the protection of a responsible adult urgently require attention.

The report highlights several serious deficiencies in current practice. These include:

1. Inadequate Data Collection

In Australia and the U.S. the statistical record kept by state authorities on unaccompanied and separated children is seriously deficient, and hampers effective monitoring of government practice or any meaningful process of public accountability in this policy area. Data collection and dissemination in the U.K. is generally far superior, and provides a model for replication by other states but even there government statistics about the number of unaccompanied and separated children who succeed on appeal from an initial negative decision on their asylum applications are not kept.

2. Access to Territory

The report documents critically the widespread use of interdiction and the institution of offshore asylum processing centers, to deflect migrants, including child asylum seekers, from access to protection. These are practices adopted by both the U.S. and Australia to avoid international and domestic constraints on their conduct. In both countries, offshore refugee status processing is markedly inferior in form and protection outcomes. The failure to institute special arrangements for unaccompanied and separated children is particularly serious, given the isolation and risks inherent in offshore placements. The problems are acute in the Australian context because of proposals to send *all* unauthorized boat arrivals to the tiny Pacific island of Nauru—including persons who have reached the Australian mainland and sought protection as refugees. The report also discusses the application of preemptive exclusionary rules to children, such as child asylum seekers who arrive via "safe third countries", and the conspicuous lack of special procedures and consideration regarding their particular vulnerability.

3. The Identification of Children at Risk

In all three countries the procedures for distinguishing unaccompanied or separated children from other populations were found to be deficient. The report documents two shortcomings within this serious lacuna in current practice: the lack of adequate mechanisms for determining a child's age where this is disputed, and the absence of clear protocols for identifying children who, while not traveling alone, are separated from parents or guardians. Both failings have had a serious impact on the treatment of child asylum seekers: unresolved or incorrectly resolved age disputes have resulted in children being wrongly detained with adults, sometimes for lengthy periods,

a particularly striking problem in the U.K. where unaccompanied or separated children are otherwise never detained and where some good practice in relation to a holistic approach to age determination has been developed. The absence of clear procedures for identifying separated children traveling with non-parental adults, including smugglers or traffickers, continues to hamper their detection and to reduce the numbers of children who receive appropriate protection from exploitative smugglers or traffickers. This is less of a problem in the U.K.—where efforts are in place at major ports of entry to identify children at risk—than it is in the U.S. and Australia.

4. Reception and Initial Assistance Procedures

Reception and initial assistance procedures are demanding and present children with significant hurdles in their access to asylum protection at very early stages in the process, when their vulnerability and need for adult guidance are greatest. Both the U.S. and Australia subject unaccompanied or separated children to "pre-screening" in order to ascertain their *prima facie* eligibility to claim asylum, without providing any form of legal assistance whatsoever. Moreover, none of the three legal systems studied provide any formal advice or briefings for children entering the asylum system. Children typically do not understand what they are applying for or what process they are entering. As a result, the process of seeking asylum is mysterious at best and can provoke deep anxiety and trauma. In the U.S. unaccompanied or separated children are placed in the care of the immigration enforcement authorities for the first 72 hours, without any access to child welfare services, legal advice, or representation. Many children agree to "voluntary return" without the benefit of legal advice, because they find the prospect of prolonged detention alarming and because they lack legal advice about their protection options. The situation in

Australia is no better: children are still interviewed at first instance without being given any advice or assistance. It is also a system that leaves vulnerable children at risk of preemptory removal. In the U.K., by contrast, the initial screening process is supposed to be a mechanism for eliciting basic information about a child. It is designed to be child-sensitive rather than demanding and punitive. The interview is conducted on the day of arrival (or shortly thereafter) by a specially trained immigration officer. Both an interpreter and a "responsible [non-adversarial] adult" are required to be present. The report recommends this as a model for the other two countries.

5. Detention

The report documents the regrettable fact that all three countries studied, to different degrees, have a history of subjecting children seeking asylum alone to detention. Whereas in the U.K. detention is a product of contested age determination, in Australia it has been mandatory, pervasive, indefinite in length, a policy that has had devastating effects on children, some of whom have engaged in repeated acts of self-harm. In the U.S., too, there has been widespread use of detention, though its use is discretionary, rather than mandatory as in Australia, and concerns have become more nuanced as detention in institutional shelters has increased over the use of secure correctional facilities. The report argues strongly against these punitive practices and points out that, in the absence of criminal charges, detention of unaccompanied and separated children constitutes a serious breach of international standards. A particularly flagrant abuse has been the U.S. government's use of restraints such as shackles, handcuffs, and leg irons when transporting or escorting unaccompanied or separated children outside detention facilities— children who are typically not charged with any criminal offence or suspected of violent behavior. The report notes some improvements in detention policy in both the U.S. and Australia, but also calls for immediate rescission of these punitive policies which continue.

6. The Legal Process

The report documents the legal procedure facing children seeking asylum alone in each country. The absence of a guardian or guardian-like figure emerges as a significant defect in all three countries. This is coupled with inadequate or non-existent legal representation, a particular problem in the U.S. and Australia, and the lack of child-specific training of officials, which results in inappropriate interviewing techniques and questions, aggressive cross examination and an intimidating and hostile atmosphere. One example of good practice is the U.S. Asylum Office "Lesson Plan" which provides an excellent vehicle for training asylum officers and a model for adoption elsewhere. The signposted U.K. asylum application form which includes special questions for children and their legal representatives is another example of good practice to be emulated. The report also notes the pervasive complaint from children and advocates about poor and confusing interpreting, including the frequent use of remote interpreters who translate over the phone or by video link, a highly problematic procedure for children. The report suggests that, taken together, these procedural problems seriously undermine the meaningful access to refugee protection for unaccompanied and separated children. Timing issues also impinge on the adequacy of legal protection for children: in some cases, especially in Australia and the U.S., long delays in decision making exacerbate the child applicant's insecurity and lack of permanency; on the other hand, overly expeditious processing can also present problems by curtailing opportunities for data collection and legal representation. Lack of high quality legal assistance in the appellate process compounds the problems facing children applying for asylum, resulting in relatively high rates of non-appearance at appeals, and in low success rates following an appeal.

7. Recognizing Children as Refugees

Another pervasive problem is the hostile climate of opinion that children seeking asylum alone have to confront. Official attitudes to unaccompanied and separated children are colored by a widespread "culture of disbelief" that undermines children's confidence in the proceedings. The report suggests that more child-friendly procedures, such as those used in the U.S. affirmative asylum system and the U.K. screening interview, both of which are non-adversarial, are preferable for processing children's asylum claims. Australia's method of questioning children at both first instance and appeal procedures is inherently problematic. Another key finding in the report is that decision makers are not making adequate use of the legal framework available for protection of asylum seeking children. In particular, where children suffer persecution specific to childhood, such as conscription as a child soldier, or forced marriage, decision makers are reluctant to acknowledge that the conduct in question constitutes "persecution"

within the meaning of the United Nations Convention on the Status of Refugees. The report draws on legal scholarship to advocate the interpretation of the Refugee Convention in a way that acknowledges harms specific to children. As a result of current restrictive interpretation, the grant of asylum under the Refugee Convention to separated or unaccompanied child applicants often represents the exception rather than the rule in all three countries studied, despite compelling and convincing evidence of persecution. In the U.K. in 2004, 98% of asylum applications by unaccompanied or separated children were initially refused by the Immigration and Nationality Directorate. This decreased marginally to 95% in 2005 and the first quarter of 2006 but the percentage remained higher than that for adult asylum seekers. The report notes how the failure to address the needs and interests of children produces a paradoxical set of obstacles for children. On the one

hand, they encounter an attitude which discredits their particular suffering and needs and assimilates their situation to that of adults. On the other, they have to overcome discriminatory assumptions about their credibility, their vulnerability to attack, and their risk of persecution. The adoption of Guidelines on Children's Asylum Applications by the U.K. and Australia, following the good example of the U.S. government, would be a positive step forward.

8. Protection Outcomes

The report also addresses the problem of long-term protection for unaccompanied and separated children seeking asylum. It discusses critically the very low grant rate of permanent refugee protection for children in the U.K, and the complete lack of such a status for children entering Australia without a valid visa. It also describes the comparatively larger number of statuses available to children applying

for protection in the U.S. and evaluates their relative strengths and weaknesses. Special Immigrant Juvenile Status is one notable U.S. model to be emulated by the other two countries and further improved by the U.S. Finally the report criticizes the failure to accord protection to child victims of trafficking in a systematic or generous way, despite the availability of specific visas for this purpose in the U.S. and Australia.

Conclusions

The report concludes that the serious protection deficit highlighted in respect of unaccompanied or separated child asylum seekers urgently requires rectification.

It has led to troubling and predictable human rights violations against children. The research undertaken for this study demonstrates that each of the three countries studied falls short of desirable child protection practice, whether in respect of statistical data collection; government procedures and legal structures; or in addressing the social needs of unaccompanied and separated children seeking asylum.

A second conclusion is that many unaccompanied or separated child migrants have a stronger claim to asylum than is generally recognized or acknowledged and that their circumstances should be addressed appropriately in light of the possibilities for protection inherent in international law. Instead, children's claims have been ignored because policy makers, administrators, and immigration judges have tended to operate with an adult-focused lens, missing the opportunity to listen to (and even to elicit) the factual basis for children's asylum claims.

The report's final claim is that the problems it identifies can be solved relatively easily, without jeopardizing states' migration management programs. The solutions proposed do not involve open

door immigration policies or reckless incentives to use children as migration anchors or investment commodities. Children need and deserve protection and where that is available in the home country, normally that is the best place for children to be. In many cases a more child-focused asylum system would allow from the speedier assessment of cases in which return is a viable option. In all cases, the views of the children in question need to be elicited with care. Trafficked children and children destined to bonded domestic service or other forms of forced labor should all have access to effective protection. Without this, governments will continue to short change some of the world's most vulnerable children, and asylum will continue to be a dangerous odyssey for them rather than a predictable and safe haven.

CHAPTER 1

The Challenge of Child Migration

1.1 Characterizing Vulnerability

Migration is part and parcel of our world today—one in every 35 persons is an international migrant.[1] As technology and the ease of international travel shrink both real and imaginary distances, so crossing national borders, even continents, has become a mass and multifaceted phenomenon.

Migrants span demographic classes from all regions of the globe. Migration outcomes include a full spectrum from "rags to riches" stories at one extreme to experiences of isolation, trauma, and debilitating discrimination on the other. Within this complex picture, one issue has gradually emerged over the last few years as a particular, worrisome challenge. Children are traveling in significant numbers, separated from family or effective adult guardians, alone and vulnerable. Some are fleeing persecution by oppressive governments or insurgent guerillas. Others are obvious victims of exploitation, caught up in a human trafficking trade

described by some as a form of modern slavery. Yet others travel in search of family reunion, survival, or a rights-respecting life without destitution and degradation. As the reasons for travel differ, so do the means. Some children travel alone, literally walking or riding enormous distances to cross borders; others are accompanied by unrelated adults, sometimes as benign escorts, but often as profiteering smugglers or traffickers. Some children are sold or handed over by their parents or adult relatives; others are separated from them by war or snatched by kidnappers. Many end up working in dangerous and degrading child labor to pay off debts

The Challenge of Child Migration | Adris's Story

Adris's first memories of the Taliban date back to when he was 12. They came into his Afghan village demanding weapons. They walked from home to home, frightening the locals in to giving up their guns. There were (false) rumors that Adris's father had a cache of weapons in his house. The rumors were enough to rouse the interest of the Taliban.

Adris's father gave the Taliban all the weapons he had yet they believed he had more. One day Adris and his father went in to the mountains to get some feed for their livestock. They came back in the evening to find Adris's mother distraught. The Taliban had come in search of weapons. They had ransacked the house. When they could find no weapons they had taken Adris's older brother who was sick in his bed. They were holding him for ransom.

Afraid of a confrontation with the Taliban, Adris's family wrote a letter asking for their son's return. His father explained that he did not have weapons but that he was happy to give them anything he possessed. He attempted to buy weapons from his neighbors to trade but everyone was too scared of the Taliban to cooperate.

Twenty-five days later, Adris was in the mountains when his cousin came to fetch him: the Taliban had returned his brother. He ran down as fast as his feet would carry him. As his village came into sight, he could see his neighbors gathering in the streets. He saw a dark figure outside his house and realized that it was his mother. She was screaming and hitting herself as family and friends attempted to restrain her. Her piercing cries tore through the village. It was then that Adris saw his brother's dead body, dumped at the doorstep of the family home. His brother was 16 years old; Adris himself was only 13.

There were rumors that Adris would be taken next. Asked about his escape Adris says:

"My father came. His eyes were full of water. Please you have to leave Afghanistan you have to go…. So I went…. Now I am here…. I didn't know where Australia was, I didn't know between countries. What could I have done? I did not have any choice."

incurred to their exploiters. The stories of three children[2] arriving on different continents illustrate the phenomenon and the complexities it represents for both the child migrants and the three countries studied.

Children have always been particularly susceptible to human rights abuse in situations of social crisis and disintegration. But their ability to move in large numbers and the variety of reasons for their journeys are more recent phenomena. Though the three child migrants described could be considered equally vulnerable, their vulnerability stems from very different causes. Adris seems to fit the classic concept of a refugee as someone fleeing state persecution, though as we shall see many decision makers are reluctant to apply this concept to separated or unaccompanied children seeking asylum alone. Melvin and Marie, however, do not fit into the classic framework. Though Melvin was clearly at risk of physical harm or persecution, this danger did not stem from the government or from any official source. Marie was not even clearly targeted for any harm, whether by the government or others—she was simply opposed to a prevailing norm within her society. Do each of these children have an equal claim to international protection or is it inappropriate to apply one legal framework to all three of them? Are Melvin and Marie refugees or are they irregular migrants who are ineligible for international protection, Melvin simply an "undocumented economic migrant" and Marie a runaway from her traditional culture?

As a matter of both international and domestic law, the characterization of children traveling alone is of critical importance. A person classified as a refugee receives a recognized status with entitlements to remain in the country of refuge for at least as long as refugee status lasts. Permanent protection is a frequent outcome. But are children on their own capable of being refugees? Are persecutors, be they

Melvin was 13 and alone when he left his native El Salvador, "running from people who already had tried to kill [him] and who promised to keep trying."[3] He fled after a knife attack by gang members intent on settling a disagreement with Melvin's negligent father by killing his son. Melvin remembers that time as feeling "like everything was just falling down on top of me."[4] Following the attack that left a scar over his left eye, Melvin embarked on a year-long journey through Guatemala and Mexico to reach the presumed safety of the U.S. When he finally reached the U.S./Mexico border, he was turned away 14 times by Mexican immigration officials. On his 15th attempt, he made it across the border and was apprehended by a U.S. Border Patrol officer who fed the starving boy and transferred him to the custody of the Immigration and Naturalization Service (INS).

Marie was born in Sierra Leone into a society where female circumcision was widely practiced and was seen as an essential part of the rite of passage into womanhood. Her own mother and her grandmother before her had been Soweis, that is, the women in the community responsible for performing the procedure, which involved the excision of parts of the female external genitalia without an anesthetic. Marie was subjected to female circumcision at the age of 15. She found it a terrifying experience. Her mother died a few days later and as the oldest daughter within her extended family group, Marie was expected to assume the role of Sowei and to take over the task of performing female circumcision on the young girls in her community. By refusing she would bring shame on her family and lose all her rights and privileges, within her own community. Marie chose to run away.

states or non-state actors, likely to target children? And what about irregular migration? The illegal migrant, in contrast to the refugee, is seen primarily as a law-breaker, to be punished, deterred, and speedily returned to the country of origin without protection. Should the undocumented *child* migrant be treated like this, on a par with similarly classified adults? Or is there something special about the status of a child which ethically demands and legally requires a different response? In short, what difference does childhood make to the rights and obligations associated with migration?

A critical problem for unaccompanied and separated children is that their protection needs do not always fit neatly into recognized legal categories. What is more, their needs are often not immediately apparent. For a variety of reasons, children at risk of persecution can slip through border control undetected.

For example, children may find it impossible to articulate their fears; or they may be passed off as the offspring of traffickers. They may rigidly follow smugglers' instructions to conceal their true circumstances and lie about who they are and where they have come from. Researchers in the U.S., the U.K., and Australia encountered instances of all these situations, as we will explore later.

The phenomenon of unaccompanied and separated children in need of protection is gradually attracting increased attention from governments and national and international organizations.

It is now acknowledged that children who are unaccompanied or separated from their families face an increased risk of military recruitment, sexual violence, exploitation and abuse, forced labor, denial of access to education and basic assistance, and detention.[5]

Public awareness of and concern about the trafficking in women and children has never been greater.[6] However, while there is growing acknowledgment of how and why vulnerable children come to be on the move, less attention has been paid to the legal and policy frameworks constructed by governments to deal with the phenomenon. To be sure, governments across the refugee-receiving world are gradually enacting legislation and drafting policies to address the problems facing unaccompanied and separated children. So are international organizations—indeed, the UN Committee on the Rights of the Child published a General Comment in 2005 devoted to this topic.[7] It remains the case nevertheless that many Western countries have not responded appropriately to the challenges presented.

This report draws together the findings of research conducted in Australia, the U.K., and the U.S. into the phenomenon of unaccompanied and separated children and their treatment under immigration and refugee law. Building on pre-existing research in Europe,[8] the study investigates where child asylum seekers are coming from; how and why they travel alone; and how receiving states address the distinctive challenges of dealing with them. This study traces children's journeys in the three countries studied, examining the legal frame-

works, the procedures, and the outcomes. It illustrates how, in each country, the legal and administrative system is shaped by a complex combination of culture, history, and domestic and international politics. A particular (although not exclusive) focus of the study is on the protections offered by refugee law.

The report represents a synthesis of a multifaceted critique. We address the central question of how countries *should* be responding to the phenomena we describe. We acknowledge that different perspectives can inform the approach taken to the challenge of children traveling alone. This type of migration may be seen as a route to safety requiring support from the destination state, a perilous venture in exploitation mandating the intervention of child support agencies as for domestic children, or an abdication of parental or state of origin responsibility demanding speedy return home of the child. The tension between migration, law enforcement, or child-rights perspective inheres in all of these scenarios. In each of the countries studied, different approaches are apparent.

In the U.K., for example, "exceptionalism" rather than legal entitlement seems to inform the legal and political response to children traveling alone. The children's cases are dealt with as exceptions, and generally managed through the exercise of discretion based on their minority rather than the application of law. A significant number of children simply do not receive refugee protection where adults faced with similar circumstances are recognized as refugees.

In the U.S., legal and procedural responses are bewilderingly varied and inconsistent. This seems to be a response in part to the wide range of child migrants who make their way to the U.S. It is also a reflection of the lack of central administrative oversight or responsibility for the process as a whole. As a result, punitive administrative responses coexist with imaginative and creative legal solutions. The product is a veritable labyrinth of laws and policies.

In contrast, the phenomenon of unaccompanied and separated children entering Australia by irregular means is recent and relatively small in scale. In this country the legal responses appear to have been poorly adapted from the perspective of both the child and the state. If there has been a tendency among Western countries to observe the experiences and responses of each to the phenomenon of forced migrants, states have also tended to copy the restrictive measures developed. In this context, Australia's laws and policies governing the reception and treatment of unaccompanied and separated children has represented something of a lowest common denominator among developed countries. With its interdiction program and its detention policies Australia has adopted some of the worst features of U.S. asylum and border control laws, while ignoring positive child-specific policies such as the Special Immigrant Juvenile Status visas.

At the heart of the problem in all three countries is the central conflict between safeguarding children at risk on the one hand, and the maintenance of immigration controls on the other.

In spite of the manifest vulnerability of unaccompanied and separated children, the tendency of all the governments studied has been to treat them as migrants first, and children a distant second, placing the issue of border control above that of child protection.

The children are thus seen first and foremost through the legal lens of exclusionary immigration law, as outsiders with no immediate claim to enter. Too many concessions made for the vulnerability of the child are considered a threat to the sovereign right of the state to determine who enters or remains on state territory. Among policy makers, children are sometimes seen as stalking horses for more broad scale incursions, the "thin edge of the wedge," a view evident in this quote from a U.K. government minister:

When we considered [the] issue [of unaccompanied and separated children] in relation to the Children Act [2004 (U.K.)], we had to be absolutely clear that the primacy in this issue has to be immigration control and immigration policy. If we had given, for example, the duty to cooperate and duty to safeguard [such children] to the Immigration Service, I think that we would have opened a loophole which would have enabled asylum-seeking families and unaccompanied asylum-seeking children to use those particular duties to override government controls and the asylum-seeking controls…. I think that we took the right route, which is that the primacy is on maintaining a fair and just immigration system but, within that, we have always to have regard to the wellbeing and safety of children.[9]

Even where the vulnerability of a separated child is recognized, and an asylum claim is made, refugee status determination systems have generally been established with adult asylum seekers as the norm. Within this context, children seeking asylum in their own right face significant procedural barriers in gaining protection. In addition to the cultural and linguistic difficulties experienced by many adult asylum seekers, the age and vulnerability of separated children place them at a particular disadvantage when attempting to navigate refugee determination systems.[10]

Another barrier faced by unaccompanied and separated children is the reach of available legal protections: questions remain as to how well the international definition of refugee accommodates the particular experiences of unaccompanied and separated children today. The UN Convention relating to the Status of Refugees and its attendant Protocol have been criticized as being too political and "Eurocentric" in their orientation.[11] This Convention was focused from its inception on problems and conflicts familiar to the Cold War era in Europe, where the label of "refugee" was applied most readily to the political and intellectual dissidents escaping to the West from the Communist Bloc countries. On its face, the definition of refugee certainly favors adults who are active dissenters of some kind. It is less easily applied to the manifold circumstances of children fleeing persecution today.

1.2 Outline of the Study

This project used both quantitative and qualitative research designs to track the physical, administrative, and legal journeys of unaccompanied and separated children through the asylum processes in the three countries studied. In each country we reviewed relevant legislation and case law; we solicited and analyzed all the available statistical data, interviewed key decision makers, administrators, advocates, and politicians; and conducted in depth open-ended interviews with unaccompanied and separated children.

The study begins in chapter 2 by setting out the available data on the number of unaccompanied and separated children who entered or who were detected in each country between 1999 and 2003 (the U.K. data is for 1999–2004). Although the United Nations High Commissioner for Refugees (UNHCR) has been able to track asylum claims lodged by children in 28 industrialized countries over this period, neither the U.S. nor Australia are included in this data. The omission of these two countries is remarkable given the substantial government resources dedicated to controlling immigration in both places—and the sophistication of the control methods employed. Having said this, UNHCR's omission reflects the difficulties also experienced by this study's researchers in obtaining reliable statistics.

Overall we were struck by the contrast in the availability of data—between the U.K., where statistics are gathered and classified meticulously; the U.S., where the data is incomplete and confusing; and Australia, where figures on unaccompanied and separated children are generally unavailable.

The deficiencies raise immediate questions about the priority that has been given to the issue of child migration in those countries.

Chapter 3 surveys the key contemporary international law instruments that govern all aspects of child asylum procedures today. These establish consensus benchmarks about appropriate treatment of unaccompanied and separated child asylum seekers. We assess the three countries' practice by examining the general legal and institutional frameworks they

have developed for dealing with these children. In each case there has been some institutional recognition of the need to link immigration enforcement and child protection measures. However, we find that child protection concerns are not given sufficient prominence in any of the three countries studied.

In none of the countries did we find coherent or streamlined child-specific processes within the asylum procedure that ensure priority and special attention to children's cases. Only in the U.K. have some preparatory steps been taken to create such a structure.

There follows in chapter 4 a more detailed review of the law and policy in each of the three states as these affect unaccompanied and separated children who claim protection as refugees. We examine the frameworks for the identification of unaccompanied and separated children, covering such matters as age determinations and the testing of national or ethnic identities. The laws governing the reception and initial assistance of such children are considered, as are the circumstances in which children are detained pending the processing of asylum or visa claims. The frameworks for processing a refugee claim are examined in three stages: in the preliminary or "screening" phase, the status determination proper and in the appeal systems used in each country. The chapter concludes with a review of protection outcomes for both children recognized as refugees and for those identified as victims of trafficking or simply as children in need of care and protection.

Chapter 5 turns from theory to practice and examines how each of the three states' laws and policies has been implemented on the ground. We review each country's screening process and whether child refugee claimants have access to assistance and legal advice in preparing their asylum applications. We compare and contrast the use (if any) of interviews in the asylum process of each country. Our research highlights problems in the decision-making processes, raising questions about the training and/or responsiveness of officials in cases involving child asylum seekers. Similar short-comings were observed at the appellate level. While we found some examples of good practice, the lack of adequately trained and publicly funded legal representation for separated and unaccompanied children stands out as a defect in all three systems. Another serious problem we find is the absence of guardians to act as trusted advisers and mentors for children navigating the complexities of the asylum process. Finally, we point out that in all three countries studied, we encountered a widespread and disturbing "culture of disbelief" directed at unaccompanied and separated children.

Chapter 6 reviews legal hurdles placed in the way of asylum seekers that are particularly harsh in their impact on children. Referred to sometimes as "pre-emptive exclusionary rules," these hurdles include pre-travel visa requirements, "safe-third-country" rules (or requirements that refugees seek protection in another state), interdiction, and off-shore processing. Particular consideration is given to a controversial interception measure used widely by both the U.S. and Australia: the interdiction of migrants, including asylum seekers, at sea and their deflection to offshore centers for the processing of any asylum applications. We argue that non-entrée and interdiction/blockade policies are particularly devastating for unaccompanied and separated children. In the harsh environment of such exercises, children are typically powerless to demand a hearing, to ensure their own physical safety, or to provide acceptable evidence in support of their claim for protection. We conclude that the fact that none of the three countries studied have child-specific policies for these particularly rights-violative procedures is of grave concern and urgently requires rectification.

Chapter 7 reviews the different interpretations that have been made of the Refugee Convention in cases involving unaccompanied and separated children. For example, we examine how the courts in each country have defined notions of persecution, discussing three distinct but general categories of what may constitute "child persecution." We look also at the five grounds for recognition as a refugee, to which the persecution must be linked. We note that the definition of "refugee" provides considerable scope for the accommodation of claims made by unaccompanied and separated children. Precedents are to be found in the way the same definition has been interpreted so as to recognize the particular needs of women refugees. In practice, however, little consideration appears to have been given to adapting the definition for children. As a result, many child asylum seekers have gone unprotected, their claims ignored or denied.

Chapter 8 examines the "outcomes" for unaccompanied and separated children, whether they are recognized as refugees or given some other status. We applaud the fact that in all three countries, the protection needs of broad classes of unaccompanied and separated children are acknowledged. For example, both the U.S. and the U.K. have settled mechanisms for providing legal status for such children purely on the basis of their minority and vulnerability (in Australia such status is dependent on the Immigration Minister's personal discretion). Special provision is made in Australia and the U.S. for victims of trafficking. Nevertheless, we argue that some children—for example those trafficked or fleeing parental abuse—are wrongly being denied protection within the scope of the refugee definition, a status that would afford them enhanced protections.

We conclude in chapter 9 by making several recommendations. We argue that the protection deficit illuminated by our research must be addressed—in particular through a more child sensitive and inclusive interpretation of the Refugee Convention definition of refugee. Finally, we conclude that the problems identified can be solved relatively easily, without jeopardizing states' migration management programs.

In each country, governments have tried in different measure to deal with the phenomenon of unaccompanied and separated child asylum seekers.

While respecting the good faith of politicians and administrators presented with situations and challenges that could never be described as easy, the legal and political responses do not as a whole measure up to each country's tradition or aspiration of child protection.

Having said this, each country exhibits some examples of good practice. Our objective is to articulate both the similarities and the differences in the approaches taken, reviewing each within the frameworks of international, multi-national, and domestic legal and policy standards. The ultimate aim is to give broader context to individual national experiences in the hope that an understanding of what other countries are doing might encourage self-reflection on domestic practices. No country may yet lay claim to having developed the perfect system.

Endnotes

1   United Nations. *World Economic and Social Survey 2004: International Migration.* Department of Economic and Social Affairs. 25.

2   Unless otherwise indicated, the stories of children used in this study are those of individuals interviewed or studied by researchers in the three participating countries. All identities have been changed in deference to the privacy rights of the young people involved.

3   McGann, Chris. "U.S. Gives Harsh Welcome to Children Seeking Asylum." *Seattle Post-Intelligencer.* 19 June 2003.

4   Ibid, Endnote 3.

5   See Cohn, Ilene and Goodwin-Gill, Guy. *Child Soldiers: The Role of Children in Armed Conflicts.* Oxford: Oxford University Press, 1994; Gallagher, Michael S. "Soldier Boy Bad: Child Soldiers, Culture and Bars to Asylum." 13(3) *International Journal of Refugee Law* 310–353 (2001); and Bhabha, Jacqueline. "Demography and Rights: Women, Children and Access to Asylum." 16 *International Journal of Refugee Law* 227–243 (2004).

6   International Organization for Migration. *Journeys of Jeopardy: A Review of Research on Trafficking in Women and Children in Europe.* IOM Migration Research Series No 11, 2002. See also International Labor Organization. *Unbearable to the Human Heart: Child Trafficking and action to eliminate it.* ILO, 2002.

7   Committee on the Rights of the Child. General Comment No. 6: Treatment of separated and unaccompanied children outside their country of origin. UN, 2005. CRC/GC/2005/6.

8   Separated Children in Europe Program, http://www.separated-children-europe-programme.org.

9   Reply from Margaret Hodge MP, Minister quoted in *Every Child Matters.* Report of the Education and Skills Committee's Inquiry. 5 April 2005. Para 207.

10 Bhabha, Jacqueline. "Inconsistent State Intervention and Separated Child Asylum-Seekers." *European Journal of Migration and Law* 3 (2001).

11 Hathaway, James. *The Law of Refugee Status.* Toronto: Butterworths, 1991.

Journeys of a Lifetime:
The Phenomenon of Unaccompanied and Separated Children Traveling Alone

Mary was a 13-year-old girl from Sierra Leone who lived in a small village in the north of the country. Her father was a teacher at a nearby Jesuit seminary. When rebel soldiers came to her compound she was forced to watch as her whole family were massacred and mutilated. She was then abducted, forced to carry the soldiers' equipment and fight for them.

As the government began to regain control of the country, the rebel group that had captured her disintegrated. Mary was too frightened to return to her village as she knew that other villagers would take revenge on her for her involvement with the rebels.

She sought the help of the seminary. Though they could not offer her shelter, they considered it imperative to find an alternative to the official refugee camps where unaccompanied girls were regularly exposed to sexual violence. They persuaded a Catholic family traveling to London to pretend that Mary was their daughter. They arranged a false passport for her with

the family name. One of the priests told the family that he had heard of an African community center in East London that helped young refugees. He suggested that when they arrived in London, they should leave her outside that center.

Mary had never left her village before and the journey to the U.K. was bewildering. She was also very cold, as she had traveled in her own clothing and no one had thought to give her a coat. By the time she was found huddled in the street outside the center, she was so terrified and confused that

she could not even give her name or explain how she came to be there.

There has been a dearth of information about the phenomenon of unaccompanied and separated children, an institutional indifference to data collection about their circumstances, and a vacuum of political will to impinge on the issue. The experience of the U.S. researcher attempting to gather quantitative and qualitative information for this project exemplifies the problem.

Each federal government office has very little data available on the situation of children in general, or separated and unaccompanied children in particular. While disappointing from the standpoint of data collection, it is emblematic of the extent to which the plight of child asylum seekers has been overlooked. Some isolated efforts have been made to improve the situation of children in this process, most notably by the Asylum Office, the Office of Refugee Resettlement, and more recently by the Office of the Chief Immigration Judge, but without a more coordinated and comprehensive approach, the overall effect is very limited. Researchers attempted, without success, to gather statistical data on children from Immigration and Customs Enforcement, Customs and Border Protection, the Executive Office for Immigration Review (the Immigration Court), the Office of the Principal Legal Advisor (which supervises the trial attorneys in Immigration Court), and the Board of Immigration Appeals. The Freedom of Information Act applications we submitted to pursue requests within the Department of Homeland Security are still outstanding.

A request to interview an Immigration and Customs Enforcement (ICE) Juvenile Coordinator in Miami, Florida, during a visit to conduct a cluster of interviews in the area, was also unsuccessful. After an initially cordial response by the appropriate ICE/Miami public relations office, no further reply was received to a written interview request. When the researcher arrived in person at the Juvenile Coordinator's office at the Krome Detention Center, following other meetings with government personnel at the same complex, the Juvenile Coordinator replied that he had been instructed by superiors not to speak with the researcher and to stay out of the hallways so as not to run into her.[1]

2.1 Historical Perspective

In their seminal work on unaccompanied children, Ressler, Boothby, and Steinbock[2] make the obvious point that wars, famines, and natural disasters have almost always resulted in children being separated from their families. The authors list some 17 examples of major conflicts or disasters between 1915 and 1980 which resulted in large numbers of children being orphaned or otherwise separated from their caregivers.

Sadly, the intervening quarter century has seen continuing distress and loss for humanity's most vulnerable members. UNICEF estimates that, by the end of 1994, more than 100,000 children had been separated from their families in Rwanda alone. The same organization cooperated with UNHCR to register more than 6,300 unaccompanied children in and from the former Yugoslavia through its Operation ReUnite.[3] Unsurprisingly, the greatest concentration of unaccompanied and separated children is to be found in developing countries that have either experienced natural or man-made disasters or that border such a country. In 2000, Wendy Ayotte listed such countries as Algeria, Armenia, the Democratic Republic of Congo, Ethiopia, Guinea, Iran, and Pakistan.[4] Since then, Iraq, the Darfur region of Sudan, and Afghanistan would have to be added to this list.

Unaccompanied and separated children have long been a feature of asylum-seeker and refugee flows in the developing world. Children who have been displaced by war often lack the funds to travel long distances; instead, many end up traveling to neighboring countries, often finding their way with other refugees who are moving on foot. The increasing extent to which civilians are the targets of violence in intra-state armed conflict has undoubtedly added to the numbers of children who lose their homes and families in the midst of war.[5]

In the developed world the majority of unaccompanied and separated children have historically arrived in the context of official resettlement programs. This has changed in the last few decades, however, as significant numbers of unaccompanied and separated children have found their way to these countries as asylum seekers. Such children travel outside the context of any planned resettlement schemes. In her report, *Separated Children Coming to Western Europe*, Wendy Ayotte cites various factors that might explain why countries in Europe have begun to see more children traveling on their own. War and instability in the former Yugoslavia, the former U.S.S.R., and elsewhere in Eastern Europe sent waves of refugees into nearby Western Europe. Children have also arrived seeking asylum from much farther away. Ayotte offers several reasons for this phenomenon: a worldwide rise in the incidence of trafficking in children; a change in the nature of modern warfare, with the increasing rate of civilian casualties;[6] instability within refugee camps in developing countries; a significant drop in the cost of air travel; and the increasing mobility of both people and information around the world. All of these factors have conspired to make unaccompanied and separated child asylum seekers a truly global—and not just regional— phenomenon.

These aspects of globalization have also fostered unprecedented growth in the business of human trafficking and smuggling. Unaccompanied and separated children, who by definition travel without primary caregivers and without the resources, contacts, and abilities of adult migrants, often become the clients or the prey in this underground economy.

The three countries examined in this report reflect these general trends. The U.K., the U.S., and Australia each have their own histories of receiving groups of unaccompanied and separated children, in most cases as part of planned humanitarian resettlement programs. Yet all three countries have also experienced the dual modern phenomena of children arriving as asylum seekers on the one hand, and of children being trafficked into a country for exploitative purposes on the other.

■ The United Kingdom

The U.K.'s proximity to continental Europe means that the migratory experience of unaccompanied and separated children has paralleled that of the

European community at large with variations being accounted for by language and colonial history. For example, England received many abandoned and orphaned Basque children who were dislocated as a result of the Spanish Civil War.[7] It took in over 10,000 Jewish children as part of the *Kindertransport* in the 1930s and 1940s; Hungarian children after the October Revolution in 1956; Korean children during the war in that country between 1950 and 1953; and a large number of Vietnamese children in the early 1990s pursuant to the Comprehensive Plan of Action[8] established to deal with the refugee fallout following the end of the Vietnam War. Like many other European countries, the U.K. has received young asylum seekers fleeing war in Sri Lanka, Ethiopia, Eritrea, Somalia, Angola, Sudan, and other countries on the African continent. It also continues to take in unaccompanied and separated children from conflicts in Europe, most notably from Kosovo, Albania, and the fractured states of the former Yugoslavia. Finally, the U.K. has taken its share of unaccompanied and separated children from the states of the Former Soviet Union, Afghanistan, Iraq, Iran, and the Middle East generally.

■ The United States

With its long land border adjoining Mexico, the U.S. stands at the end of a bridge for migration from an entire, developing world continent. If only for this reason, the U.S. has a long and varied experience of unaccompanied and separated child migrants.

It has admitted thousands of such children from crisis areas and refugee camps since World War II. Until 1980, when the Refugee Act 1980 (U.S.) became law, the admission of these children was facilitated through *ad hoc* and situation-specific programs.[9] These programs seem to have had three overriding

objectives. The first was the evacuation of children in direct danger of harm or persecution. Examples of such programs are the U.S. evacuation of 1,300 British children in 1940; the evacuation of over 14,000 Cuban children in 1961–1962; and the evacuation of 2,547 Vietnamese children to the U.S. in Operation Babylift of 1975.

A second objective of these programs has been the resettlement of unaccompanied and separated children from countries into which the children had been displaced by war or disaster. Since World War II, unaccompanied and separated child refugees have been resettled by the U.S. from countries of first asylum in several crises. Examples include the resettlement of Hungarian unaccompanied children in 1956–1957 and of Indochinese children in both 1975 and from 1979 onwards. In fact, one of the most significant reasons for the enactment of the Refugee

Act 1980 was the admission of over 400,000 Indo-chinese refugees between 1975 and 1976.[10]

A third objective has been the facilitation of inter-country adoption by Americans. Operation Babylift is an example in point. This began as an effort by private adoption agencies, with the cooperation of the U.S. government, to remove from South Vietnam children who were already being processed for adoption abroad. Americans also adopted many Korean children after the Korean War.

In contrast to the above programs, the Refugee Act 1980 established a permanent mechanism for the admission of unaccompanied and separated children. In general U.S. policies have worked best for pre-screened children from overseas, whereas onshore child asylum applicants have, with some exceptions described in later chapters of this report, had to fit into a system designed for adults and ill suited to their needs.

▪ **Australia**

As a country built on immigration, Australia has a long history of taking in groups of unaccompanied and separated children for resettlement purposes. History records the presence of unaccompanied children on the First Fleet.[11] In the early years following Federation—indeed until the end of the Second World War—private (usually religious) organizations undertook the "recruitment," reception, settlement, and guardianship of unaccompanied and separated children under programs targeted at Empire settlement and rural development.[12] Child migrants, drawn mainly from the U.K. and Ireland, were housed on rural properties run by private organizations and raised to perform rural or domestic labor.

Until the conclusion of World War II, the Commonwealth government had very limited involvement in child migration. Each Australian state had its own immigration department and

managed its own schemes. In 1946 the Immigration (Guardianship of Children) Act 1946 (Australia) came into force, designating the Minister for Immigration as guardian of unaccompanied child migrants. Australia's first large-scale government-run program to accept unaccompanied and separated children involved orphaned or destitute children from the U.K. living in children's homes or other state institutions. It included children who had lost their parents during World War II. The stories of the 10,000 children taken in under this scheme were tragic. In addition to the sometimes scandalous circumstances in which the young immigrants were selected,[13] many of the children suffered horrendous physical, sexual, and other abuse in the Australian institutions to which they were consigned.[14]

In spite of the new legislative basis for federal government involvement in settlement and care arrangements, powers were ceded immediately to state and territory governments and then outsourced to the same private agencies that had dominated the scene prior to the conclusion of the Second World War. These organizations continued to house the children in appalling conditions, subjecting them to systematic abuse and using them as a source of cheap and easily exploitable labor. Vigorous campaigning about the plight of these victims of private "care" arrangements eventually led to their abandonment in the late 1970s, with a renewed emphasis on government control over all aspects of the child migration program.

Australia's second major experience with the resettlement of unaccompanied child migrants occurred in the years following the Vietnam War. In 1975, Australia evacuated 2,000 refugees from Vietnam and instituted the first of what were to be a series of programs for the admission and resettlement of Vietnamese nationals. By the end of 1975 Australia had also selected about 400 Vietnamese refugees from Guam, Hong Kong, Singapore, and Malaysia. In 1976, a small boat carrying five refugees from Vietnam reached Australia, the first of 56 boats that were to make the journey to Australia over the next six years. In June 1980, Australia took in many unaccompanied and separated refugee children as part of its intake from South East Asia.[15]

The violent civil war in East Timor in 1975 also led Australia to accommodate a number of evacuees from that conflict, among them unaccompanied and separated children. Apart from the major resettlement schemes, Australia has also accepted children at various stages from Malta and from the former Yugoslavia. Attempts were also made from as early as 1939 to bring in unaccompanied and separated Jewish children.

2.2 The Scale of Movement Today

Historically, separated and unaccompanied children arriving in developed countries under planned resettlement programs did not pose a special dilemma for policy makers. Easily subsumed into the larger category of pre-screened refugees with whom they traveled, their reception and treatment in their new countries were dictated by the terms of the resettlement programs under which they came.[16] The phenomenon of children traveling to seek asylum *outside* such programs— either on their own or in the company of traffickers, smugglers, or other non-parental companions— similarly received little attention until quite recently, despite their unique and extreme vulnerability. Only in the past few years have countries begun to recognize this as a serious oversight, and to see this population as one that merits particular consideration.

Accordingly, there is very little longitudinal data available on separated and unaccompanied child asylum seekers. A concerted international

effort to collect data on this population only began in the late 1990s and early 2000s. It is consequently difficult to say *how many* more children are now traveling to seek asylum on their own, without their primary caregivers, than in years past.[17] What is clear is that, today, unaccompanied and separated children constitute a small but significant percentage of all asylum-seeker flows in developed countries.

■ International Data Gathering

UNHCR began collecting annual statistics on unaccompanied and separated child asylum seekers in developed countries in 2001. It currently collects statistics from 28 European countries (these being the only governments that make comparable data available).[18]

Although incomplete, these figures—last updated in 2004—suggest that between 4% and 5% of all asylum applications received in these industrialized countries each year are from children seeking asylum on their own, without parents or guardians.[19]

In 2003, 12,800 unaccompanied and separated children applied for asylum in the 28 industrialized countries for which UNHCR collects data. This is down from a peak in 2002, when, out of a total of 379,196 asylum applications, 20,252 (or 5.3%) were submitted by children.[20] While the absolute number of child asylum seekers has declined since 2002, so has the absolute number of asylum applications in general. Therefore, unaccompanied and separated children have remained fairly steady as a percentage of the total asylum-seeking population in recent years (although, of course, asylum flows to individual asylum countries have changed during the period under review).[21]

The U.K. produces monthly and quarterly figures on the asylum applications it receives from

children as principal applicants: these figures are included in the UNHCR database. In contrast, due to problems with comparability, UNHCR does not collect data on unaccompanied and separated children for either the U.S. or Australia. This study sets out in part to fill some of these gaps—to sketch the outlines of the phenomenon, despite the imperfections in data availability and the problems of differing definitions across jurisdictions. The data we were able to collect is generally consistent with the broader picture of the industrialized world painted by UNHCR's statistical report. By gathering statistics from the various agencies that interact with children at different points on their journey, we have attempted to create a composite picture of the number of children seeking asylum alone in the U.K., the U.S., and Australia.

■ **The United Kingdom**

Since 2002 comprehensive statistics about the numbers and characteristics of unaccompanied and separated children claiming asylum in the U.K. have been collected by the Home Office.[22]

The table below indicates that between 2003 and 2004 there was a 2.2% increase of unaccompanied and separated child applicants among the total number of asylum seekers. Moreover, these figures may underestimate the phenomenon of child asylum seekers: according to Home Office figures, in 2004 alone, 2,345 cases gave rise to age disputes, with the Home Office refusing to accept the applicant's claim to be a child. Research carried out by the Refugee Council and Cambridgeshire County Council at Oakington Reception Centre indicates that around 50% of age-disputed individuals are in fact unaccompanied or separated children.[23]

Anecdotal evidence from non-governmental organizations, social workers, and legal representatives working with unaccompanied and separated children collected by the U.K. researchers suggests that a substantial number of children are being trafficked into the U.K. for domestic slavery or for use in prostitution and child pornography or other exploitative situations. Many of these children do not come to the attention of the Immigration Service on entry as they travel with agents who pass them off as their own children or the children of those settled in the U.K. Thus, the true number of unaccompanied children entering the U.K. is likely to be much higher.

Unaccompanied and Separated Child Asylum Seekers (U.K.)

	2002	2003	2004
Total Asylum Seekers	**84,130**	**49,405**	**33,960**
Total Children	**6,200**	**3,180**	**2,990**
% of Children	7.3%	6.4%	8.8%
% of Children, 16–17 yrs	63%*	60%	62%
% of Children, under 16	36%*	40%	38%

Source: U.K. Home Office   ★ 1% UNCLASSIFIED

■ The United States

With its size and formidable administrative complexity, the U.S. presents real challenges in terms of data collection. There are no comprehensive government statistics on how many children enter the U.S. alone every year; and since the Executive Office of Immigration Review (EOIR) does not track birth dates, there is no annual data on how many children go through Immigration Court proceedings. There are, however, a number of access points in the immigration system where the authorities come in contact with unaccompanied and separated children, and where partial information can be found.

The first access points are with the reception and interception agencies. One such agency is the U.S. Coast Guard, whose officials patrol U.S. waters and interdict boats of asylum seekers. In 2004, the Coast Guard interdicted 10,899 asylum seekers at sea. This number includes both adults and children. If the UNHCR's findings for 28 European countries can be extrapolated and applied to the U.S.—that is, if we can assume that unaccompanied and separated child asylum seekers constitute between 4% and 5% of any given asylum-seeker population in the industrialized world—then we can estimate that the U.S. Coast Guard intercepted and returned about 500 unaccompanied children in 2004. This is, however, an unusually high number of interdictions. The average number of interdicted migrants for the preceding five years (1999 to 2003) was approximately 4,631. If unaccompanied and separated children constituted 4% of that total, that would amount to an average of 185 unaccompanied and separated children picked up by the Coast Guard each year.[24]

The other two reception and interception agencies are Customs and Border Protection (CBP) (whose officials are stationed at airports and points of entry) and Border Patrol (whose officers are stationed along the land borders of Mexico and

Canada between official points of entry). The children these officials meet are often physically located on U.S. territory, but not considered legally "present." Some of those who lack valid visas will be turned away immediately before ever being admitted to the country.[25] Neither CBP nor the Border Patrol provided statistical information, but what patchy evidence is available suggests that quite large numbers of unaccompanied children are intercepted by U.S. officials while attempting to enter the U.S. via the southern border. The U.S. Department of Justice noted that in fiscal year 2000, the Border Patrol apprehended and repatriated a total of 94,823 Mexican minors at the southern border. This number includes both accompanied and unaccompanied children, but excludes all nationalities other than Mexican. Hence, it does not represent the total number of unaccompanied and separated children turned back at the border. The figures do, however, give some indication of the scale of migration involved.[26]

Other children, instead of being turned away at the border, come into contact with government officials once they have already entered the U.S. This is either because they have managed to cross the border without being detected, or because they have entered the country on a valid visa that has since expired, and are later discovered. Once apprehended, these children are usually[27] detained in federal custody while their asylum eligibility is determined or while the government puts them through removal proceedings. Detention is therefore another potential source of quantitative data. The U.S. Office of Refugee Resettlement (ORR), which is charged with the care and custody of children in removal proceedings,[28] reported that it had between 750 and 900 unaccompanied and separated children in care at any one time during fiscal year 2004. A total of 6,200 unaccompanied and separated children were referred to ORR during that year.[29]

All of the children who are detected by the various interception and reception agencies must make their claims for asylum or withholding of deportation in Immigration Court (these procedures are explained in chapter 5). But the court is not a source of quantitative data on unaccompanied and separated child applicants because it does not record the ages and birthdates of the petitioners who come before it. As a result we were unable to find any information on how many children are awarded asylum or withholding of deportation in court. There is only slightly more information available regarding other forms of protection for unaccompanied and separated children. The principal sources are "Trafficking" or T-Visas[30] and Special Immigrant Juvenile Status (SIJS).[31] Between the fiscal years 2002 and 2004, 32 unaccompanied children were certified as victims of trafficking[32] and therefore eligible for the T-Visa.[33] The numbers of children who applied for and were granted SIJS are unknown, but the Yearbook of Immigration Statistics states that in 2002, a total of 521 juvenile court dependants were granted permanent residency (presumably

because they had been granted SIJS).[34]

Even if it were available, any data collected by the Coast Guard, CBP, Border Patrol, the ORR, and the Immigration Court would only capture part of the unaccompanied and separated child population in the U.S., namely those children who entered or attempted to enter the country *without* valid documents, and who were apprehended by government officials. Other children, however, enter the asylum channel by choosing to present themselves to the authorities. These children include those who are living in the U.S. on valid visas, as well as those who entered the country clandestinely or whose visas have expired, but who have still not been detected by immigration officials. These children are allowed to make their claims affirmatively, through the Asylum Office. Only if they are denied asylum by the Asylum Office do they then revert to the same position as children apprehended without documents by the authorities and have the option of appealing to the Immigration Court to seek to reverse the refusal of asylum.

Unlike most other government agencies we contacted, the Asylum Office does collect data on unaccompanied and separated children. It stated that out of 46,945 total onshore asylum applications in 2003, 500 were submitted by children as the principal applicants. The five-year average (1999–2003) is 524 applications per year.[35]

A final cohort of unaccompanied and separated children comes to the U.S. through the refugee resettlement program, having been pre-screened and approved overseas. In 2003, 400 unaccompanied children entered the U.S. in this way.[36]

The numbers of resettled refugees dropped dramatically after 11 September 2001, but have since begun to find equilibrium again. The five-year average per year for 1999–2003 was 460 cases headed by children.

A separate specialized program is in place for Cuban and Haitian entrants, with 47 unaccompanied and separated children from those countries resettled in the fiscal year 2003.[37]

While it is difficult to extrapolate exact totals from these disparate figures, the clear message is that the number of children coming to the U.S. on their own each year is far from insignificant.

■ Australia

Australia presents a rather different statistical profile. Unlike the U.S. and the U.K. where unaccompanied and separated children consistently represent a small but significant proportion of the asylum seekers arriving each year, Australia had no sizeable experience of child asylum seekers arriving at its shores until the late 1990s. During the late 1980s, one or two children appeared as stowaways or among groups of boat people, but Australia's inaccessibility kept larger numbers away.[38] Of all groups of asylum seekers, children traveling without guardians found it particularly difficult to collect the money needed for the airfare and documentation (passports and visas) necessary to board a plane.

This changed at the very end of the 1990s.

Between 1999 and 2002 Australia became the destination for a significant number of undocumented asylum seekers traveling by boat, including unaccompanied and separated children, though it has proved difficult to determine their numbers precisely.

The Department of Immigration, Multicultural and Indigenous Affairs (DIMIA) reported that a cohort of 283 unaccompanied and separated children arrived in Australia between 1999 and 2002. Over the same period of time, an additional seven unaccompanied children arrived by plane and claimed asylum—three with visas and four without.[39] In more recent years, unaccompanied children have continued to present as a small percentage of the asylum-seeker/irregular-migrant population. In February 2006, for example, 13 unaccompanied or separated children were reported to be detained either in community detention on Christmas Island or in hotel accommodation.[40]

These figures reflect only those asylum seekers who managed to disembark on the Australian mainland. They do not include children interdicted at sea and deflected to Nauru, New Zealand, or the excised zones for offshore processing, as part of the "Pacific Strategy" devised in response to the *Tampa* Affair in 2001 (see chapter 6). Obtaining accurate statistics for this population was extremely difficult. Data provided to the Human Rights and Equal Opportunity Commission (HREOC) suggest that a total of 66 unaccompanied or separated children traveling by boat were deflected from Australia between 1999 and 2003. These included 36 accepted by New Zealand from the *Tampa* and 30 redirected to Nauru or Manus Island. HREOC stated that the vast majority of these young people (91.2%) were recognized as refugees over this period.[41] How this statement relates to the apparently high number of young people returning to Afghanistan is not clear.[42] According to statistics supplied by the International Organization of Migration (IOM), 55 children were registered as unaccompanied upon arrival on Nauru. Of these, 32 were to return to Afghanistan in 2002–2003. This suggests that well over half of the unaccompanied children detained on Nauru and Manus Island were sent back to Afghanistan in 2002 and 2003. On this point, IOM pointed out that all returnees departed voluntarily and that only nine of the 32 were still recorded as unattached minors at time of departure (suggesting that many of the young people were aged 16 or 17 at time of arrival).[43]

Apart from the unaccompanied and separated children recorded as asylum seekers, it has been alleged that children are brought to Australia by

traffickers each year (principally for sexual exploitation). Estimates of the size of this population vary dramatically. In response to our request for information on trafficking, the official response was that before 1994 there had been only one incident in 1995 involving a 14-year-old girl from Thailand.[44] On the other hand, a research team for the U.S. Trafficking in Persons Report found around 300 non-national women and children forced into bonded sex work in Australia in 2004.[45] That report does not give a breakdown for the number of children detected, and appears to be based on estimates.

As noted earlier, Australia has a long history of refugee resettlement programs. In this context, it continues to receive unaccompanied and separated children, who are categorized as refugees prior to their arrival, from many of the world's most troubled countries. Although programs have been created to offer sanctuary to women at risk,[46] the offshore humanitarian program has no specific program

for orphaned or separated children. Even so, there appears to have been a tendency in the years since the *Tampa* Affair to target particularly vulnerable groups when selecting migrants under the offshore humanitarian scheme. In this climate, orphaned and separated children appear to have been beneficiaries, with sharp increases apparent in the number of such children being selected for admission.

2.3 Who are These Children?

■ Gender

UNHCR calculates that, in the 28 European countries for which it collected statistics between 2001 and 2003, 28% of unaccompanied and separated children were female, while 72% were male.[47] Across all three countries studied for this report, males outnumbered females, though the proportions varied significantly. In the U.K., boys constituted 77% of the unaccompanied/separated asylum-seeking population in 2002, 67% in 2003, and 67% in 2004.[48] In the U.S., the average gender breakdown for child asylum applicants between 1999 and 2003 was 57% male, 43% female.[49] In Australia, the gender difference was far more pronounced: of the 290 unaccompanied and separated children who arrived between 1999 and 2002, only four were female: two from Iraq and two from Afghanistan.[50]

Despite fluctuations across years and countries, male children appear to be universally more likely to become unaccompanied and separated asylum seekers than females. These ratios correspond with the gender breakdown among asylum seekers of all ages. Although the global refugee population (including those who have received refugee status and those who are living in UNHCR-administered camps) is about half female, the global population of asylum seekers (that is, those who submit onshore applications directly in receiving countries) is predominantly male.[51]

Why are boys more likely to seek asylum alone than girls? One reason is that boys are more often directly involved in conflict situations, and thus are more likely to be targeted by fighting or forced into child soldiering (although, as the story of Mary from Sierra Leone shows and also the experiences of many girls throughout Africa, not only boys are vulnerable to this threat). Another reason is that many parents who want to send a child abroad to earn money will send a boy rather than a girl, believing boys to be more capable of traveling alone and finding work.[52] Of course, there are other factors which counteract the tendency for boys to travel and girls to stay home. Girls are particularly at risk of sexually discriminatory practices (such as forced genital mutilation or forced marriage) and sexual violence during conflict situations (when they may be raped or kidnapped to serve as soldiers' "wives") which might cause them to flee. This may account for the relatively high number of Somali girls who flee to claim asylum in the U.K. Young girls are also increasingly being trafficked or smuggled abroad for domestic servitude or sex work, sometimes with their parents' knowledge and acquiescence.

Breaking the data down further reveals that certain countries of origin produce disproportionately more girl asylum seekers than others. In 2002 and 2003, for example, there were 10 sending states from which more than 50% of the unaccompanied children fleeing to the U.K. were female. Of these countries, nine out of 10 were in Africa. Unusual gender ratios like this may tell us something about the sorts of gender-specific persecution these children have been fleeing in their countries of origin, and suggest that any protection strategies must be sensitive to their needs both as children and as females.

▪ Age

Age determination procedures vary from country to country and even, sometimes, within countries. In the U.S., for example, the Office for Refugee Resettlement looks to the preponderance of documentary evidence (including birth certificates, school enrolment papers, etc.) in order to establish a child's age when it is in dispute, while Immigration and Customs Enforcement still relies primarily upon the outmoded method of analyzing dental x-rays.[53] Combined with the differing definitions of a "child" in various jurisdictions[54] and the neglect of some government agencies to keep records of ages and birthdates at all,[55] the variety of approaches to age determination makes it difficult to gather comparable data on age breakdowns.

However, we can make some general observations. UNHCR notes that, in the 11 European countries that submitted comparable information on age in 2003, 65.3% of all unaccompanied and separated child asylum seekers were 16 or 17 years old.

In the two preceding years as well, more than half of the children submitting asylum applications in those countries were either 16 or 17 years old.[56] This is not surprising, given the considerable physical demands and dangers confronting children on their journeys.

This age breakdown holds true for the three countries studied in this report. While the U.S. media has alerted public attention to the plight of very young unaccompanied and separated children (most famously, the six-year-old Elian Gonzales), the majority of children seeking asylum alone appear to be teenagers. According to the ORR, the average age of children in federal custody in 2004 was 15. In the U.K., out of 2,990 new applications submitted by children in 2004, 62% were from children aged 16 or 17; 28% were from 14 or 15 year olds; and 10% were from children younger than 14.[57] And among the group of 290 unaccompanied and separated children arriving in Australia between the calendar years of 1999 to 2002, 54.5% were 16 or 17 years old; 39% were 13 to 15 years old; and 6.5%

were below the age of 13.[58] The youngest member of the Australian cohort was eight years old.

■ Countries of Origin

It is difficult and probably unhelpful to make global generalizations about the countries of origin for unaccompanied and separated child asylum seekers. Country-of-origin demographics among these children can differ substantially between receiving countries and years, reflecting not only changes in the situations of sending countries (that is, the flaring up or resolution of conflicts) but also the diverse geographical realities and economic, social, political, and linguistic factors that lead children to head for one receiving country rather than another. Parents who send their children abroad for protection may prefer to send them to a country where they speak the language, or where they will be more likely to find communities of co-nationals to care for them. For example, many of Poland's asylum seekers come from Russia. Similarly Belgium receives a large number of child asylum seekers from the Democratic Republic of Congo, and a large percentage of Portugal's child asylum seekers come from Angola. Even where there are no colonial, historical, or linguistic ties, the existence of an established refugee community in a receiving country may provide an incentive for more asylum seekers to follow them there—like Somali children seeking asylum in Finland, Denmark, and Sweden.[59]

In some receiving countries, the country-of-origin profiles of unaccompanied and separated child asylum seekers are no different from the patterns to be seen among asylum seekers of all ages. In other receiving countries they are noticeably different. Where they are different, this can indicate the existence of widespread child-specific threats and forms of persecution. For example, UNHCR noted that Afghanistan was a major source of unaccompanied and separated child asylum

seekers arriving in Europe between 2001 and 2003. While Afghan nationals made up only 7% of all claims (adults and children) submitted in this period, they made up 13% of all unaccompanied and separated child asylum seekers. This may suggest that children were selected by families with insufficient resources to travel together either because they were at particular risk of recruitment by the Taliban or because families considered their survival most critical. In both the U.K. and Australia a large proportion of the unaccompanied Afghan children were aged 14 years and up, the optimum age for forced recruitment. Angola presents an even starker example of the disproportionate effects of conflict on children: an astonishing 27% of all asylum seekers leaving Angola for Europe between 2001 and 2003 were unaccompanied and separated children. This accords with what the world knows about the Angolan civil war: the pervasive use of landmines; the displacement, abduction, and deliberate targeting of civilians which left many children orphans; and the widespread use of child soldiers, all of which put children at special risk. Other major source countries for unaccompanied and separated children were Somalia, Sierra Leone, Serbia and Montenegro, Guinea, China, the Democratic Republic of Congo, and Nigeria.[60] The number of children from Nigeria is thought to be related to the high incidence of child trafficking for child prostitution and domestic slavery from that country.

Like many countries in Europe, the U.K. receives unaccompanied and separated children from a number of conflict and post-conflict zones. Two of the top three countries of origin in 2004 were areas of generalized insecurity in the wake of conflict: Afghanistan (producing 10% of all unaccompanied or separated child asylum applicants in the U.K.) and Somalia (producing 8% of all unaccompanied or separated child asylum applicants). In Afghanistan it is clear that young boys are still being sent out of the country—this may well be because the warlords and their followers continue to seek revenge on other groups or those connected with the previous Najibullah government and this includes revenge on sons. Countries experiencing prolonged war in Africa also figure prominently among the major countries of origin (see Figure 1).

For geographical reasons, the U.S. presents a somewhat different profile. The long and porous land border with Mexico—combined with the stark economic asymmetry which that border demarcates—means that a large proportion of unaccompanied and separated child asylum seekers come by land to the U.S. from Mexico or elsewhere in Latin America. Of all unaccompanied children in U.S. custody, 86% come from Honduras, El Salvador, Guatemala, or Mexico. (See figure 1.) While not fleeing "hot war," many of the children from Central America have been displaced by the lingering effects of civil wars in the region: continuing instability, economic deprivation, the collapse of government infrastructure, endemic corruption, or political persecution. Children from Mexico—who are undoubtedly underrepresented among the unaccompanied child population, since so many would-be asylum seekers are turned away at the border without ever reaching federal custody—are most often migrating to escape poverty, although it should be noted that this does not necessarily mean that the threats to their lives are less acute than for children of other nationalities.

In Australia, throughout the 1980s and early 1990s, most children who arrived by boat were from Southeast Asia (specifically Vietnam and Cambodia) and China. In more recent years, the demographic profile has shifted: most separated child asylum seekers arriving in Australia between 1999 and 2003 came from Afghanistan (86.7%) and Iraq (10.5%), with smaller proportions coming from Iran, the Palestinian Territories, and Sri Lanka. This is consistent with the nationality patterns among adult asylum seekers.[61]

2.4 How and Why Do They Travel?

Children who cross borders alone to seek asylum are a diverse group who begin their journeys for a variety of reasons. While unaccompanied and separated children are often met in receiving countries with suspicion—cast as untrustworthy opportunity seekers or as the "anchors" for other, adult family members who are waiting in the wings to gain access to the country—the truth is always far more complex. We found great diversity in the reasons for migrating, and in the degree to which children themselves chose to migrate and understood what was happening to them.

Some children are completely alone, having been orphaned or abandoned, and they cross borders to seek asylum of their own volition. Many others make the journey not on their own initiative, but because their adult caregivers believe it is their best option (for bare physical safety, for economic opportunities and a better life, or for some combination of the two).

However; no matter how benevolent or apparently voluntary the reasons for travel, children invariably suffer when sent abroad with no family to care for

Journeys of a Lifetime | Juan Pablo's Story

Juan Pablo, a boy from Honduras, suffered extreme physical and emotional abuse from his mother throughout his childhood. At the age of 16 he fled his home country for the U.S. He walked north through El Salvador to Guatemala, catching rides on buses when he could, and covering the rest of the distance on foot.

Along the way he encountered large groups of other migrants who, like himself, were headed north. As they traveled they were periodically approached by "coyotes" who offered to transport them across borders and difficult terrain.

By the time Juan Pablo reached the Mexico border, he was ill from hunger. He recalls walking day and night, trekking through cities, swamps and farmland without a thought to where he was going, only worrying about where his next meal or drink of water would come from. By this time, he had lost or sold all his belongings except for a backpack, a pair of pants, a shirt and a prayer that his grandmother had given him "on a piece of paper." Eventually he caught a ride to Mexico City on a crowded bus filled with oranges and other migrants like him.

Upon arrival in Mexico City, Juan Pablo grew desperate. He recalls sitting by the highway and throwing rocks at passing cars in the hopes of getting arrested. No police came, but eventually he found a coyote who agreed to put him on a bus north to the U.S. border. In his exhaustion he fell asleep on the bus, only to be awakened near the border when a Mexican official demanded to see his documents. Juan Pablo suggested that if he won a card game, the official would allow him to continue on to the border. He lost. But after some pleading, the official let him go anyway.

Juan Pablo and another young migrant he had met in Mexico waited for nightfall before attempting

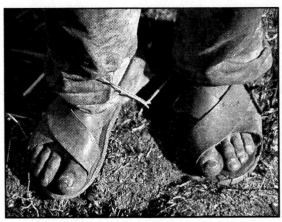

to cross the border into Arizona. Juan Pablo recalls running through wire, tearing his shirt, trying to reach a coyote's truck he saw in the distance. Before he could reach it, the U.S. Border Patrol caught him. He remembers helicopters and dogs. The guards took his shoes, belt, and everything else he had, and brought him to jail. When immigration officers questioned him the following day, he told them he was from Mexico. "I was very scared because the coyotes had told me that no matter what you did, you could not tell them the truth."

In all, Juan Pablo's journey lasted three months. He arrived in the U.S. ill, alone, and frightened. He recovered from malnourishment while in immigration detention, but has since been diagnosed with Post-Traumatic Stress Disorder from the abuse he suffered from his mother at home and from the journey he endured to escape it.[62]

them. Child protection issues inevitably arise when children are sent alone across great distances to countries of which their parents or guardians have little knowledge or experience.

■ Reasons for Leaving: Persecution and the Five Grounds for Asylum

Our research showed that children travel for a wide variety of reasons, not all of which are recognized by the current dominant readings of international refugee law. Some children are forced to flee on account of a fear of persecution based on one of the traditional five grounds outlined in the 1951 Refugee Convention: race, religion, nationality, membership in a particular social group, or political opinion. Persecution based on race, nationality, or religion can affect children just as it does adults. Children can also be persecuted as political activists in their own right, or they may be targeted on account of the political activities of a family member. They may also suffer persecution because of their membership in a social group—whether that be their family affiliation, gang membership, disability, or other affiliation.[63] While the U.K. and the U.S. are beginning to acknowledge some of these affiliations as legitimate readings of the "particular social group" clause, the evidential burden is relatively high. In the U.K., for instance, it is necessary to show that not only will the individual child face persecution but that as a child he or she will not receive the necessary protection under the law or by society in his or her country of origin. Gang members and street children in particular face considerable stigma in receiving countries, and their attempts to claim asylum on these grounds have had mixed results.

Children may also be targeted for persecution on account of child-specific vulnerabilities that were not necessarily foreseen by the Refugee Convention's drafters. Some situations that might not constitute persecution because they involve consenting adults

are persecutory when applied to children, who may not be in a position to give real or meaningful consent. These include marriage, manual labor, and conscription into armed forces. Other forms of persecution—including gang violence and sexual exploitation—target children especially.

Another group that may not easily fit into the Convention definition of refugee is that made up of those children who are escaping the random destruction of war, but who cannot prove they would be specifically targeted for persecution by virtue of one of the five protected grounds. Judging from the country-of-origin breakdowns described above, generalized conflict is a major cause of child displacement. Children without guardians to care for them face particularly bleak odds in war zones, being vulnerable to abduction, sexual exploitation, and child slavery. The Convention as it is normally construed does not extend refugee status to those who flee generalized violence, although children who have been orphaned by war and who cannot claim asylum on any of the five protected grounds may be eligible for some form of humanitarian status in receiving countries.

Undoubtedly, economic motivations also play a role in the decision to leave for some children—or perhaps, more often, in the decisions that adults (parents, relatives, and guardians) make on their behalf. The desire for a better life is a common theme in children's accounts of why they travel (or are sent) abroad. Still, our research suggests that the so-called "anchor child" phenomenon—whereby parents allegedly send their children to a receiving country first to establish him or herself, hoping that this will open a path for the rest of the family to migrate later—is unlikely to play anything but a secondary role in most unaccompanied and separated children's migration. It is also clear from the accounts given by many unaccompanied and separated children that their parents or guardians may have minimized the dangers faced by the family as a whole in the country of origin in order to persuade the child to leave the rest of the family behind.

In both the U.K. and Australia country-of-origin statistics show that most unaccompanied children come from conflict or post-conflict zones, or from countries where political repression is widespread. For these children, economic motivations for travel are probably secondary to bare survival. As Ayotte's research in Western Europe has suggested, while economic motives may be present, the precipitating event that causes children to flee most often involves violence or persecution.[64] The Australian research findings point to the same conclusion: the vast majority of children studied claimed to have fled in response to very immediate threats of harm. Many were the oldest surviving siblings or had lost family members.

International research has found that very few separated children are granted family reunion and,

in most cases, they lose contact with their parents.[65] Thus, it appears that public anxiety about "anchor children" is not borne out by the facts. Even among Mexican and Central American migrants in the U.S.—who are usually cast purely as economic migrants in the public discourse—the unaccompanied and separated children we interviewed described mixed motives leading to their flight. They spoke not only of poverty and lack of opportunity but also of child abuse, gang persecution, and other threats to their lives.

■ By Air, Land, and Sea

In the U.K., asylum seekers from Africa and Asia tend to arrive by air while asylum seekers from Turkey, Eastern Europe, the Baltic, and the former Yugoslavia tend to enter through sea ports. Between 2002 and 2004 approximately one quarter of all asylum applications by unaccompanied and separated children were made or notified at ports of entry (airports or harbors). The other three quarters were submitted after the children had entered the country.[66] Of the latter group, most had entered clandestinely. In Australia virtually every unaccompanied and separated child seeking asylum between 1999 and 2003 was smuggled into the country and identified immediately as an asylum seeker. This reliance on clandestine entry can be explained by a number of factors. First, an unaccompanied child is unlikely to be able to meet the criteria to obtain a valid visa as a student, visitor, or skilled migrant worker. Second, children—especially those who have been separated from their parents even before departure—often find it difficult to obtain other types of valid travel documents like passports, which may be costly and available only to those with the sort of contacts that a child on his or her own is unlikely to possess. Young children traveling alone may also arouse the suspicion of airport liaisons or airport officials and thus become more prone to arrest. For these reasons, many children are forced to enter the country clandestinely, or else to travel in the company of a smuggler who arranges fake documents or who poses as the child's parent or guardian. Our interviews with advocates confirmed that many unaccompanied and separated children coming to the U.K. use the services of a smuggler at some point in their journey.

In Australia, the vast majority of adult asylum seekers arrive by air. Most travel on a valid tourist or work visa and apply for protection only after entering the country.[67] As discussed earlier, this mode of entry is difficult for children. Therefore, the unaccompanied and separated child asylum seekers who arrived between 1999 and 2003 traveled predominantly by boat, since this option was cheaper and did not require the procurement of travel documents. Of the cohort of 290 child asylum seekers this report examines, all but seven arrived by boat without a visa.[68] Smugglers also played a large role in their journeys to Australia. The voyage involved such dangers that it would have been nearly impossible for a child to navigate without some sort of assistance. Many of the child asylum applicants in Australia described how they left their homes under cover of darkness, using a variety of disguises, hiding places and vehicles to escape. For the majority of these children, this was their first experience of modern transport and of transcontinental and oceanic travel. Their apprehension and even terror can only be imagined.

The departure of one of the children fleeing Afghanistan was particularly dramatic. He traveled in a coffin-shaped space beneath a pile of bricks (strewn with offensive smelling material to disguise any scent) where he lay motionless for hours. As he made his way from Afghanistan to Pakistan, and then to Singapore in a cargo container, he was given succor by a crew member but barely survived the experience. He spoke of being nurtured back to health in Singapore, where he hid for six weeks before making his way to

Indonesia and a boat bound for Australia. He was 16 years of age when he arrived in Australia.

The situation in the U.S. is different. Though many asylum seekers arrive by airplane, particularly those coming from Africa, Asia, and Europe, anecdotal evidence suggests that the majority of unaccompanied and separated children arrive overland, by foot, train, or motor vehicles, via the Mexican border. Again, it appears that many, if not most, are accompanied at some point in their journey by an adult, whether that is a relative, family friend, or professional smuggler. As the story of Jose from Honduras illustrates, children often put their lives in the hands of an adult — or even a series of adults — whom they have never met before. The advice of these smugglers may be the only adult guidance children have during their journey. Children from Central and South America, for example, often report being "coached" by smugglers to tell U.S. authorities that their country of origin is Mexico, since that way, if they are caught and returned, they will not have so far to go before attempting another border crossing. Many children make multiple attempts before they succeed in entering the U.S.

■ Choice and Consent

Determining whether asylum seekers have embarked on their journey through coercion or consent is often difficult and entails complex evaluations regarding the factors that impinge on the decision to migrate. Assessing the motivational background to children's quest for asylum is even more challenging. The children we interviewed ran the gamut of maturity and agency, some displaying remarkable resourcefulness and resilience, others being utterly bewildered by their situation. Many of the young people interviewed claimed that they had no say in either the decision to leave or the mode of their departure. Ali, for example, expressed his anger and frustration at having been "sent into exile" from Afghanistan to

Australia by his father. By contrast, Jose planned his escape from his abusive mother in Honduras all by himself, displaying remarkable determination in his long and demanding three-month trek north to the U.S. border.

Our research confirmed that children who seek asylum alone are a diverse group, displaying considerable variety in terms of their agency and their understanding of what is happening to them. Some children flee because of their active involvement in political groups; others flee because of the persecution of a family member; still others flee threats to their lives from generalized war or economic deprivation. Some children have only a vague understanding of the precipitating events that caused them to flee in the first place; others express a keen awareness of the threats they have fled, and have clear goals for a better life in their destination country. Some are sent abroad by their parents, having had no say in the timing or mode of travel and no idea of their intended destination; some of them have been lied to in order to persuade or induce them to leave and will suffer the added trauma of betrayal; others plan their journeys themselves, through their own ingenuity. Some travel with an adult; others are totally alone.

Despite the variety of children's experiences as they travel in search of asylum, however, one constant theme is visible throughout: their need of protection and guardianship. This is as true of children who planned their journeys themselves as it is of those whose journeys were arranged by adult caregivers. No matter whose choice it was in the first place, it is the child who must brave the risks of the journey. For many children, the memory of the trauma they left in their home countries is compounded by the trauma of the movement itself, which can be scary, confusing, physically demanding, and often exploitative.

Even when the mode of travel involves no exploitation and minimal physical risk, it can be

an extremely emotionally difficult experience. Children may have special difficulty in appreciating the permanent nature of their movement and in anticipating the linguistic and cultural isolation they may face in the receiving country. And, until they find themselves in detention or removal proceedings, most children have no way to comprehend the dire legal implications of their undocumented border crossing. Whatever the mode of their travel, children who seek asylum alone frequently express surprise, fear, and disappointment at their reception in what they hoped would be a better country than the one they had fled.

Figure 1: Countries of Origin: U.S.

Unaccompanied and separated children in U.S. federal custody (ORR), 2005

■ Honduras	30%
■ El Salvador	26%
■ Guatemala	20%
■ Mexico	10%
■ Brazil	3%
■ China	2%
■ Ecuador	2%
■ Nicaragua	.82%
■ Costa Rica	.47%
■ Other Countries	5.71%

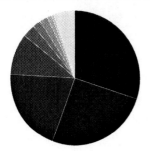

Endnotes

1 Bhabha, Jacqueline and Schmidt, Susan. *Seeking Asylum Alone, United States*. Cambridge, MA: Bhabha and Schmidt, 2006. (U.S. Report.) ch. 1.2.

2 Steinbock, Daniel, Ressler, Everett and Boothby, Neil. *Unaccompanied Children: Care and Protection in Wars, Natural Disasters and Refugee Movements*. Oxford: Oxford University Press, 1988.

3 See United Nations. *Impact of Armed Conflict on Children*. Report of Graca Machel, Expert of the Secretary-General of the United Nations. UN, 1996. Available at http://www.unicef.org/graca/.

4 Ayotte, Wendy. *Separated Children Coming to Western Europe: Why They Travel and How They Arrive*. London: Save the Children, 2000. 13.

5 Ibid, Endnote 3.

6 On this point, see also Ibid, Endnote 3.

7 Bell, Adrian. *Only For Three Months: The Basque Children in Exile*. Norwich: Mousehould Press, 1996.

8 International Conference on Indo-Chinese Refugees, Office of the United Nations High Commissioner for Refugees. UN GAOR, 44th Sess, Annex 1, UN Doc. A/44/523 (1989).

9 Steinbock, Daniel J. "The Admission of Unaccompanied Children into the United States." *Yale Law and Policy Review* 7 (1989): 142.

10 Bucci, Maria. "Young, Alone and Fleeing Terror: The Human Rights Emergency of Unaccompanied Immigrant Children Seeking Asylum in the United States." *New England Journal on Criminal and Civil Confinement* 30 (2004): 287.

11 See Holden, Robert. *Orphans of history: the forgotten children of the First Fleet*. Melbourne: Text Publishing, 2000. It is uncertain whether these children were in fact "orphans" or were simply taken into British institutional care at a young age.

12 National Archives of Australia. *Good British Stock: Child and Youth Migration to Australia, 1901–83*. Research Guide No. 11, 1999. Ch 3.

13 See Humphreys, Margaret. *Empty Cradles: One Woman's Fight to Uncover Britain's Most Shameful Secret*. London: Doubleday, 1994; and *The Leaving of Liverpool*. BBC Television, 1993.

14 This scandal laid the groundwork for the Immigration (Guardianship of Children) Act of 1946. Senate Community Affairs References Committee. *Lost Innocents: Righting the Record—Report on child migration*. 2001. 2.42.

15 Department of Education and Youth Affairs. *Immigrant and Refugee Youth in the Transition from School to Work or Further Study*. 1983.

16 This is consistent with a general tendency among policy makers and immigration officials to view children as mere accessories in international migration, rather than as movers in their own right. See Faulstich Orellana, et al. "Transnational Childhoods: The Participation of Children in Processes of Family Migration." *Social Problems* 48 (November 2001).

17 The Separated Children in Europe Programme, a joint effort of UNHCR and Save the Children, claims there has been a "steady rise" in separated and unaccompanied child asylum seekers arriving in Europe in "recent years." See "About Us." Available at http://www.separated-

children-europe-programme.org/separated_children/
about_us/scep_programme.html.

18 UNHCR Population Data Unit. *Trends in Unaccompanied and Separated Children Seeking Asylum in Industrialized Countries, 2001–2003.* Geneva: UNHCR, July 2004. 2. UNHCR does not collect data from the U.S., Canada, Australia, France, and Italy.

19 Ibid, Endnote 18, 4. This percentage can fluctuate dramatically between countries. In 2000, for example, the Netherlands reported that unaccompanied and separated children constituted over 15% of all asylum seekers (Ibid, 7).

20 Ibid, Endnote 18, 9, table 1.

21 Ibid, Endnote 18, 4.

22 Up until 2002, its statistics were not complete as unaccompanied or separated children claiming asylum at local enforcement offices or by post as opposed to making claims at ports of entry or in country at Asylum Screening Units were not included in the overall total of unaccompanied child asylum applicants.

23 U.K. Home Office.

24 U.S. Coast Guard Maritime Interdiction Statistics, 10 February 2004. See also U.S. Report, Ibid, Endnote 1, 15–16 and 195.

25 In 2004, The Department of Homeland Security gave Border Patrol the power (previously exercised only by CBP and the Coast Guard) to turn away undocumented migrants at the border without allowing them access to U.S. Immigration Courts, so long as Border Patrol officers are satisfied that the migrants do not have a genuine fear of persecution. Although unaccompanied children are technically exempt from this policy of "expedited removal" on land (but not at sea), they may nevertheless find themselves at greater risk because of it. The speed with which migrants are processed and returned may allow Border Patrol officers to misidentify children as adults, and to turn them away before they have a chance to prove their age or to make an asylum claim. See Swarns, Rachel L. "U.S. to Give Border Patrol Agents the Power to Deport Illegal Aliens." *The New York Times.* 11 August 2004: Section A, Column 3. See also Ortiz Miranda, Carlos,

Associate General Counsel of the U.S. Conference of Catholic Bishops. "Open Letter to Customs and Border Protection." 12 October 2004. Available at http://www.usccb.org/mrs/usccbexpedremcom.shtml.

26 U.S. DOJ/Office of the Inspector General. "Juvenile Repatriation Practices at Border Patrol Sectors on the Southwest Border." Report Number I-2001-010, September 2001. p. 1 of the Introduction.

27 The major exception here are Mexican children, who are, most of the time, returned immediately or within 72 hours of apprehension without ever coming into ORR custody. In contrast, "OTMs" (or "other-than-Mexicans") are typically kept in federal custody while they go through removal proceedings.

28 Children who are apprehended upon attempted entry but cannot be immediately returned may also be referred to ORR.

29 Data from "ORR/DUCS FY 2004 Summary," courtesy of Maureen Dunn, Director, Division of Unaccompanied Children's Services, Office of Refugee Resettlement, U.S. Department of Health and Human Services. 5 November 2004.

30 T-Visas are available to victims of severe forms of trafficking in persons.

31 SIJS is available to child victims of abuse, abandonment, or neglect.

32 These statistics represent all children certified as trafficking victims in the U.S. who were unaccompanied by adults able to care for them, for the period 10/1/01 through 01/31/05 (three years and four months). Data provided by Margaret MacDonnell, U.S. Conference of Catholic Bishops/Migration and Refugee Services. 14 February 2005.

33 However, in this time period, only seven children actually obtained their visas (defining "children" as those under age 18, though data was provided for those under age 21). "Child Principles and Derivatives," provided by Rebecca Story, U.S. Citizenship and Immigration Services, DHS. 25 March 2005.

34 *2002 Yearbook of Immigration Statistics* (formerly the *Statistical Yearbook of the Immigration and Naturalization Service* prior to the 2002 edition). The Department

of Homeland Security. Available at http://uscis.gov/ graphics/shared/aboutus/statistics/IMM02yrbk/ IMM2002.pdf. 24.

35 "Principal Applicants Under Age 18 at Application" provided by Christine Davidson, Asylum Office Headquarters, U.S. Citizenship and Immigration Services, DHS (personal correspondence dated 26 May 2004).

36 Data provided by the Refugee Processing Center, under contract with the Bureau for Population, Refugees and Migration, U.S. Department of State. 25 June 2004.

37 Statistics provided by the Miami office of the U.S. Conference of Catholic Bishops/Migration and Refugee Services (USCCB/MRS). Cuban and Haitian child entrants overlap with the numbers of children in ORR custody, since they are put into federal care upon arrival.

38 There were exceptions from earlier days, however. One such was a young Chinese boy named Bas Wie, who stowed himself in the wheel carriage of a DC3 that flew in to Darwin at the end of the Second World War. Aged only 12 years upon his arrival, he was adopted by the Chief Administrator (Governor) of the Northern Territory and grew to his majority in Government House in Darwin. See ABC TV. *7.30 Report*. 7 July 2004.

39 These figures are close but not identical to the information provided to the Human Rights and Equal Opportunity Commission (HREOC) in the context of that body's inquiry into children in immigration detention. That agency reported a total number of 285 unaccompanied children, constituting 14% of all child asylum seekers who arrived in Australia without a valid visa between 1 July 1999 and 30 June 2003. Compare HREOC. *A Last Resort? National Inquiry into Children in Immigration Detention*. 2004. Section 3 at 71. Available at http://www.hreoc.gov.au/human_ rights/children_detention_report/report/pdf.htm, with DIMIA, response to questions on notice from Senator Harradine. Additional Senate Estimates Hearing. Commonwealth Government of Australia, 11 February 2003. Available at http://www.aph.gov.au/ senate/committee/legcon_ctte/estimates/add_0203/ dimiafeb03/qon53-69.doc. Statistics provided at different stages in the Australian research for this

report have all varied. See further Crock, Mary. *Seeking Asylum Alone, Australia*. Sydney: Themis Press, 2006. (Australian Report.) 2.2.3.

40 Statistics provided by Alanna Hector (ChilOut), and by Charlene Thompson, Social Worker, Christmas Island. 6 February 2006. The young people detained in hotel accommodation reflect the fact that many boats caught fishing illegally in Australian waters include children as crew members.

41 Commonwealth Ombudsman. *Submission to National Inquiry into Children in Immigration Detention*. 2002. 2.5. Available at www.humanrights.gov.au. These figures again do not tally with DIMIA data. See Australian Report, Ibid, Endnote 39, 2.2.3.

42 Ibid, Endnote 39, HREOC 71, para 3.5.1.

43 The figure of 55 unaccompanied children may not be reliable as it records information at point of registration. Some children were found later to have relatives in the group. Anecdotal evidence from other sources suggests that there were also children who were not recognized as "unattached" at this initial stage. See Australian Report, Ibid, Endnote 39, Chapter 2.2.3.

44 Research notes for Australian Report, Ibid, Endnote 39.

45 O'Brien, Natalie. "The U.S. Government for the first time has named Australia as a 'destination' country for sex slaves, putting the nation on a par with countries such as Morocco, Colombia and Lithuania." *The Australian*. 16 June 2004. Available at http://www.theaustralian .news.com.au.

46 For a discussion of this program, see Manderson, Lenore et al. "A Woman without a Man is a Woman at Risk: Women at Risk in Australian Humanitarian Programs." *Journal of Refugee Studies* 11 (1998): 267.

47 Ibid, Endnote 18, 6.

48 Ibid, Endnote 18, 6.

49 Data used to compile this statistic was provided by Christine Davidson, Asylum Office Headquarters, U.S. Citizenship and Immigration Services, DHS. Personal correspondence dated 26 May 2004. Based on affirmative asylum applications between 1999 and 2003 where a child was the principal applicant. The gender breakdown in the U.S. is slightly unusual. Compare this with gender breakdown among asylum seekers of all ages in the U.S. (F=37%; M=63%). The relatively high proportion of females among unaccompanied and separated children may be because increasing protection opportunities for victims of gender-related violence in the U.S. (including T-Visas and VAWA) encourage female children who might otherwise not come forward to apply for asylum as well. It should be noted that this proportion does not mean that so many females *arrive* in the U.S., but only that so many females *apply for asylum once inside* the U.S. How many female children are arriving in the U.S. is more difficult to estimate.

50 Ibid, Endnote 39, HREOC 3.5.1.

51 UNHCR. *2003 Global Refugee Trends*. Geneva, 2004. Population Data Unit/PDGS, Division of Operational Support, UNHCR Geneva, 15 June 2004. Para. 32. Available at http://www.unhcr.ch/cgi-bin/texis/vtx/home/ opendoc.pdf?tbl=STATISTICS&id=40d015fb4&page= statistics. Bhabha, Jacqueline. "Demography and Rights: Women, Children and Access to Asylum." *International Journal of Refugee Law* 16 (April 2004).

52 Ibid, Endnote 4, 17.

53 Physicians for Human Rights and the Bellevue/ NYU Program for Survivors of Torture discuss the unreliability of dental x-rays in judging age in From Persecution to Prison: The Health Consequences of Detention for Asylum Seekers. Boston and New York City, 2003 June. 189.

54 For example, in contradiction to international law, Germany defines "unaccompanied child" as 0–16 (not 18) years of age.

55 For example, the U.S. Immigration Court.

56 Ibid, Endnote 18, 6–7.

57 Statistics provided by the Home Office's Research, Development and Statistics Directorate.

58 Ibid, Endnote 39, HREOC.

59 Ibid, Endnote 18, 6 and table 3.

60 Ibid, Endnote 18, 5.

61 Ibid, Endnote 39, HREOC 76.

62 Interview with Honduran youth who was 16 at the time he entered the U.S. Interview by Joanne Kelsey, interpreted by Judith Wing from Holland and Knight. 12 July 2004.

63 See Ibid, Endnote 4.

64 Ibid, Endnote 4.

65 See Renland, Astrid. "Trafficking of Children and Minors to Norway for Sexual Exploitation." ECPAT Norway/Save the Children Norway, 2001.

66 These statistics were presented to the Home Office's Unaccompanied Asylum Seeking Children's User Group meetings and are subject to adjustment. (Home Office figures are subjected to adjustment year on year but as a snapshot view are accurate).

67 DIMIA, Fact Sheet 74. Accessed December 2004.

68 DIMIA. Response to questions on notice from Senator Harradine. Additional Senate Estimates Hearing. Commonwealth Government of Australia, 11 February 2003.

Responding to the Needs
of Unaccompanied and Separated Children:
International Benchmarks for Protection

3.1 The Recognition of Vulnerable Children under International Law

If the establishment of an international legal framework guaranteed realization of the rights protected, many of the problems facing children seeking asylum alone today would have been solved years ago. The special vulnerability of unaccompanied and separated child refugees has long been recognized.

Since the early 20th century international law has acknowledged their double claim to state protection, as particularly vulnerable children (because they are refugees) and as a special subset of refugees (because they are children). Indeed the first ever international document to address children's rights, the Declaration of the Rights of the Child (drafted in 1924), was as a response to the particular problems facing refugee children during and after war. The 1946 Constitution of the International Refugee Organization, the founding document of the precursor to today's international

refugee organization, UNHCR, similarly highlighted the plight of a group of child refugees: war orphans under 16 years of age. In their separate domains and very early on, both child welfare and refugee law—the two directly relevant areas of international law—recognized the particular hardships facing unaccompanied and separated children in need of asylum.

This early vision has since been crystallized in several key contemporary international law instruments. We survey them, not because they govern all aspects of child asylum procedures today, but because they establish consensus benchmarks about appropriate treatment that are relevant to an assessment of current practice. Today's applicable international law, like that of half a century ago, is divided between child welfare and immigration control.

Regrettably, no international body or senior official, no UN department, institute or treaty body, is charged with responsibility for migrant children *per se*. As a result such children have tended to fall through the cracks of protective safety nets, victims of an almost complete lack of political will to address their situation.

There has been a striking institutional indifference to the need for data collection about their circumstances. The familiar political marginalization of both refugees and of children as minority constituencies is simply compounded in the case of this population.

Having said this, in recent years, international concern about children traveling alone in search of asylum has grown—in large measure because the phenomenon has become so widespread and visible. As a result, both refugee and child-rights organizations have issued guidelines and policy recommendations. Most recently, the UN Committee on the Rights of the Child, the treaty body that oversees implementation of the UN Convention on the Rights of the Child, has issued a General Comment on the treatment of unaccompanied and separated children outside their country of origin.[1] Moreover, concern over a subset of migrant children, those trafficked or smuggled by illegal migration networks, has spawned a whole new body of international law.

In this chapter, we set the scene for an analysis of the way the three countries studied have responded to this phenomenon by outlining the major frameworks for the protection of child migrants under international law. We examine in particular the Convention on the Rights of the Child, the Refugee Convention, and the Anti-Trafficking and Anti-Smuggling Protocols of 2000. Some remarks are made also about other relevant human rights instruments such as the UN Convention Against Torture and the European Convention on Human Rights. Part 3.2 of the chapter then examines the extent to which the three countries have acted to incorporate these international standards in their domestic legislation and policies. Subsequent chapters highlight startling gaps between legal obligations and established norms, on the one hand, and rights enforcement and protection in practice on the other.

3.2 International Legal Frameworks

Children who travel without the protection of a responsible adult confront policy makers and administrators with two sets of issues. The first and most obvious is their substantive need for physical assistance; the second is the question of procedural propriety, and the extent to which the fact of childhood itself requires a modification in the normal migration and refugee determination process. Procedural accommodation is particularly important in eliciting the "voice" of the child migrant him or herself.

International law has, to some extent, addressed both the substantive and procedural aspects of child migration. However, translating international legal obligations into binding policies under domestic law has proved difficult and elusive, as chapters 4 and 5 demonstrate. On the one hand, distinctions are drawn between the duties assumed by states which are signatories to an international instrument and those which assume full obligations under a treaty (by way of accession or ratification). Mere signatories are obliged to refrain from any action that may frustrate the object and purpose of the treaty, while full state parties are obliged to fulfill the obligations that they have accepted under the treaty.[2] As will be seen, while the U.K. and Australia have generally signed and ratified all of the major international instruments, the U.S. has not taken this step in some cases. On the other hand, the situation is complicated further by the fact that the U.K. has entered reservations in respect of some treaties, while Australia has signed and ratified treaties but refused to give domestic effect to its obligations by enacting relevant provisions into statute law.

■ The United Nations Convention on the Rights of the Child

The most comprehensive articulation of the rights of children seeking asylum is that set out in the 1989 Convention on the Rights of the Child (CRC). This convention is a central human rights convention for children. More widely signed and ratified than any other human rights instrument (only the U.S. and Somalia among UN states have not become full parties[3]) the CRC brings together (and in some cases amplifies) all the protections relevant to children

that are to be found in earlier international human rights instruments, starting with the 1948 Universal Declaration of Human Rights. Measures include both general human rights protections such as the prohibition on torture or inhuman or degrading treatment, but also more child-specific provisions relating to child labor, traditional child-specific cultural practices, and transnational adoption. The centerpiece of the Convention is Article 3, which requires states to take into account "the best interests of the child" in all actions concerning the child. These "actions" clearly include asylum and other immigration and child welfare matters relating to the protection and care of unaccompanied and separated children.

At the same time as the Convention stipulates protective measures, it also addresses issues of process. It requires states to pay attention to the views of children, treating them as agents rather than objects of adult care. In other words the "best interests" or protection principle must be combined with a requirement to elicit the child's opinion and attend to it where possible. Protection must go

with a recognition of agency, of the child as an independent, rational person. In addition to these general provisions which apply to all children, the Convention requires states to provide special care to children who lack a family environment, and to assist and protect children seeking asylum (both before and after a formal grant of refugee status[4]), to contribute to international efforts to trace family members from whom the child may be separated, and most important, to afford asylum-seeking children the same protection as domestic children deprived of parental care. In short, international children's law requires states dealing with unaccompanied and separated children seeking asylum to adopt a child-centered lens and not to discriminate against them in any way in their child welfare provision. These seemingly innocuous requirements in fact set a high standard for states that are parties to the Convention.

In June 2005, the Committee on the Rights of the Child, the treaty body that oversees implementation of the CRC, published a General Comment on separated and unaccompanied children.[5]

This Comment calls on states to take seriously their obligations not to discriminate against these children because of their alien status but to make available to them the full range of protective services offered to vulnerable domestic children, including education, shelter, and health provision. The General Comment also urges states to balance the requirements of best interest, through appointment of a guardian for each separated or unaccompanied child, with the complementary need to accord careful attention to the expressed wishes and views of the children themselves.

The Comment contains critical statements about the inadequacy of state information and data collection regarding unaccompanied and separated children, about the inappropriate and widespread use of detention (which, according to the Committee, is only to be used exceptionally as a last resort where this is in the best interests of the child), and about each child's need for access to competent legal representation. Finally, the Comment urges states to prioritize family reunification, in the state of origin if that is safe and feasible, but if not, within the destination country, and warns states about the dangers of returning children home without careful investigation of available support structures and protection from harm. The General Comment provides an excellent distillation of the considerations that states need to take into account in order to bring their policies regarding separated and unaccompanied children into compliance with prevailing legal standards.

■ The United Nations Convention Relating to the Status of Refugees

Exclusion, control, and management are the main goals of migration law today, as states erect increasingly impenetrable borders against unwanted or unplanned migrants. However, despite the growing fortification of external frontiers and the escalating militancy of domestic anti-migrant policies, official recognition of the entitlement to refugee protection for those fleeing persecution remains universal. No state, however xenophobic or nativist its rhetoric, has proposed withdrawing its protection for refugees. The system of international refugee protection, erected in the mid-20th century to cater to post World War II forced migrants, still exists.

Under the Refugee Convention, the ability of states to draw distinctions among migrants on the basis of their immigration status is tightly circumscribed. Article 31(1) provides (albeit with provisos) that a migrant's lack of documents, illegal entry or unauthorized presence in a receiving state should not influence negatively the migrant's claim to asylum:

The Contracting states shall not impose penalties, on account of their illegal entry or presence, on refugees who, coming directly from a territory where their life or freedom was threatened in the sense of Article 1, enter or are present in their territory without authorization, provided they present themselves without delay to the authorities and show good cause for their illegal entry or presence.

In fact, states do routinely accord different treatment to undocumented asylum seekers who have arrived in the receiving state by way of another state (a "third" or transit state) or who delayed in presenting their asylum applications to the appropriate authorities. These measures are justified as purely administrative rather than penal, in that they do not deprive asylum seekers of access to an asylum determination process, but rather require them to present their asylum application in the first safe state entered. This state practice is legitimated by explicit agreements within the European Union's harmonized asylum policy, as well as by the U.S.-Canada Safe Third Country Agreement.[6]

The most universally accepted principle enshrined in the Refugee Convention is contained in Article 33. This prohibits *refoulement* or forced return to torture or ill treatment. It applies to *all* persons who could qualify as refugees under Article 1(A), including those who would be eligible for refugee status, but who have not yet received a positive status determination. This is because the recognition of a refugee under Article 1A(2) does not "create" refugees—it merely acknowledges their existing status as refugees. As we will see, this is significant for many unaccompanied and separated children. Ignorant or fearful of the practicalities of seeking refugee status, such children may not be in a position to access refugee status determination processes. Yet, they may still be refugees under international law, placing countries which return them to danger in breach of the Refugee Convention.

One shortcoming with international refugee law is that the Refugee Convention contains no provisions analogous to the CRC's Article 22, which directly addresses the protection needs of unaccompanied and separated children seeking asylum. In fact, the Refugee Convention is age-neutral; it makes no mention at all of children, leaving the circumstances of children to be covered by default, so to speak. The key provisions of the Convention, namely the definition of a refugee and the prohibition on return to danger, apply irrespective of the age of the refugee and are therefore implicitly applicable to children.

Thus, like adults, children with a "well founded fear of persecution" because of their race, nationality, religion, political opinion, or "membership of a particular social group" are refugees, and accordingly entitled to international protection and non-discriminatory treatment. How these categories apply to children is not specified in the Refugee Convention or in any implementing rules. So the extent of the protection—the persecutory conduct covered, the degree of fear required, the group membership implied—all these are to some extent open questions, matters to be argued by advocates and decided by adjudicators in practice. There is no debate or disagreement, however, regarding the cardinal principle that anyone falling within this group is protected from return or *refoulement* back to the persecuting country. And yet, consider the case of Edgar Chocoy:

A Guatemalan boy attempting to flee gang life, Edgar entered the U.S. alone, seeking reunification in Los Angeles with his mother who had abandoned him as an infant. He found his mother, but was also drawn into gang activity in Los Angeles and wound up in a juvenile detention facility. He ultimately applied for asylum at the age of 16, stating in his asylum application, "I know that they will kill me if I am returned to Guatemala. They will kill me because I left their gang."

A judge denied his request for asylum and ordered him deported. Despite his attorney's urging that he appeal the decision, Edgar could no longer bear detention, having already attempted to hang himself with a pair of shoelaces. Edgar was deported to Guatemala on 10 March 2004, and 17 days later he was murdered by the gang members he had fled two years earlier.[7]

Though the Refugee Convention does not contain child-specific provisions or categories, the international organization responsible for the Convention, the UNHCR *has* addressed some of the specific needs of refugee and asylum-seeking children.[8]

UNHCR's widely respected and quoted "Handbook on Procedures and Criteria for Determining Refugee Status" (1979) emphasizes three key points:

1   The importance of "enrol[ling] the services of experts conversant with child mentality" to assess maturity and mental development in relation to the asylum claim.
2   The receiving state's responsibility "to ensure that the interests of an applicant for refugee status who is a minor are fully safeguarded, and the importance of appointing a guardian as an appropriate measure to this end.
3   The need for a "liberal application of the benefit of the doubt" by states in determining whether the "well founded fear" standard has been met by a minor.

These provisions set a sensible but somewhat ambitious standard on a range of substantive and procedural aspects of child asylum. Several, such as the appointment of a guardian, or the liberal application of the benefit of the doubt in favor of children, will emerge as central deficiencies in all three states studied: see further below.

An Australian immigration lawyer interviewed for this study commented:

"I think that what occurred was that there was... a profound pervasive bureaucratic paranoia developed... about Afghans.... Some bureaucrats would say in all seriousness that possibly 90% of Afghans were not from Afghanistan but were from Pakistan. There was a really strong sense that there were a huge amount of people... defrauding the department and I think that that attitude grew and grew.... And that's why we saw the toughening up... of attitudes and questions and more detailed questions about identity." [9]

In the 1990s, following on from the earlier work with war orphans, UNHCR promulgated a series of guidelines aimed specifically at children, beginning with the needs and protection norms applicable to children in refugee camps (1994) and moving on to unaccompanied and separated child asylum seekers (1997). The latter, "Guidelines on Policies and Procedures in dealing with Unaccompanied Minors Seeking Asylum," direct attention to key child-specific protection issues such as the initial identification and interviewing of unaccompanied children by suitably trained personnel; the importance of appointing a guardian for unaccompanied and separated children; their need for interim care; specific aspects of the refugee determination process as it impinges on children, including prioritizing children's applications and availability of suitably trained representatives; and finally, the importance of implementing durable solutions for these children.

The recommendations made in these guidelines (particularly regarding the importance of training and the appointment of guardians) are replicated in other authoritative international documents such as the conclusions of UNHCR's Executive Committee[10] and of its Global Consultation study.[11] The latter study recommends that unaccompanied and separated children whose asylum claims are unsuccessful should not be returned to their country of origin without a final ruling on their broader need for international protection. The study recommends that such return should also be subject to the identification of a willing and suitable family member to receive the child. All of these normative benchmarks remain critical issues to this day.

The U.K. government has been working on an Early Returns Program which would return children to their countries of origin at the point at which their applications for asylum are refused and they have exhausted any relevant appeal rights. However return would not necessarily be to a family setting and the government would not be required to establish that it was in the child's best interests to return. Plans for returning a group of 16- and 17-year-old boys to Albania were in their final stages in late 2005. By 2006 plans were also being drawn up to return much younger children of both genders to Vietnam and also Angola. The arrangements envisioned would not even appear to comply with UNHCR's Guidelines. For example, in relation to returns to Albania, policy documents state:

When an unaccompanied child arrives back in Tirana, he or she will be met by [someone from a locally based but international NGO] and an Albanian border guard. He or she will then be taken to an office and issued with a "starter pack" of food and clothing. Within the next twenty four hours he or she will also be placed in short or medium term accommodation.[12]

This draconian and profoundly disruptive program appears to be exactly the kind of return policy UNHCR's Executive Committee has sought to discourage.

■ The Anti-Trafficking and Anti-Smuggling Protocols

Apart from children's rights and refugee law, there is one other area of international law that is directly relevant to the rights of unaccompanied and separated child asylum seekers. This is international criminal law and, in particular, recent developments in this field concerning trafficking and smuggling in persons. In December 2000, a UN Convention on Transnational Organized Crime (UNTOC), was concluded to promote international cooperation in tackling a broad spectrum of cross-border criminal activities, including smuggling and trafficking in persons. While the primary goal of the Convention was to criminalize these activities, the Convention also addressed the protection needs of the migrants affected. Two Protocols to the Convention are directly relevant to unaccompanied and separated children seeking asylum: the Protocol to Prevent, Suppress and Punish Trafficking in Persons, Especially Women and Children (the Trafficking Protocol) and the Protocol against the Smuggling of Migrants by Land, Sea and Air (the Smuggling Protocol). The Trafficking Protocol covers "victims of trafficking" who are forcibly transported for purposes of exploitation. It makes special provision for the support, protection, rehabilitation, and even the regularization of immigration status of trafficked persons (including children). The Smuggling Protocol, which covers irregular migrants who consensually enter into a financial agreement to get assistance with border crossing, makes no special mention of children. Nor does it include the detailed package of differentiated human rights protections, including provision for accommodation, counseling, and even the possibility of long-term residence, that are included in the Trafficking Protocol. However, the Smuggling Protocol does also encourage states to take into account the basic human rights and needs of vulnerable migrants. Thus, while both Protocols are primarily driven by states' desires to curb and criminalize irregular migration, they also signal acknowledgment of the importance of human rights protections for vulnerable migrants, even where the latter have no regular or lawful migration status.

In practice the distinction between trafficked and smuggled migrants is problematic, since the divide between chosen and coercive exploitative situations is rarely clear-cut. Many migrants embark on commercial migration agreements by consent, seeking escape from oppressive or unlivable situations. However, in the course of the migration, they may find themselves in exploitative situations which are far more serious than those initially envisaged or to which they never consented at all. For children executing the wishes and plans of parents or other adults, this shift from a simple migration-related agreement to post-migration exploitation is pervasive. Many of the smuggling arrangements in which they are implicated rely on post-migration labor to repay the smuggling fee (with onerous interest if payments are late).

A Chinese girl smuggled to the U.S. by snakeheads whose fee was paid in advance by a relative of hers explained to the Federal Appeals Court: "If I can come to the U.S.... Then I can earn money to repay my relative."[13]

Often families can only afford to make a partial down payment, leaving the balance of the fee to be repaid to the smuggler from exploitative labor, arranged by the smuggling network. It seems that a number of unaccompanied and separated child asylum seekers are trapped in such situations, as sex workers, domestic workers, or manual labor in clothing or catering establishments. Such exploitative, often bonded, working situations bring the children within the definition of trafficking. They also constitute persecution and can justify asylum claims, though to date many advocates have been slow to recognize and act on this: see further chapter 7 below.

An additional issue arises in relation to the concept of "consent" itself as it applies to children. Even if children initiate, choose, or agree to the smuggled journeys they embark on (for whatever reasons, be they obedience to parents, fear, or desperation), the very fact of being engaged in exploitative labor after the journey to repay the smuggling fee brings them directly within the definition of "trafficking" set out in the Protocol. This is because, as a matter of international law and policy agreed by the signatory states, children are simply not considered capable of consenting to these exploitative situations. The Trafficking Protocol clearly states that "the recruitment, transportation, transfer, harboring, or receipt of a child for the purposes of exploitation shall be considered trafficking in persons" even if the child consents. To secure their fee, the transportation professionals (traffickers, snakeheads, or smugglers) have to ensure that the migrant children are converted into income generating commodities post-migra-

tion: ensuring that exploitation is therefore their purpose in arranging the transportation. Children can be considered smuggled and not trafficked if and only if, the smuggling fee is paid in full prior to the journey and the child has no responsibility to earn money to cover the fee. Trafficked children are entitled to the additional human rights protections set out in the Trafficking Protocol. This approach has been adopted by the trial division of the Canadian Federal Court:

In granting refugee status to a 13-year-old Chinese boy who had been smuggled into Canada as a result of arrangements made between the boy's parents and the smugglers, the court held that the child was persecuted by virtue of having been "trafficked," that he had a well-founded fear of future trafficking and that, as a matter of international law (irrespective of Chinese customs) he was incapable of "consenting" to being trafficked. The government had opposed the asylum claim on the basis that the child, an adolescent and therefore not "of tender years," had consented to being smuggled in the hope of economic betterment.[14]

■ **Other International Human Rights Instruments**
There are many other international human rights instruments that are relevant to the protection of unaccompanied and separated children. These have gained increasing prominence in recent years as states have increasingly accepted the need to extend the central tenets of the Refugee Convention—in particular the notion that people should not be returned (*refouled*) to a broader range of situations of grave personal danger. The Convention against Torture and the European Convention on Human Rights (ECHR) (Article 3) provide far-reaching protections against *refoulement*, since neither treaty restricts the protection to those who fall within the Refugee Convention definition. Rather it is enough

that the individual is at risk of serious ill treatment in his or her home country. Moreover, these protections are "non-derogable"—in other words, states cannot use national security or other public policy arguments to qualify the protection; it is absolute, irrespective of circumstances. This system includes children within its scope, just as it does irregular migrants or others with less than full legal capacity.

3.3 The Implementation of International Law in the Three States

Unaccompanied and separated migrant children have had to fit into legal systems designed by and for adults, systems that are complex, confusing, and adversarial. Our research suggests that none of the three countries studied has a coherent legal framework specifically directed at the international protection rights and welfare needs of children traveling alone. However, there is an emerging acknowledgment in all three countries that the phenomenon is significant and that it requires systematic attention. While the U.K. and the U.S. have already made some special legal and administrative provisions to address children's distinctive needs, Australian migration law has been slower to respond.

For different reasons, none of the three states in this study consider themselves fully bound by the most important of the international conventions relevant to children—the Convention on the Rights of the Child. Both the U.K. and Australia have ratified this Convention, but the U.K. has entered a reservation excluding immigration and nationality matters from compliance and Australia has failed to incorporate the CRC into its domestic law and so has not implemented the Convention in full. Indeed, the Australian courts have confirmed that

the "best interests of the child" principle enshrined in the Convention is neither a constraint on the detention of children nor the basis for requiring effective guardianship for unaccompanied and separated children seeking asylum.[15] As noted earlier, the U.S. has failed to ratify the Convention, which in practice places it in a similar position to Australia.[16] Since all three countries have signed this Convention, they should not legislate to contradict its provisions, even if they are not legally required to enforce it in full.[17]

In spite of these formal restrictions on the CRC's legal relevance, it has played and continues to play a role in all three countries, if only as a normative and widely accepted standard setter. In the U.K., the Court of Appeal has held that the CRC, as an element of international treaty law, is relevant in construing the government's human rights obligations when the European Convention on Human Rights is already engaged, as in cases where children are being detained with their parents in an immigration removal center.[18] This led Lord Justice Brooke to find that:

"If a court judges that in making his decision to detain, an immigration officer failed to take into account matters of material significance (viz he has overlooked relevant features of internal policy or paid no regard to the fact that the prospective detainee is a child protected by Art. 37(b) of the UN Convention on the Rights of the Child) then he will have strayed outside his wide ranging powers."[19]

Moreover, the internationally recognized "best interests of the child" principle is a useful measure for determining appropriate interview procedures for child asylum seekers.[20]

In the U.S., the government implicitly refers to the normative framework established by the CRC by using this principle in two sets of official immigration

manuals: the asylum officers' "Guidelines for Children's Asylum Claims" and the immigration judges' "Guidelines for Immigration Court Cases Involving Unaccompanied Alien Children." A weaker acknowledgment of this principle is to be found also in the Homeland Security Act 2002 (U.S.), which stipulates that "the interests" (albeit not quite the "best interests") of the child must be considered in decisions and actions relating to the care and custody of unaccompanied and separated children. In Australia, key cases concerned with the protection of unaccompanied and separated children seeking asylum have drawn on CRC principles in their analyses. The Convention was the centerpiece for a major report into the detention of children by immigration authorities in 2004[21] and was a clear basis for the eventual relaxation by the Australian government of its mandatory detention laws in July 2005.

For vulnerable children traveling without the care of a responsible adult, a pervasive problem in all three countries is the failure to link issues of child welfare with the structures of immigration or refugee law.

In Australia and the U.S., two quite discrete bodies of domestic law have developed—migration on the one hand and child welfare on the other. Neither fully encompasses the needs of unaccompanied and separated children seeking asylum, though in the U.S., as discussed later, there is a special status for immigrant children who have been abandoned, abused, or neglected. In general, migration law is adult-centered, and child welfare law privileges citizens, with the result that unaccompanied and separated children tend to fall through a series of significant cracks. This is not true in the U.K., where a local authority owes the same duty of care to any child within its geographical jurisdiction regardless of his or her immigration status. This was the point of principle behind the judgment in *Behre & Others v. London Borough of Hillingdon*[22] which held that asylum-seeking children and young people were entitled to that same provision as they approached and became adults as any other child looked after by a local authority.

■ **The United Kingdom**

Of the three countries studied, the U.K. has made the most significant and successful moves to recognize the special status of such children under international law. In addition to mechanisms for the protection of children who meet the international definition of refugee, it has established systems for the protection of all child migrants traveling without a responsible adult. However, unless the child is granted refugee status and while they remain minors, they will be at best granted discretionary leave for an initial period of one or three years dependent upon their country of origin. In the future they may also be returned to their countries of origin at the point at which their application for asylum is refused and any appeal rights exhausted if adequate care and reception arrangements have been made for them there.

Immigration control (including decisions relating to asylum seekers) is governed principally by the Immigration Act 1971 (U.K.), the Immigration and Asylum Act 1999 (U.K.), the Nationality, Immigration and Asylum Act 2002 (U.K.), and the Asylum and Immigration (Treatment of Claimants etc) Act 2004 (U.K.). The Immigration Act confers power on the Secretary of State for the Home Department to make rules governing arrival, entry, residence, and removal: see the Immigration Rules (U.K.). The Immigration and Asylum Act incorporates the majority of the U.K.'s obligations under the Refugee Convention, with the legislation passed in 2002 and 2004 refining or restricting interpretation of that Convention. The Human Rights Act 1998 (U.K.) incorporates in U.K. law the European Convention on Human Rights. By way of aside, it is worth noting that the U.K. has not enacted the UN Torture Convention into its domestic law. It is conceivable that the Torture Convention could provide additional protection to some children not eligible for refugee status, such as child soldiers who have been implicated in serious human rights violations and

violations of the laws of war during combat.

The responsibility for screening in-country applicants and for deciding whether or not to grant asylum to a child rests with the Immigration and Nationality Directorate of the Home Office. The Home Office's Immigration Service is responsible for accepting applications at ports of entry and local enforcements offices around the country and for the initial screening of such applicants. A child's eligibility for asylum depends on meeting the requirements of the definition of refugee in the 1951 Refugee Convention. When considering this definition, decision makers will also take into account the guidance contained in the 1979 UNHCR Handbook (see 3.2 above).

The Immigration Rules explicitly acknowledge the right of unaccompanied and separated children to apply for asylum and state that particular priority and care should be given to their cases. Special guidelines on dealing with unaccompanied and separated children have been issued by the Home Office to assist case workers and are updated from time to time. The actual procedures used by U.K.

officials also reflect the benchmarks of international best practice guidelines. Child asylum seekers are not interviewed directly beyond the initial screening; longer application deadlines are set for children as opposed to adults; special screening is done to identify at-risk children; and even where children are refused recognition as refugees the normal practice is to grant discretionary leave to remain for a time limited period which is dependent upon their country of origin.

The U.K. asylum system provides for a right of appeal in most cases to the Asylum and Immigration Tribunal. If the tribunal dismisses an initial appeal an unaccompanied or separated child can seek a reconsideration of this decision. If the tribunal maintains its refusal after this reconsideration, it may be possible in some cases to appeal on a point of law to the Court of Appeal or even to the House of Lords.

As noted earlier, U.K. practice is also governed by EU standards. Of particular relevance is the EU Directive "Laying down Minimum Standards for the Reception of Asylum Seekers." This embodies the spirit of the CRC, stating that the best interests of the child shall be a primary consideration for member states in all matters concerning children. The Home Office has adopted a number of internal policies to guide its case workers and immigration officers on best practice in children's cases.[23] The Immigration Appeal Tribunal (which has been known as the Asylum and Immigration Tribunal since April 2005) has also produced guidance for immigration judges (referred to as adjudicators prior to April 2005) in the form of "Adjudicator Guidance Note No. 8 April 2004 on Unaccompanied Children". The responsibility for ensuring that unaccompanied and separated children are suitably accommodated and protected has also been delegated to local authorities who already have the experience and skills to look after for children who have been separated from their parents, albeit for other reasons.

Questions about the general welfare and protection of such children in the U.K. are governed by the Children Act 1989 (U.K.). The responsibility to support, accommodate, and protect children established under this Act applies to all children irrespective of nationality or immigration status. Hence, under U.K. law, unaccompanied and separated children have the same rights to state protection as domestic children. This Act does not impose any duties on the Immigration Service or the Immigration and Nationality Directorate. Nor does it refer specifically to the rights of unaccompanied and separated children to accommodation and financial support. However, these rights have been confirmed by the High Court in a number of cases involving the judicial review of decisions by local authorities which had sought to limit the rights of unaccompanied and separated children. One area in which the U.K. parts company with the other countries studied is in the presumption that all children should have access to free legal assistance in their dealings with government authorities (see further chapters 4 and 5 below).

The legal obligations of the U.K. government to support, accommodate, and protect children are distributed across different ministries.[24] For example, the Department of Education and Skills is responsible for ensuring that unaccompanied and separated children are supported by local authorities while their protection applications are being decided. The Department of Constitutional Affairs provides public funding for legal representation and is responsible for the authority that hears asylum appeals. Despite this broad range of institutional responsibilities, no government entity or individual in the U.K. is charged with legal guardianship of unaccompanied and separated children.

The U.S. system for ensuring immigration control (including access to asylum and other protections available to people fleeing persecution) is the most complex of the three countries studied.

The U.S. provides several major forms of protection for those, including children, who apply for protection from persecution at a port of entry or from within the country. They are (i) asylum, for those claiming a well-founded fear of persecution; (ii) withholding of removal for those facing a probability of harm if returned; and (iii) relief under the 1984 Torture Convention.

The Refugee Act 1980 (U.S.) incorporates into U.S. law most of the provisions of the 1951 Refugee Convention, including the refugee definition and the prohibition against *refoulement*. This lies at the core of both asylum and the U.S. statutory "withholding of removal" protection. The latter remedy requires a higher burden of proof than asylum: claimants must show a *probability* as opposed to a *possibility* of threat to life or freedom if returned. "Withholding" is available to applicants who are ineligible for asylum, either because they do not fit into one of the five grounds set out in the refugee definition or because the authorities choose not to exercise their discretion in the applicant's favor.[25] Relief under the Torture Convention is limited to those threatened with torture, which covers only one subset of forms of "persecution." However, in cases where this threat is proved, the protection is available irrespective of the individual's personal conduct. Child soldiers, for example, might be excluded from a grant of asylum as war criminals, but not from Torture Convention relief (even if they have perpetrated war crimes).

A fourth form of protection for separated and unaccompanied children is encouraging, though it does not carry the weight of federal policy guidance. In a letter to the American Bar Association, the Chief of the Office of Border Patrol states:

Expedited removal (ER) is not applied to unaccompanied juveniles, citizens and nationals of Cuba and El Salvador, and aliens who are members of the class action settlement in American Baptist Churches v. Thornburg.... I have issued instructions, to every Border Patrol sector that is performing ER, reiterating that unaccompanied minors may not be processed for ER.[26]

While hopeful, this personal letter has neither the force of law nor policy. All these forms of relief are governed by the Immigration and Nationality Act (INA) which stipulates both the criteria that must be satisfied and the way in which the process is to be conducted. As in the other countries studied, U.S. administrators have supplemented the INA with various policy memos, guidelines, and specific pieces of legislation relevant to unaccompanied and separated children. The first official memorandum on the topic, relating to the release from detention of unaccompanied minors, was issued in 1984, in response to class action litigation initiated by child advocacy groups. Guidelines on children seeking asylum were issued in 1998. Four years later, the Child Status Protection Act 2002 (U.S.) was passed to protect from "aging out," children with age-sensitive applications for immigration status (including asylum and refugee status) derived from a parent's status. The legislation protected the child from becoming ineligible due to bureaucratic delays.[27]

In addition to these forms of protection, which apply to all protection seekers irrespective of age, a child-specific protection, called Special Immigrant Juvenile Status (SIJS), has been created for abused, abandoned, and neglected children who have sought refuge in the U.S. This allows for the grant of permanent protection (with conditions) for children

under the age of 18 who lack a parental caregiver. Other forms of protection are discussed in chapter 6 below.

Until 2002, the Immigration and Naturalization Service (INS) was responsible for both the immigration and the child welfare elements of unaccompanied and separated children's asylum cases. The conflict of interest inherent in this dual set of responsibilities —analogous to the dual roles vested in the Australian Minister for Immigration—resulted in *de facto* primacy for immigration enforcement over child welfare considerations. This was a much criticized aspect of the system for dealing with unaccompanied and separated children seeking asylum. As a result of far-reaching administrative changes consequent upon the terrorist attacks in the U.S. on 11 September 2001, the INS (once a part of the Department of Justice) was abolished, and its functions spread between two agencies: the very large new Department of Homeland Security (DHS) and the U.S. Department of Health and Human Services. Most

INS functions were divided between two sections of DHS, the service-oriented U.S. Citizenship and Immigration Services (CIS) and the enforcement-oriented U.S. Immigration and Customs Enforcement (ICE). Responsibility for the care and custody of "unaccompanied alien children" was transferred to the Office of Refugee Resettlement (ORR), a federal agency within the Department of Health and Human Services. This is a very positive development that has addressed the conflict of interest problem inherent in the previous system. The ORR has a social service mandate and a background in serving foreign-born children outside the care of their parents. The new U.S. structure is now similar to the U.K. division of competence between immigration and child welfare government departments. ORR is responsible for the care and custody of unaccompanied and separated children from the time they are handed over by the immigration enforcement agents until they are removed, released from detention, or awarded asylum or some other legal status.

In the U.S., unaccompanied and separated children can seek asylum in two ways. If they are in the U.S. legally or are in the country but have not come to the attention of the authorities, they can initiate the process by proactively presenting themselves to an immigration office and requesting asylum. This is known as the affirmative process. A corps of specially trained asylum officers within CIS decides most of the affirmative cases at first instance. The second method, known as the defensive process, is the only avenue open to children who attempt to enter the U.S. without legal documentation and who are apprehended either at a U.S. border, a port of entry, or within the U.S. territory (before making an affirmative claim). These applicants are not eligible for the affirmative asylum application process and are automatically placed in "removal proceedings" in the Immigration Court, where they may seek "deportation relief," in the form of asylum or withholding of removal. These proceedings take place in the setting of a court and are adversarial. The DHS is represented by a DHS trial attorney who operates as a prosecutor for immigration enforcement purposes. Unlike the government, children are not guaranteed a legal representative in Immigration Court. As with adults, children are permitted a legal advocate, but they must arrange for it themselves at no cost to the government. Immigration judges, under the Executive Office of Immigration Review (EOIR), decide these defensive applications.[28] They also decide appeals lodged by children whose original, affirmative applications have been refused by the asylum officer. The Board of Immigration Appeals (BIA—also part of EOIR) hears appeals against decisions of the immigration judge. Decisions by the Board of Immigration Appeals can be further appealed to the federal courts on points of law.

Responsibility for dealing with unaccompanied and separated child asylum seekers in the U.S. is thus shared between a bewildering range of federal agencies. The most important are the Asylum Office (for affirmative asylum claims); the EOIR (the Immigration Court system, which includes the immigration judges and the BIA); and the ORR. In addition, children seeking asylum may come into contact with several other branches of the DHS, such as the Customs and Border Protection service (that has initial contact with children at major ports of entry); the Office of Border Patrol (the agency that apprehends children at land borders between major ports of entry, for example, if they are attempting to enter through the Arizona desert); the Coast Guard (responsible for interdicting migrants at sea); and the Office of Chief Counsel in CIS (that deals with special protective visas for children who have been trafficked or subjected to serious human rights abuses). Some children, about whom little is known, also end up in the custody of the U.S. Marshal's Service, which is part of the U.S.

Department of Justice, if they are to serve as government witnesses against smugglers, traffickers, or other criminal agents. As we will explore further in chapters 4 to 6, there are many aspects of U.S. border control law and practice that are difficult to reconcile with the obligations the U.S. has assumed under international refugee law.

▪ Australia

In Australia, the structures and the procedures for dealing with unaccompanied and separated children are not as complex as those in either the U.K. or the U.S. Unfortunately, however, the relative simplicity of the system has not produced superior protection outcomes in practice. As noted earlier, there has been a tendency for Australia to adopt some of the worst features of U.S. law and practice, without interposing some of the ameliorating concessions made for immigrant children in that country.

Both the immigration process and refugee status determinations are governed by the Migration Act 1958 (Australia) and its attendant Migration Regulations 1994 (Australia). This legislation implements some of Australia's obligations under the Refugee Convention (including the definition of refugee) but makes few distinctions between adult and child applicants. No special provision is made for unaccompanied and separated children. For such children to gain protection as refugees, they must meet the same criteria as adult asylum seekers.[29] While the law has been changed in recent times to provide for the grant of both temporary and permanent visas to victims of trafficking (in response to international initiatives), again no special provision has been made within this scheme for children.

Towards the end of the 1990s, a steep rise in the number of asylum seekers arriving by boat without authority lead Australia to adopt various measures to discourage and deflect refugees from its territory.

These included the decision to grant temporary protection only (with no rights to family reunification) to refugees entering without the authorization of a visa. In 2001 a full-scale program was instituted for intercepting and deflecting boat people to other countries in the Asian-Pacific region. The program was modeled on U.S. interdiction practices and has had a particularly harsh impact on unaccompanied and separated children: see chapter 6 below. Few aspects of any of these measures can be described as either good international practice or even as being consistent with norms of international human rights law.

A major source of complaint with the Australian laws is that there is no longer a formalized regime for the grant of visas in cases involving special compassionate or humanitarian circumstances.[30] No legislation has been passed to give effect to the *non-refoulement* obligations assumed by Australia as a party to the UN Torture Convention. The only available mechanism for relief is for unsuccessful claimants to petition the Minister for Immigration to intercede personally. However, the minister cannot

be forced to consider a petition and a decision not to intervene cannot be reviewed by any court or other authority. This "residual discretion" in the minister is a matter of acute importance to unaccompanied and separated children who may be unable to meet the tough criteria for recognition as a Convention refugee.

As in the U.K., the process of setting, implementing, and enforcing immigration law and policy is the responsibility of a designated member of government (a minister). The administering authority is the Department of Immigration and Multicultural Affairs (DIMA),[31] which handles all matters pertaining to immigration status—from temporary visas through to the grant of Australian citizenship. As noted in chapter 2, the Minister for Immigration has held the titular position of guardian of unaccompanied and separated immigrant children since 1946. In practice, this has meant that immigration authorities have often been in the conflicted position of being charged with enforcing immigration control and simultaneously carrying the responsibility for the welfare of vulnerable immigrant children.[32] The Australian research suggests that the Minister for Immigration and the administration in general have not handled these dual functions well: see further chapter 4 below.

Therefore, in both the U.K. and Australia a serious protection deficit exists in the legal framework for protecting unaccompanied and separated child asylum seekers. In the U.K. no official legal guardian exists and local authorities merely have a duty to provide these children with accommodation and the support necessary to meet their physical, emotional, social, and intellectual needs while they are in the U.K. In Australia, no official child welfare body has responsibility for ensuring the best interests or nurturing needs of children entering the asylum process, although formal legal guardianship is vested in the Minister for Immigration and children are allocated advisers (or "immigration assistance") once they have been through an initial screening process. This is in spite of the fact that such children desperately need counsel at the time of entry since they must immediately express any fear of return or lose access to protective measures. It is only upon the release of the child from detention that state welfare authorities become involved (pursuant to Memoranda of Understanding with the federal government).

One of the greatest challenges facing asylum seekers in Australia is the statutory requirement that all non-citizens in the country hold a valid visa. Those entering without a visa *must* be detained until they either leave the country or are granted permission to remain. The scheme is known colloquially as Australia's "mandatory detention" regime.

It operates to require the incarceration of persons who hold no visa and who are not eligible for the grant of a visa, even where there is no reasonable possibility that the person might be deported or removed to another country. While children arriving without authorization are eligible for release from immigration detention, the general practice until late 2003 was to keep all un-visaed children—whether accompanied or not—in custody. It was not until late June 2005 that the Migration Act 1958 was amended to provide that children generally should not be detained.[33]

The policy of detaining unaccompanied and separated children meant in turn that they were subject to the same restrictive processing regime as adults. The Migration Act 1958 contains no provisions requiring government officials to provide "application assistance," and actually stipulates that non-citizens have no right to an application form or to an adviser unless they request it. The practical ramifications of this regime are that, in order to

access Australia's asylum procedures, a child who enters Australia without a valid visa must demonstrate *without legal assistance of any kind* that he or she is a person in respect of whom Australia owes "protection obligations": see further 4.2 below.

Governmental policies regarding the interpretation of the Migration Act 1958 and the Migration Regulations 1994 are set out in various policy documents, of which the most important is the Procedures Advice Manual (PAM) and the Migration Series Instructions (MSI) (a form of interim policy direction). The PAMs and MSIs are guidelines addressed to officers administering migration law, in particular decision makers who are delegates of the Immigration Minister. The first occasion on which DIMIA (DIMA's predecessor) outlined the specific care arrangements required for unaccompanied and separated children in policy guidelines was in September 2002. This was several years after the arrival of most of the children who have sought asylum alone in recent years.[34] These guidelines address the position of children under the age of 18 who make claims for protection in their own right rather than as part of a family unit, covering such matters as applications for a protection visa, processing claims for protection, assessing claims, determining age, and post-decision appeals. The guidelines now stipulate that all minors (including unaccompanied wards) should be received by staff with appropriate expertise in child welfare. The guidelines also state that a "mentor" in the form of a "suitable adult" may be appointed from within the detainee community to provide "guidance and support" for a child. These mentors are not responsible for the "care and safety" of the unaccompanied ward. Although a good idea in theory, the fact remains that children are still not appointed a formal guardian apart from the Immigration Minister or detention center manager during the initial reception process. Nor do the guidelines provide for the appointment of a legal adviser, or for anyone to explain the nature of the process to the child, until after the "screening in" process is completed. The guidelines are silent on the critical matter of how the definition of refugee should be interpreted in cases involving children.

The care of children in immigration detention (until the 2005 changes) was governed by the Immigration Detention Standards. These standards were spelled out in the contract between the Immigration Department and relevant detention center management companies.[35] These stipulated that the "special needs of particular groups or individuals must be identified and addressed."[36] Unaccompanied and separated children constituted one such group. The use of private companies to perform functions required of government by statute has been the subject of considerable criticism by child-rights advocates.

The Migration Act 1958 provides for administrative appeals in respect of most decisions affecting unaccompanied and separated children. For those seeking protection as refugees, the main appeal authority is the Refugee Review Tribunal (RRT). This tribunal is described as "quasi-inquisitorial," and operates with single (non-judicial) members who conduct hearings by asking claimants a series of questions. The RRT followed DIMA's lead and produced guidelines applicable to separated children in 2002. The tribunal also seems to have instituted training programs for members in that year.[37] These guidelines address the giving of oaths, the competency of minors to give evidence, rights of representation, the elicitation of evidence, the assessment of evidence, and the particular issues associated with child witnesses.[38]

Unlike the Migration Act 1958 (and attendant Regulations), guidelines, Procedures Advice Manuals, and instructions are not binding on the delegates of the minister. As explored further in chapters 4 and 5, difficulty of enforcement leads inevitably to uneven applications of the measures outlined. Moreover,

the policy guidelines for children are not nearly as detailed as those prepared on issues relating to women and to victims of torture and trauma.[39]

Another problem in the Australian context has been the adequacy of external oversight of the immigration process. Of particular concern in this regard is the trend in successive governments to restrict access to judicial review—the most important and immediate recourse for individuals affected by the operation of the system. Following a series of scandals involving the wrongful detention and even removal of Australian citizens and permanent residents, the government moved to confer a more formal supervisory function on the federal ombudsman: by 2006 hopeful signs were emerging that regard might be had to the recommendations made by this office on the handling of individual cases. Although Australia has signed optional Protocols enabling individuals to make complaints to both the UN Human Rights Committee and the Committee Against Torture, there is no requirement under Australian law that the opinions issued by those committees have any binding effect in Australia.[40]

Having said this, it is fair to say that DIMA is one of the most highly scrutinized government agencies. Recent years have seen the publication of numerous reports by parliamentary committees, the Human Rights and Equal Opportunity Commission, the federal ombudsman, the Australian National Audit Authority, and privately appointed commissioners. DIMA points out also that "UNHCR plays an active role in accordance with its mandate in overseeing all aspects of Australia's arrangements to implement its obligations under the Refugees Convention, including issues relating to asylum seekers. The UNHCR also plays an active role in relation to specific cases."[41] If the changes made to the system in 2006 are any indication, the many inquiries and critical reports may ultimately be having an impact of sorts.

3.4 Conclusion

This brief summary of the legal and institutional framework for dealing with unaccompanied and separated child asylum seekers in the three countries studied highlights several key points. First, it is clear that in each country domestic concerns about immigration control have tended to predominate in spite of the acceptance of international obligations respecting the human rights of vulnerable children. With the exception of the U.K. (which stands apart somewhat in this regard), the default starting point is immigration enforcement: the acute needs of traumatized children emerge as a secondary consideration. However, in none of the three countries studied is an independent or effective guardian, "trusted adult," or advocate routinely allocated to act in *loco parentis* when the child is first identified. As a result, no entity is specifically charged with protecting the best interests of these children and, among other consequences, access to competent legal representation is compromised and inconsistent." Second, within the legal system for allocating asylum, no coherent or streamlined child-specific processes have been established to ensure priority, special attention, and child-sensitive approaches to children's cases. Guidelines or instructions addressed to government agents working with unaccompanied and separated children suggest accommodations or modifications within the adult asylum system, rather than an alternative child-targeted procedure for arriving at just decisions. Again, compliance with the benchmarks established under international law has been uneven across the three countries studied.

Having said this, the experience over the past decade with unaccompanied and separated child migration has left clear traces in all three countries, forcing institutional recognition of the need to link enforcement and child protection measures. In the

U.K., for example, the normal (adult) legal framework for asylum has been modified piecemeal over time to take account of the specific needs of children. While problems of identification and age determination, exclusion from long-term protection, and discrimination in access to comprehensive care provision remain (see chapter 4 below), the U.K. legal framework certainly reflects a serious engagement with the child protection issues that arise with this population of asylum seekers.

In the U.S., too, several innovative legal measures are gradually being developed to complement the adult-centered legal framework and afford special provision for unaccompanied and separated children in need of protection. Some immigration statuses (such as the Special Immigrant Juvenile Status visa, the T-Visa and the U-Visa: see chapter 8 below) are targeted at particularly vulnerable categories of children, such as children who have been trafficked, or children who have been abused, abandoned, or neglected.

Later in this report we document some innovative jurisprudence expanding the scope of refugee protection for child-specific persecution which is being developed in immigration and appeal courts across the three countries studied: see chapter 7. We also describe an innovative and experimental local scheme in the U.S. to allocate specially trained child advisers to provide guardian-like assistance through the asylum process to unaccompanied and separated children who are in detention. This pilot program may possibly seed a greatly improved national system in the U.S., something that child advocates have been pressing for in the past several years. Finally, it is noteworthy, as much for the substance as for the recognition of current gaps within the U.S. system, that two sets of child-specific guidelines have been officially promulgated by the DHS and EOIR to encourage decision makers—in Asylum Offices and Immigration Courts—to attend to child-specific needs and interests.

In Australia, the system has throughout been characterized by a rigid imbalance between the migration and child welfare domains of law, with unaccompanied and separated child asylum seekers governed firmly by the former. This has had devastating consequences for child asylum seekers in the area of processing protection claims, which we document in chapters 4 and 5 below. Despite acknowledgment of the obligations arising from the Refugee Convention, migration law in Australia has been, and to a certain extent continues to be, focused on exclusion and deterrence. The mismatch between international standards and domestic law drew this comment from an Australian judge:

"The question of unaccompanied minors seeking asylum is a pressing, current issue…. The [Migration] Act provides little in the way of the kinds of protections contemplated by the UNHCR Guidelines. At the very least, there is a case for considering the provision of legal advice and assistance to unaccompanied minors up to and including the point of judicial review. It is of concern that the application for judicial review in this case was lodged by a 15-year-old non-citizen and lodged out of time, thus depriving him of such limited rights of review as he would otherwise have enjoyed." [42]

The child welfare regime, meanwhile, is addressed to citizen children and no senior child welfare official has comprehensive child protection responsibilities for child asylum seekers in Australia. As a result, unaccompanied and separated children are subjected to punitive regimes developed for adults, and lack any child-specific legal protections. It may be that recently promulgated guidelines will soften and improve this situation. The situation is nevertheless a stark illustration of the extent to which the interests of vulnerable children can be (and indeed have been) subordinated to states' concerns about border control and migration management, even where human rights violations are evident and acute.

Endnotes

1   Committee on the Rights of the Child. General Comment No. 6: Treatment of separated and unaccompanied children outside their country of origin. UN, 2005. CRC/GC/2005/6.

2   See Vienna Convention on the Law of Treaties, Article 18.

3   See, however, the discussion in part 3.3. The U.S. has signed but not ratified the CRC. The U.K. has made a reservation to the Convention in respect of immigration matters. For its part, Australia has been slow to implement the terms of the instrument in its domestic laws.

4   Note that Article 22 of the CRC treats as "refugee children" both recognized refugees and asylum-seeker children whose legal status has yet to be determined.

5   General Comment No. 6, Ibid, Endnote 1.

6   U.S.-Canada Agreement Regarding Asylum Claims Made at Land Borders. 5 September 2002. See Joint

statement on Cooperation on Border Security and Regional Migration Issues, Adopted by the Solicitor General of Canada, the Minister of Citizenship and Immigration, and the Attorney General of the U.S. on 3 December 2001. Available at http://www.cic.gc.ca/english/press/01/0126-pre.html.

7   Finley, Bruce. "Death of a deportee: Back in Guatemala, teen slain by gang he tried to escape." *Denver Post*, 5 April 2004. See also: *Seeking Asylum Alone, United States.* Cambridge, MA: Bhabha and Schmidt, 2006. (U.S. Report.) 132.

8   This organization is governed in part by an Executive Committee which meets each year and which issues "Recommendations" about the interpretation of the Refugee Convention and about the many issues that arise relating to the administration of the instrument. These recommendations and the guidelines or policies that UNHCR publish in response are regarded as "soft" (non-binding) international law. UNHCR has addressed the plight of unaccompanied and separated children, acknowledging both their substantive protection needs and the necessity of adapting administrative procedures so as to enable children to tell their stories.

9   Interview with David Manne. Crock, Mary. *Seeking Asylum Alone, Australia.* Sydney: Themis Press, 2006. (Australian Report.) 11.1.

10 For information on the UNHCR's Executive Committee, see www.unhcr.ch/cgi-bin/texis/vtx/excom.

11 Global Commission on International Migration. *Migration in an interconnected world: New directions for action.* Available at http://www.gcim.org/en/finalreport.html.

12 Bhabha, Jacqueline and Finch, Nadine. *Seeking Asylum Alone, United Kingdom.* Cambridge, MA: Bhabha and Finch, 2006. (U.K. Report.), 11.5.

13 See *Zhang v. Gonzalez*, 9th Cir. (26 May 2005), 11.

14 *Bian v. Canada* (Minister of Citizenship and Immigration) Federal Court of Canada—Trial Division, Judgment of Givson J, 11 December 2000—IMM 1640–00, IMM 932–00.

15 See *Odhiambo v. MIMA* (2002) 122 FCR 29; *X v. MIMA* (1999) 92 FCR 524 and other cases discussed in Crock, Mary. "Lonely Refuge: Judicial Responses to Separated Children Seeking Refugee Protection in Australia." *Law in Context* 22 (2005): 120. Note that changes were made to the law in June 2005 with the insertion into the Migration Act 1958 (Cth) of a provision stating that in principle children should only be detained as a last resort: see s 4AA, inserted by Act No 79 of 2005, opn 29 June 2005.

16 Note that under U.S. law, treaties that are ratified automatically pass into domestic law. Under Australian law, treaties must be signed, ratified, and then incorporated into domestic law through the passage of an Act of Parliament: *Minister for Immigration and Ethnic Affairs v. Teoh* (1995) 183 CLR 273 at 287 (Mason CJ and Deane J, Gaudron J concurring).

17 See Vienna Convention on the Law of Treaties, Article 18.

18 *ID & Others v. Home Office* [2005] EWCA Civ 38. See also *T v. United Kingdom* (2000) 30 EHRR 121 at [76].

19 *ID & Others v. The Home Office* [2005] EWCA Civ 38 at [111].

20 U.S. Department of Justice. "Guidelines for Children's Asylum Claims." 10 December 1998. 2.

21 Human Rights and Equal Opportunity Commission. *A Last Resort? National Inquiry into Children in Immigration Detention.* 2004. Available at http://www.hreoc.gov.au/human_rights/children_detention_report/report/pdf.htm.

22 *Behre & Others v. London Borough of Hillingdon* [2003] EWHC 2075 (Admin).

23 Three such government guidelines at present: The IND has re-drafted its "Asylum Policy Instruction on Children". In addition the Immigration Service has published guidance entitled "Best Practice: Unaccompanied Minors" and *"Children Arriving in the U.K."* for immigration officers at ports of entry and enforcement officers and the Immigration and Nationality Directorate has issued guidance on *"Processing Applications from Children"* as part of its Operational Processes Manual for its caseworkers. A more comprehensive set of Children's Guidelines produced by a leading U.K. immigration practitioners NGO has not been adopted by the Home Office but it has been circulated to all

immigration judges sitting in the Asylum and Immigration Tribunal and been distributed to many legal practitioners and non-governmental organizations. See Immigration Law Practitioners Association (ILPA). *Working with Children and Young People Subject to Immigration Control.* London: ILPA, 2004.

24 Australia has a similar system. Elected members of parliament are allocated responsibility for the conduct of departments. By contrast, the administration of state functions is carried out by agencies in the U.S., under the umbrella of large state departments, such as the Department of Justice or the State Department. Appointed officials head these departments.

25 See Anker, Deborah E. *The Law of Asylum in the United States.* 3rd ed. Boston: Refugee Law Center, 1999. 2.

26 Letter from David V. Aguilar, Chief, Office of Border Patrol, CBP/DHS, addressed to, and in response to a letter from, Robert D. Evans, Director, Governmental Affairs Office, American Bar Association. 14 June 2005.

27 Ironically, the Child Status Protection Act only served to protect children attached to a parent, without extending similar age-out protection to children who are alone. There appears even to be a double standard here, in that the Child Status Protection Act raised the age of eligibility from 18 to 21, for children attached to a parent, while the Unaccompanied Alien Child Protection Act (pending in the U.S. Congress), ostensibly created to protect unaccompanied children, would set a maximum age of eligibility at 18 for Special Immigrant Juvenile Status applicants, who by definition lack a parental caregiver.

28 EOIR is a part of the Department of Justice.

29 The provisions relevant to the grant of humanitarian visas are set out in Schedule 2 of the Migration Regulations 1994, and are subject to ss 40, 65 of the Migration Act 1958.

30 This has been the case since 1989 when the Migration Act 1958 and Regulations were transformed by the codification of decision making into rules that leave few discretions in decision makers to deal with unusual or hard cases. See Crock, Mary. *Immigration and Refugee Law in Australia.* Sydney: Federation Press, 1998. Chapter 3.

31 Between 1997 and 2006, this department included the portfolio of Indigenous Affairs and so was known as the Department of Immigration, Multicultural and Indigenous Affairs (DIMIA).

32 Note that where children are not placed in immigration detention, the minister has delegated the guardianship function to state and territory welfare authorities. This matter is discussed further below.

33 See Migration Amendment (Detention Arrangements) Act 2005 (Australia), amending the Migration Act 1958.

34 The policy guidelines for both the care of unaccompanied children and for their processing are discussed in the Australian Report, Ibid, Endote 8, 6.3.

35 The management of the immigration detention facilities in Australia was privatized in 1997. During the period relevant to the young people in this project, the contractor was Australian Correctional Management Limited, a subsidiary of the global Group 4 detention company. In 2003–2004 a new tender was called and let to GSL. See DIMIA. *Immigration Detention Contract.* Available at http://www.dimia.gov.au/detention/group4/index.htm. Accessed 10 October 2005.

36 See http://www.immi.gov.au/detention/group4/002_schedule_2.pdf. Para 1.10. Accessed 11 February 2005.

37 See the RRT's "Guidelines on the Giving of Evidence by Children." 2002.

38 On the practices adopted by the RRT, see chapter 5 below.

39 On this point, see Human Rights and Equal Opportunity Commission. *A Last Resort? National Inquiry into Children in Immigration Detention.* 2004. 7.5.2 and 7.6.1.

40 See Charlesworth, Hilary et al. "Deep Anxieties: Australia and the International Legal Order." *Sydney Law Review* 25 (2004): 436–437.

41 Letter from Robert Illingworth to Mary Crock. 10 March 2006. On file with authors.

42 Australian Report, Ibid, Endote 8, 4.3.

CHAPTER 4

Law and Policy in State Practice:

The Reception, Identification, and Treatment of Unaccompanied and Separated Children

In this chapter we examine the processes in each country for access, initial reception and identification of unaccompanied and separated children. We review the procedures the three countries use for identifying children—as children at risk and as children *per se* (determining age). We describe the arrangements made for guardianship, and care; and the laws and policies governing immigration detention.

4.1 Access to Territory: Border Controls and In-Country Apprehension

The point at which an unaccompanied or separated child first comes to the attention of government authorities significantly affects how well that child is treated by a destination state. Both the U.S. and Australia have active maritime interdiction programs,[1] and available evidence suggests that children apprehended after entry generally fared better than those apprehended before they reached the country (for example, at sea or while boarding a plane) or at the point of entry. The U.K. by contrast does not patrol surrounding waters. However, all three countries engage operatives in foreign countries to "pre-screen" individuals wishing to make their way to their territories. The U.K. places immigration officers at ports and Eurostar railway stations in France and Belgium and at some airports in other countries to check the immigration status of those wishing to travel to the U.K. If travelers are not eligible they are simply turned back without having the opportunity of claiming asylum. The U.K. Immigration Service is not presently recording whether any of those refused permission to travel are unaccompanied or separated children.[2] The lack of oversight of the foreign operations make it difficult to assess definitively the concessions made for vulnerable children, but the few indications available suggest that the regimes studied do not take account of child-specific needs in practice: see further chapter 7 below.

"When I arrived in Waterloo [at Waterloo Station, London] I was so confused—no one explained what to do. I did not ask either. I don't know what I was thinking of but for months we were all waiting to get out by any way possible, but we never talked about after getting out."[3]

There is no age limit for claiming asylum; in theory, therefore, children are in the same position as adult refugees. The practice, however, is that children often slip through without being noticed. There are two difficulties with the legislative apparatus at this preliminary stage. First, none of the domestic legal systems studied provide any advice or briefings for children entering the asylum system. Children may not know what they are applying for or what process they are entering.

"The words for applying for asylum in my language are translated as 'giving up your hand' [surrendering]. That was what I was told to do once I got to London. The picture I had was that I would surrender to someone with guns."[4]

Second, as we have noted already, the law and policy in each country is so focused on immigration control that the particular protection needs of children *as refugees* are not recognized. A child-rights perspective is absent and instead the officials who first encounter the unaccompanied and separated children seeking asylum have to balance a dual role. They are charged with enforcing immigration control but they also have a responsibility to identify and if necessary protect the children from harm. In practice none of the three countries studied deals adequately with this dual responsibility at the point of arrival. This is why so many trafficked children slip through the cracks, an issue to which we return later in this report.

▪ The United Kingdom

Of the three countries studied, the U.K. comes closest to adopting a child-rights perspective: child protection concerns are written into U.K. procedure from the outset. If a child is under 10 years of age, the child is not be given a formal screening interview but is merely asked a few questions to find out who he or she is and who they are traveling with. If it is clear that he or she is alone or if there is any doubt about the suitability of any adult who may be traveling with or meeting the child, he or she will be placed immediately in local authority care and will be entitled to government funded legal representation. It will be the responsibility of the legal representative to ascertain whether an asylum application should be made on behalf of the child or whether some other sort of application under immigration or family law legislation would be more appropriate. If a child is aged 10 years or more, he or she will be given a preliminary screening interview, designed to elicit basic identity information and to ascertain whether the child has passed through a safe third country en route to the U.K. This interview is conducted on the day of arrival or shortly thereafter by a specially trained immigration officer, in the presence of an interpreter and a "responsible adult".

Despite these child-sensitive elements, the U.K. system still has its flaws. Though unaccompanied and separated children are entitled to free legal representation at screening interviews, in practice they are unlikely to have time to instruct a solicitor if they are screened at ports of entry. Unless evidence of trafficking or some other special circumstance emerges, the screening interview is meant to be restricted to preliminary information and not to delve into the substance of the child's case. However, this is not always the situation in practice. Some immigration officers question unaccompanied and separated children about the substance of their applications on the pretext that there is a doubt about their nationality or age.

"They asked me who my president was, what flag of my country is, why I have problems and why my father was killed by the government. I felt very bad so I started crying. At that point the Home Office interviewer stopped the interview. I was afraid because I didn't understand what asylum and refugees were.... She kept asking me questions that I didn't understand."[5]

In the U.K. the Immigration and Nationality Directorate (IND) is obliged to notify the Refugee Council's Panel of Advisers of all children, including age-disputed children who claim asylum. The IND or Immigration Service will also contact social services so that they provide accommodation for any child. The Panel is responsible for obtaining legal representation, if the child does not already have a representative. New safeguards proposed by the Legal Services Commission in 2005 would ensure that every child applying for asylum at the Asylum Screening Unit in Croydon or Liverpool would be allocated a legal representative from a panel of suitably qualified contractors who would represent them at any screening interview. These on site legal representatives would then refer the unaccompanied or separated children on to immigration and child law specialists from a specialists' panel who would then take their cases further and deal with both immigration and child law aspects of their cases. While promising this scheme was not yet in operation in early 2006.

▪ The United States

In the U.S., the system for dealing with unaccompanied and separated children on arrival is flawed and problematic. The agencies that first come into contact with these children at the point of entry to the U.S. have enforcement mandates and lack well-articulated, child-specific procedures. Generally, only children who are completely alone come to the attention of the authorities, not those who are accompanied by non-parental adults. The research for this study did not (despite requests) uncover any written rules to assist Coast Guard, Border Patrol, and Customs and Border Protection officers interviewing children in deciding on the *bona fides* of accompanying adults. Nor is training in child welfare and child development provided despite the complex assessments required. For example, if a child is traveling with an "uncle," how should the officer assess the validity of the relationship or whether that adult should remain present during an interview with the child?

An asylum officer who conducts preliminary screenings of would-be entrants highlighted this difficulty and recalled one case where a mother, who was present during a child's interview to provide moral support, had in fact given the child "dirty looks" or said "that's stupid" to the child's comments.[6]

Asylum officers receive thorough training on interviewing children. However, asylum officers are not the first officials to encounter unaccompanied and separated children, nor is more in-depth training provided to officers who are.

Unaccompanied and separated children apprehended by Border Patrol are supposed to be referred promptly to Office of Refugee Resettlement (ORR) for care, after which their legal case will proceed before the Immigration Court. However, there are disturbing exceptions to this in practice. One *pro bono* attorney working in Arizona reported that children held in the Tucson sector are taken to Immigration Court while still in Border Patrol custody, where they appear in court without an attorney and most often have removal orders issued against them. They are finally transferred to ORR custody after this process. The children themselves report being advised by Immigration and Customs Enforcement (ICE) agents that they have no chance of winning in court, and that if they fight their case in court they will remain in jail for months or years.[7] These practices are an affront to due process and effectively deny such children access to meaningful protection.

While border enforcement agents do not engage in full status-determination interviews with children, they are the first source of information gathering

with children and their actions are consequential. One widespread current U.S. practice at the border is particularly worrisome. Children who are picked up by Customs and Border Protection (CBP) or the Border Patrol trying to enter the U.S. without permission are usually given a choice by their arresting officers: they may either sign a "voluntary return" form or elect to go before a judge to seek permission to remain in the U.S. No attorney or adviser is present to counsel the child regarding the consequences of this critical decision.

Children who choose a hearing with a judge may apply for asylum, or they may choose voluntary departure if they are not eligible for legal relief. However, here again children are penalized for their dependency on adults. In a practice that appears to vary from jurisdiction to jurisdiction, some ICE districts require children with a voluntary departure order to pay for their own travel home, while other districts waive this requirement for children. When children are required to pay for their own travel and cannot do so, they must be issued a formal removal order by an immigration judge in order for the government to cover their return travel.[8] This results in a permanent removal order that precludes reentry to the U.S. for 10 years. Ultimately, the outcome is the same for the government either way, but it is the children who are penalized for financial dependence beyond their control.

One child interviewed described her experience in the Border Patrol office by saying, "Lots of paper; I didn't know what the papers said, but I signed them."[9] Clearly, children should be allowed to speak with an attorney and a family member before being made to decide whether to choose between voluntary return or a hearing before a judge. Moreover, in cases where a child initially opts for a court hearing but later changes his or her mind and decides to choose voluntary return after consultation with legal representatives, this should be accepted expeditiously, without requiring the child—as at present—to go through lengthy court proceedings.

Another worrying practice relates to the classification of children as "unaccompanied." An attorney working in Arizona reported that Border Patrol agents are sometimes overly generous in classifying a child as accompanied, even when stated relationships are dubious or distant, so that the duly classified child can be subjected to expedited removal procedures.[10]

However, current U.S. procedure is not entirely neglectful of children's special needs. One positive aspect is that, though U.S. immigration law provides for "expedited removal proceedings" for entrants who are not in possession of proper entry documents, unaccompanied and separated children normally bypass these proceedings unless they have been involved in criminal activity or have previously been removed, excluded, or deported from the U.S.

This is a positive acknowledgment of child-specific circumstances and an illustration that child-sensitive timing is not synonymous with speed. Though delays and open-ended decision making without a set timetable are unacceptable and disturbing for children, so too are procedures which hurry the process and militate against careful preparation of the child's case.

Despite the general exemption from preliminary screening procedures for unaccompanied and separated children, some specialized U.S. entry procedures contradict this. The Visa Waiver Program (VWP) enables citizens of 27 specific countries to enter the U.S. for up to 90 days without first securing a visa.[11] Those who enter under the VWP cannot change their status once in the U.S. unless it is to apply for asylum. Surprisingly, children entering under the VWP, as well as child stowaways on boats or planes, are not exempt from pre-screening procedures. Instead they undergo an exacting interview to establish their fear and thus their eligibility to claim asylum at all. Furthermore, again for no good reason, these groups of children are not eligible to apply for protective statuses such as the Special Immigrant Juvenile Status (for abused, abandoned or neglected children needing foster care) or T-Visas (for trafficking victims)—asylum is the only form of relief available to them. Not only do these provisions contradict the principle of excluding children from pre-screening measures; also, given children's general lack of responsibility for their migration arrangements, these disqualifications seem inappropriate and clearly against the child's best interests.

■ **Care and Custody**

As far as the physical care and custody of unaccompanied and separated children seeking asylum is concerned, the three countries studied vary considerably. In the U.S., custody will first rest with either the Customs and Border Protection if the child is at a port of entry, or the Border Patrol if the child attempts entry elsewhere along the border; both agencies lack clear policy for addressing the specific protection needs of children in their custody. The responsibility for unaccompanied and separated children passes (or is supposed to pass) from these immigration enforcement authorities to the ORR, the welfare-oriented refugee resettlement authority, within 72 hours of apprehension. This transfer of custody lasts until the child is removed from the U.S. or released into the care of relatives or other carers. While an improvement over pre-2002 arrangements, in which the Immigration and Naturalization Service remained the custodian of such children, advocates still complain of mistreatment and inadequate care of children during the initial period in which they remain in the hands of enforcement agencies such as Border Patrol or Customs and Border Protection.

A Department of Homeland Security (DHS) Office of Inspector General report expresses concern about the length of time that children are spending in Border Patrol and ICE detention, before transfer to ORR custody, noting that 35% of children's cases examined exceeded the mandatory maximum of 24 hours in an initial CBP processing facility.[12] Regarding children detained by ICE, the report noted:

Our analysis showed that 224 (12.1 percent) of the 1,857 juveniles were held longer than five days before placement in a longer-term detention facility. According to the…data, these lengths of time ranged from 6 to 225 days. The records did not reflect the reasons for the delays or who approved them.[13]

This Office of Inspector General (OIG) data is unsettling considering that Border Patrol policy is that children should not be held more than 12 hours at Border Patrol stations (as opposed to 24 hours), and that three days (rather than five days) is usually the maximum under the *Flores* Stipulated Settlement Agreement that children should be held in ICE custody before placement in an appropriate facility.[14] While shackling children in federal custody has been reduced, it has not disappeared. One advocate reports that children in ORR custody held at the Marin County Juvenile Hall are shackled when they come to Immigration Court.[15]

▪ Australia

In Australia children have no right to an adviser, "responsible adult," or any other representative at the initial, "screening in" stage, even though the screening interview is recorded and establishes whether a full asylum claim can be made. Here, it is not just a question of lack of assistance with an unfamiliar procedure: the Australian system mandates detention of all non-citizens in the country without a valid visa. This deprivation of liberty without any prior opportunity for legal advice affects all asylum seekers, including children. In theory, under Australian law, children can be released from detention if it is in their best interests, but during the period relevant to the children interviewed for the Australian Report, this had not occurred. Australian law thus in effect has required the mandatory detention of all unaccompanied and separated child asylum seekers at the point of arrival. As noted earlier, important changes were introduced in late June 2005 such that children are no longer placed in immigration detention centers but are released into "community housing" arrangements. The arrangements for the screening of unaccompanied and separated children for refugee claims remain unchanged, however.

Where an unaccompanied or separated child arrives in Australia without a visa or is otherwise refused "immigration clearance" at point of entry,[16] the child is taken immediately into what is known as "questioning" and then "separation" detention.

The process deliberately takes a person aside so as to allow immigration officials to interrogate that person in relation to issues such as identity and purpose of visit, without permitting contact with anyone who might provide "coaching" on how to get through immigration controls. No special arrangements are made for children. If the nationality of the child or the circumstances of their arrival suggest that they may wish to claim asylum, they are referred for what is known as a "screening in" interview: see further chapter 5 below.

Since late June 2005, longer-term detention of children has ceased to be the norm. The likelihood is that the Australian system will operate in the future in much the same way as its U.S. counterpart. While children are referred to (state) welfare authorities under delegation from the Immigration Minister, children "screened out" of the refugee process will remain at risk of being removed from the country without gaining access to advice of any kind.

■ Conclusion and Recommendations

The contrast between the legal systems of the three countries is marked. In the U.K., where the screening process is simply a mechanism for eliciting basic information about a child, a protective, non-adversarial adult is required to be present. The child is then placed in local authority care while he or she instructs a legal representative and provides the details to substantiate his or her asylum claim. In the U.S., the unaccompanied or separated child is placed initially in the care of the immigration enforcement authorities without access to child welfare services, legal advice, or representation for the first 72 hours. Within the first three days, children may agree to "voluntary return" without the benefit of legal advice. In the case of Mexican children, they may simply be returned across the U.S./Mexico border without formality or any record of their arrival. In Australia, on the other hand, the screening inter-

view is a substantive process designed to establish whether the child has a *prima facie* case for seeking asylum. It is only if the child successfully articulates a need for protection at this first screening interview that he or she can carry on to the next stage of the asylum procedure. Both the U.S. and Australian systems thus present children with key hurdles in their access to asylum protection at very early stages in the process, when their vulnerability and need for adult guidance are greatest.

In Australia and the U.S. the inadequacies of the initial government contact with unaccompanied and separated children should be remedied. The identification of unaccompanied and separated children should immediately engage the welfare agencies of the state in question. Such children should only be interviewed after being given access to independent advice.

4.2 The Identification of Unaccompanied and Separated Children

Perhaps the most important step in the establishment of a system in which the human rights of children are safeguarded is the identification of a person as a child and as a child at risk.

■ Identifying Children At Risk

Of the three countries studied, the U.K. is the only one that seems to have a program for training immigration officials in the identification of children likely to be at risk. In this regard, the U.K. stands out for the efforts that it has made to institute programs to target trafficking in children through training of in-country border officials on profiling children who may have been trafficked. Also, research has been undertaken at Heathrow Airport between August and November 2003, as part of a study of child migration entitled *Paladin Child*, into whether children arriving alone to meet adults who were not their parents may have been trafficked. The research was carried out by Reflex (a multi agency task force set up by the U.K. government to tackle organized immigration crime) in partnership with the Immigration Service, the Metropolitan Police, London Borough of Hillingdon, and the National Society for the Prevention of Cruelty to Children. It did not identify a high proportion of trafficked children but did alert the authorities to the need to adopt further safeguards.[17]

In both the U.S. and in Australia, as noted earlier, it is generally only children who travel completely alone who come to the attention of the authorities—not those who are accompanied by non-parental adults. Indeed, the Australian research indicates that no child has been identified at the point of arrival as a victim of trafficking, a fact that gives rise to at least some concern that officers may not be identifying separated children traveling in the company of unrelated adults.

■ Recommendation

Both the U.S. and Australian governments should institute training and operational programs to assist immigration officials to identify separated children who may be being trafficked or otherwise in an abusive situation.

■ Age Determinations

In spite of the differences and deficiencies in the treatment of unaccompanied and separated children in the three countries studied, minority is a basis for preferential treatment of one kind or another in each. Our research suggests that the more concrete the benefits flowing from identification of minority, the greater the controversy that has developed over the determination of age. In the U.K., children are given discretionary leave to remain on the basis of their minority for at least one year where there are no adequate care or reception arrangements in place in their countries of origin (see 4.5 below). As a result, age determinations have been a major focus of contention. For young asylum seekers adverse age findings can be linked also with general adverse findings on the credibility of a refugee claim. In Australia, confusion about age can be particularly damaging in the context of initial interviews because of the (legislated) ability of immigration officials to use both general demeanor and/or later contradictions as evidence of adverse credibility.[18] In many instances children sent for age testing in Australia were also challenged about their stated origins and were referred for expert language testing.

One problem is that unaccompanied or separated children apprehended by immigration authorities often lack any identification documents at all, or if they have them, the documents are fraudulent. In some instances, U.K. immigration officers simply refuse to accept the validity of any birth certificates or other documents from certain countries on the basis that other documents from that country are regularly found to have been forged. In both the U.S. and Australia, where identification as a minor brings with it concrete benefits in terms of detention conditions and sometimes release options, immigration authorities often assume that young adults claim to be younger than they are. However, when asked about this, a U.S. Border Patrol officer said he has only noticed this phenomenon among smugglers who pretend to be minors, thinking that they will receive a lesser criminal penalty than as an adult.[19] Alternately, children are also known to overstate their age to match fraudulent identity documents, to meet eligibility requirements for work permits, or because they simply do not want to be treated as children.[20]

In February 2002, the U.K. government stated that it "needed to identify children in genuine need at the earliest possible stage, to sift out adults posing as children and to deter those seeking to abuse the system."[21] It noted that Home Office staff were "already taking steps to challenge older applicants and divert them to the adult asylum process so that adults posing as children do not become a problem for local authorities."[22] Although U.K. researchers found some cases where adults had indeed posed as children as claimed by the authorities,[23] they found a substantial amount of other evidence of children being wrongfully classified as adults. In such cases, children were excluded from an age appropriate asylum determination process or placed in physical or psychological jeopardy by being housed with adults either in detention or National Asylum Support Service (NASS)[24] accommodation. Other children were found who had been wrongly age disputed and rendered homeless and destitute by having their age disputed late on a Friday afternoon. This left them unable to access assistance

from the Refugee Council or a social services department until the following Monday morning.

In the U.K., six out of the nine children interviewed in depth about their experiences of the asylum determination process had initially been age disputed. The Refugee Council keeps a record of the number of separated children referred to its Children's Panel each year. In 2001, 11% of these children had their age disputed. This rose to 28% in 2002, decreasing slightly to 25% in 2003. In 2004 there was a significant increase again of 37% with 1,456 of 3,867 referrals being age disputed.[25]

The Home Office also started to publish statistics on the number of age disputes which had occurred in 2004. These showed that in that year alone, 1,950 individuals claiming to be children were allocated to the adult asylum determination process.

Establishing someone's age exactly in the absence of reliable documentation or contemporaneous evidence of birth is impossible. Many unaccompanied and separated children come from countries which do not generate records of births. Birthdays may not be celebrated and dates, years,

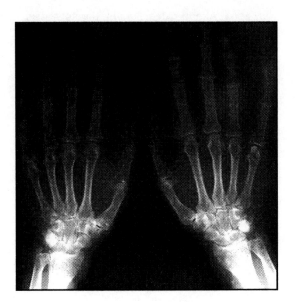

and even seasons may be recorded using calendars that do not equate with the Julian calendar favored in the West. Australian researchers found that many of the young Afghan people interviewed could not supply a date of birth. The immigration authorities in that country responded by allocating random birthdays such as 1 January or 31 December in a given year.[26]

No one-to-one correlation can be established between appearance and chronological age because both physical and behavioral traits are context dependent. Diet, heredity, social mores all impact on the full range of personal attributes, from bone

structure to language skill. Given the centrality of age as an indicator of identity and status in the immigration determination system, this radical indeterminacy presents both a serious administrative problem and a possible source of a child protection deficit.

In all three countries studied, disputes about age were settled using mechanisms to supplement visual assessment. In Australia, the favored supplemental method appears to be the examination of wrist x-rays.[27] U.S. researchers recorded reliance being placed on dental x-rays and examinations, with occasional recourse to wrist x-rays. While a

Law and Policy in State Practice | One Boy's Story

"I lost my birth certificate in Puerto Rico when it fell in the water.... I was at Boystown [a children's detention facility] for one month when they brought me to the dentist.... They did not do wrist x-rays, just a dental exam. They said that I was 19 years old. I tell people [I am 17], but they don't listen."

"**When I was first picked up**, Krome [adult detention center] took all of the papers.... Joe has a copy of the medico [sic]. They took me to the medico on 5 May 2004. After the dental exam, Boystown said that they believed me, but [said] "you don't have your birth certificate, so you have to go to Krome and then maybe you can come back." I went from the doctor to Boystown just long enough to pack my clothes and things and then I was handcuffed and put in the van alone and driven to Krome. I'm lost, a child, I was 17. People lied to me. I was in Georgia; Immigration Officer would come from Atlanta. They should know if I am 19. It doesn't make sense.... I told the judge that I was 17; the IJ looked at the file and said "You are 17," but he

said to the INS lawyer, "Do you believe he's 17?" The INS [Immigration and Naturalization Service] lawyer says "but the medicals say he's 19."[29]

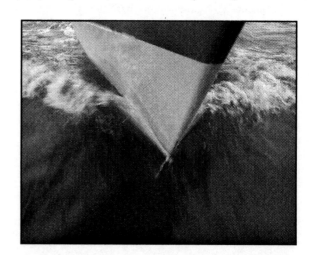

"preponderance of the evidence" test is used in questions of age for children who have entered the U.S. with refugee status,[28] children who enter the U.S. without legal status, and usually without documentation, are held to a more rigid, and medically questionable, standard.

The U.K. has made considerable strides forward in comparison with these crude approaches. In that country one dimensional physical tests are no longer acceptable as proxies for age.

According to the Royal College of Pediatricians and Child Health (U.K.):

"[A]n age determination is extremely difficult to do with certainty, and no single approach to this can be relied on. Moreover, for young people aged 15–18, it is even less possible to be certain about age.... Age determination is an inexact science and the margin of error can sometimes be as much as 5 years either side.... Estimates of a child's physical age from his or her dental development are [only] accurate to within + or − 2 years for 95% of the population."[30]

The Royal College of Radiologists (U.K.) has also advised its members that a request by an immigration officer for a radiograph to confirm chronological age would be unjustified both on grounds of accuracy and also because of the risks attached to using ionizing radiation for non-clinical purposes.[31]

In the U.K., it is now best practice for social services departments to carry out age assessments using an eight page *pro-forma*[32] which was developed by the London Borough of Hillingdon in conjunction with Refugee Council, Save the Children and the Refugee Arrivals Project and other local authority practitioners. The *pro-forma* has been designed to ensure that the social worker undertaking the assessment does not just rely on the child's physical appearance, the Home Office's opinion, or any documents he or she may be able to produce. Instead a holistic approach is recommended which takes into account a child's demeanor, ability to interact with an adult, cultural background, social history and family composition, life experiences, and educational history. Medical evidence of probable age is also considered useful, as are the views of adults with whom the child has had contact such as foster carers, residential workers, teachers, Refugee Council Panel Advisers, interpreters, and legal representatives. The ability of the age-disputed child to provide information must also be taken into account as there will be cases where a child is too traumatized to provide an accurate and coherent account of his or her past.[33] In the U.K., the courts have also stressed the fact that both the Immigration and Nationality Directorate and local authorities must give full weight to the medical opinions of experienced consultant pediatricians.[34]

■ **Recommendations**

Accurate assessment of age should be viewed as a child welfare issue, rather than an enforcement issue. The assessment should be used to determine the type of care to be given to the child, rather than the credibility of his or her claim to refugee protection.

In contested cases, the benefit of the doubt should always be given to the minor, given the importance of the "best interests of the child" principle. Finally, age assessment must be based on the totality of the evidence, taking account of both physical and psychological maturity[35] and including documents, evaluations of healthcare professionals and case workers, information from family members, and any scientific exams.[36] In the U.S. and Australia, consideration should be given to following the best practice now developed in the U.K. In all three countries the individuals charged with determining age should not also be responsible for funding the care of the individual if he or she is deemed to be a minor.

4.3 Guardianship and Care Arrangements

In the three countries studied, the challenge of balancing immigration control and child welfare interests in the response to unaccompanied and separated children is addressed quite differently. Australia is the only country that allocates both functions to the immigration authorities. As explained in chapter 3, the Australian Minister for Immigration is both guardian of unaccompanied and separated immigrant children and at the same time their jailer and prosecutor. By contrast, in the U.S. the dissolution of the INS in 2002 has led to a welcome functional separation of roles between two agencies: the newly formed DHS, through its sub-agency ICE, charged with enforcement on the one hand, and the Department of Health and Human Services' (DHHS) Office of Refugee Resettlement (ORR), through its Division of Unaccompanied Children's Services (DUCS), responsible for child care and custody on the other. U.S. researchers ascribe to this change the recent and dramatic drop in the percentage of unaccompanied children held in secure detention facilities (such as those used for youth accused of delinquent acts) and the abolition of the much criticized conflict of interest inherent in the INS for so long. The U.K., in sharp contrast to both Australia and the U.S., has always drawn a clear distinction between the local authorities, who have responsibility for the immediate care and protection of unaccompanied children, and the immigration authorities, charged with immigration control and determining their asylum applications.

All children require adult care and supervision. But children who are separated from parents and a familiar social context, alone in a foreign country, require such support and guidance with particular urgency. The issue of guardianship is thus a central one for this population. It is distinct from the question of legal representation, because what is at issue is not advocacy regarding immigration status but a more holistic responsibility for the best interests of the child. It emerged clearly from the research that the availability of a person to ensure that an unaccompanied or separated child's legal and welfare needs were being met often made the difference between success versus failure of the child's asylum application and between positive future prospects versus mere survival. Yet, all three countries studied are seriously deficient in the provision of guardians for unaccompanied and separated child asylum seekers. This is one of the key lacunae in current policy and one of the clearest indicators of the neglectful attitude towards vulnerable non-citizen children in all three countries.

■ The United Kingdom

In the U.K. the responsibility for the care of unaccompanied and separated children is conferred on local authorities, but in practice the research revealed that very few unaccompanied or separated children had an adult who was responsible for overseeing their progress through the asylum determination process, arguably the most fundamental response to his or her child protection needs.

An older child may live with local authority foster carers, have an allocated social worker they meet occasionally, have a Student Welfare Officer[37] at his or her school or college, or have a "Connexions" worker[38] and a key worker supplied by the child's accommodation provider.[39] The plethora of services provided are in reality a far cry from effective guardianship that is responsive to the best interests of the child. First, this multiplicity of supportive personnel can lead to confusion and the absence of any emotional bond with a trusted or caring adult figure in *loco parentis*. Secondly, the plethora of different agencies leads to "buck passing" between them. For example, some local authorities appear to expect Connexions' Personal Advisers to undertake a substantive welfare role more usually played by a local authority social worker and are reported to do no more than give an unaccompanied child a telephone number to call without any further explanation.[40] While Connexions plays a vital role in advising young people between 13 and 19 about educational, employment, social, and emotional problems, it does not have an effective child protection role or any formal responsibility for those who have been separated from their families.

The lack of effective adult support can have a negative affect on the child's ability to comply with the requirements of the refugee status determination process, both in terms of articulating a full story and in complying with administrative procedures.

In one case, two very young children arrived for their appeal hearing on their own and the Regional Adjudicator had to call the police in order to ensure their safety, even though they were technically in the care of a local authority.[41] In another, a young boy was accompanied to court by a mini-cab driver paid to bring him to court by the local authority.[42]

The U.K. researchers identified the absence of an effective guardian as a problem for children too young to have either the legal or practical ability to properly engage with the asylum process. Under U.K. law, only persons over 18 are deemed legally competent in domestic law. With no adult to give instructions to the children's legal representatives or act as their litigation friend,[43] legal representatives were concerned that they were being asked to take on two potentially conflicting roles. They were both required to take best interest decisions on behalf of the child but at the same time to follow the child client's instructions. Some complained that this dual role distracted them from their primary duty to promote the child's legal interests and that they were neither trained nor legally entitled to make best interest decisions which affected the child in other contexts.

■ **The United States**

Despite the very different institutional picture, identical problems arise in the U.S. system. Concerns were expressed to the researchers conducting this study about the lack of adequate guardianship arrangements in the daily lives of unaccompanied and separated children; and child asylum advocates are torn between their obligations as legal representatives of their child clients, on the one hand, and as untrained mentors and parental advisers on the other. This tension is most acute where the advocate's best interest judgment conflicts with the child's expressed wishes or where the child's instructions are unclear.

In the words of a child asylum attorney in Phoenix, Arizona: "As their attorney I'm supposed to represent their wishes, but often I don't think it is what's best for them."[44] A shelter care director in the same community noted the need for a guardian *ad litem* in cases where a child says conflicting

things: **"A guardian *ad litem* would be especially useful in cases where it is unclear whether a child wants to go home. Sometimes children go back and forth between: 'I want to go home; no I want to apply for political asylum.'"**[45]

In financial terms, the day to day responsibility for children apprehended by the federal government for immigration violations (for example, at the border or as undocumented migrants) is typically not disputed: the federal government pays for the care of such children and is responsible for their treatment. This clarity of responsibility disappears when children come to the attention of state or county child welfare entities (for example, if they are in need of foster care, or other welfare services due to abuse, abandonment, or neglect). The willingness of these local systems to accept unaccompanied or separated children into custody can vary greatly by location, and by the financial resources of a particular community.

A Chinese girl was granted dependency in Florida days before her 18th birthday, a successful outcome since this saved her from returning to abusive parents and a forced marriage to an older man.[46] **However, the local child welfare authorities refused to provide services for the adolescent, on the grounds that she was the financial responsibility of the federal government which originally placed her in a Florida facility for detained children.**[47] **In a sad commentary on the dereliction of duty by public entities, services were provided to her by neither state nor federally funded programs. It fell to a privately run shelter for homeless and runaway youth to care for this traumatized child.**

Since the reorganization of the U.S. immigration system, there has been some acknowledgment of the importance of adult guidance for unaccompa-

nied and separated children. The post-2002 system represents a compromise between the desire to assist vulnerable immigrant children, and the reluctance to allow such children to be a charge on the public purse. The Director of ORR can develop *pro bono* legal representation, and guardian *ad litem* schemes, but cannot fund or support direct legal representation, even for children.

An example of the sort of project undertaken by ORR is the pilot Immigrant Children's Advocacy Program in Chicago, Illinois. The project recruits and trains "Child Advocates" for certain categories of children in ORR custody, including all children in federal custody in Chicago who are seeking asylum in Immigration Court proceedings.[48] **Child advocates meet their assigned child on a weekly basis and, to the extent possible, speak the same language. The child advocate's responsibilities include many of the functions associated with the role of guardian, such as forming a personal relationship; offering counsel; liaising with the legal system; helping to assemble evidence; and generally advocating for the best interest of the child.**

In the U.S., the extent of the required access to legal counsel consists of giving children a list of free legal service providers at the time of apprehension and expecting children to find their own attorneys. In an examination of legal service lists distributed by three Border Patrol sectors, a DHS OIG report noted that these lists were not "consistently accurate," with more than 50% of the attorneys listed ultimately unavailable (of 29 offices contacted, eight did not represent children, three phone numbers were not in service and four offices were unable to be contacted despite multiple attempts).[49]

The inaccuracies of these lists are troubling, but this examination misses a more critical question: how can it be reasonable, or even responsible, to give children a list of phone numbers and leave it to them to find their own attorney? It is unlikely that U.S. society would find this an acceptable means of providing legal counsel for children in domestic court proceedings, yet it has been allowed to persist in Immigration Court proceedings. Typically in domestic juvenile justice proceedings, children are assigned an attorney and a guardian *ad litem*, to ensure that children in court have an adult adviser looking out for their best interests. In contrast, children in U.S. immigration proceedings must look out for themselves.

▪ Australia

The greatest shortcomings in the guardianship system were found in Australia. While the mechanisms established to confer guardianship on the Minister for Immigration would make sense in the context of an ordered migration program where unaccompanied and separated children are admitted as legal migrants, they were unsatisfactory when applied to children entering the country alone without a legal immigration status. There are several reasons for this. First, although the Immigration Minister has primary care as well as immigration control responsibilities, it is invariably the control function that dominates. In practice the minister has delegated his or her role as carer to the managers of the privately owned detention centers who had custody of "screened-in" asylum seekers. Conditions within the detention centers nullified the possibility of effective child-centered care as regards basic custodial arrangements. Second, access to effective legal representation is compromised by the minister's dual role. He or she acts both on behalf of the child asylum applicant and as the decision maker in the child's application, a fundamental conflict of interest and breach of the principles of natural justice. An independent guardian (delegated to state welfare authorities) is only appointed to children outside of

immigration detention, though even here variations within state and territory welfare systems result in a wide range of standards of involvement. Although children in and out of detention are appointed advisers under the Immigration Advice and Application Assistance Scheme, such advisers cannot operate effectively as both adviser and guardian. These two roles are distinct: the first is focused on legal entitlements, the second on the physical and mental welfare of the child in all the circumstances of a case.

At the height of the influx of children in and after 1999, some advocates raised concerns about whether very young children could be regarded as having the legal capacity to make refugee claims. But the Australian Federal Court ruled that the capacity of children to both lodge asylum claims and to institute legal challenges is one of fact to be determined in each case. The court declined to rule that the minister could be compelled to appoint an independent guardian[50] or that the minister was under a legal obligation to provide for the physical welfare of the children.[51]

The nature of the Australian minister's guardianship obligations remains a matter of contention. The failings of the system were particularly evident in the cases of unaccompanied and separated children transferred to Nauru in 2001–2002, a strategy plainly against the interests of the children in question, and one that led to years of deprivation, anguish, and uncertainty for many children.[52]

▪ Recommendation

In all three countries studied, the presence of a responsible adult to advocate on behalf of the unaccompanied or separated child vastly improved the child's access to justice and sense of emotional wellbeing. It also enhanced the quality of legal representation provided. The findings of this research therefore corroborate the recommendation in the General Comment of the Committee on the Rights of the Child:

States should appoint a guardian or adviser as soon as the unaccompanied or separated child is identified and maintain such guardianship arrangements until the child has either reached the age of majority or has permanently left the territory and/or jurisdiction of the state in compliance with the Convention and other international obligations. The guardian should be consulted and informed regarding all actions taken in relation to the child. The guardian should have the authority to be present in all planning and decision-making processes, including immigration and appeal hearings, care arrangements and all efforts to search for a durable solution. The guardian or adviser should have the necessary expertise in the field of child care, so as to ensure that the interests of the child are safeguarded and that the child's legal, social, health, psychological, material and educational needs are appropriately covered by, inter alia, the guardian acting as a link between the child and existing specialist agencies/individuals who provide the continuum of care required by the child.[53]

4.4 Interim Care Pending a Decision—Guardianship and Legal Custody

Some of the children in greatest need [are] unaccompanied asylum seekers [who] may have left their homes and communities in violent and traumatic circumstances and [suffer] poor health.[54]

The arrival of unaccompanied and separated children forces receiving states to cater to their needs and to consider how the absence of parents or legal guardians is to be addressed. Each of the countries studied has developed different strategies, but none of them, as will become clear, adequately cater to the children's best interests.

■ The United Kingdom

In the U.K., the Children Act 1989 requires local authorities to protect and support all children in need, irrespective of nationality or immigration status. Unaccompanied and separated children therefore have a right to accommodation and financial support by a local authority while their asylum application is considered. However, the local authority does not acquire legal custody of or parental responsibility for unaccompanied or separated children. It would only be granted parental responsibility by a family court if there were child protection concerns about the child's situation in the U.K. over and above the fact that he or she was an asylum seeker. If there are such concerns, the local authority will apply for a care order under section 31 of the Children Act 1989. This could occur where a child had been rescued from traffickers and there was a danger that other members of the trafficking gang may try to harm or abduct him or her. (This is an important improvement on the practice in some places in the U.S., where, as discussed above, local child welfare entities may be reluctant to take responsibility for unaccompanied and separated children in need of care because they have no explicit statutory obligation to non-citizen children, reserving limited resources for children who are perceived as "from here.")

Under the EU Council Directive laying down minimum standards for the reception of asylum seekers (hereafter EU Directive)[55] the U.K. also has an obligation to ensure representation of unaccompanied and separated children by a legal guardian or by an organization which is responsible for the care and wellbeing of minors or by any other appropriate representation. At one time the U.K. government was intending to create a form of legal guardianship for unaccompanied and separated children. However, no such provision was included in either the Asylum and Immigration (Treatment of Claimants etc) Act 2004

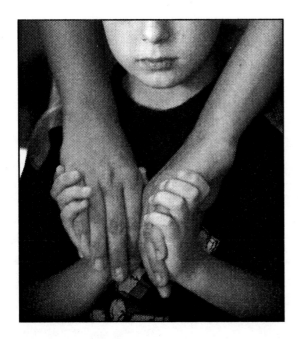

vacuum in law, and a deficit compared to the provision made for citizen children without parental protection. This affects the entire asylum-seeking process as separated or unaccompanied children lack anyone acting on their behalf in *loco parentis*. This protection deficit clearly contradicts the requirements of the Convention on the Rights of the Child which requires states to provide children seeking asylum with "appropriate protection and humanitarian assistance" and "the same protection as any other child permanently or temporarily deprived of his or her family environment."[58]

In addition to these guardianship obligations, the U.K. also has a legal obligation, under the EU Directive on minimum standards for asylum seekers, to trace families of unaccompanied and separated children in a manner which will not place the child or any family member at risk. In practice nothing happens about tracing. The latest Asylum Policy Instructions (2005) state:

If there are any details regarding the parents' whereabouts, such as a last known address, the case worker should begin enquiries by contacting the relevant British diplomatic post. However, as of yet, the returns program has not started tracing. The British Red Cross runs a limited tracing service but will only accept referrals from a child and not the IND.

■ **The United States**

Within the U.S., ORR now oversees the care and custody of unaccompanied alien children from the time when they are referred by the Border Patrol or other immigration enforcement agents (usually within 72 hours of apprehension at a border or entry point), until removal or release to family or other care arrangements. This represents a significant improvement on the previous system where custodial care for unaccompanied and separated children rested with the INS authorities, also

(U.K.) or the Children Act 2004 (U.K.). Instead, the U.K. has sought to comply with the directive by relying on the fact that local authority social services departments provide accommodation for unaccompanied and separated children and that it is funding the Refugee Council's Panel of Advisers. The inadequacy of this response is exemplified by the fact that in 2004 this panel only had funding to allocate an adviser to 1,082 children although 3,862 unaccompanied or separated children were referred to the panel.[56] The Refugee Council also doubts its ability to act as a legal guardian in the light of its lack of statutory status.[57]

If the obligations set out in the EU Directive have not been realized, neither has the recommendation by the Committee on the Rights of the Child that the U.K. consider appointing guardians for unaccompanied and separated children seeking asylum. Though social services have the power to do what is reasonable to safeguard and promote the unaccompanied or separated child's welfare, neither they nor anyone else acquires parental responsibility for the child. There is, thus, a serious protection charged with enforcing immigration control. ORR has responsibility for deciding on the release of separated or unaccompanied children from detention and sometimes even remains involved for several months after release.

■ Australia

In Australia, legal guardianship rests with the Minister for Immigration throughout the asylum process until the child is recognized as a refugee. The minister thus has all the rights, duties, and obligations of a guardian in general law. Unlike any public official in the U.K. the minister is able to incur both equitable and statutory liability on behalf of all separated and unaccompanied children seeking asylum in Australia, whether they are in detention, in offshore locations or within the community. The allocation of clear legal guardianship is a positive feature of the Australian system, most particularly when the role is delegated to appropriate welfare authorities. However, as noted earlier, the conflicting roles combined in that office—guardian, immigration law enforcer, and detention instigator—compromise its efficacy for child protection.

As a Brisbane lawyer representing unaccompanied and separated children commented: "I can probably say that the [children] weren't thinking of the minister as their legal guardian at any stage…. The minister in their eyes was this person who was either going to grant them a visa or not grant them a visa. That is all they saw in the minister."[59]

4.5 The Detention of Unaccompanied and Separated Children

I think I am totally broken and I'll be in this cage forever.

> — 15-year-old Afghan boy detained in Woomera, South Australia

The issue that has rightly provoked most public criticism of child asylum policy is the widespread use of detention of unaccompanied and separated children seeking protection. Of the three countries studied, only the U.K. has a firmly established policy that children under 18 should not normally be detained. In the U.S. the use of detention is widespread, though the punitive detention of unaccompanied and separated children in juvenile jails is much less common now than it was prior to the INS reorganization, when approximately one-third of the 5,000 children annually detained were held in secure facilities for youth with criminal offences. Single purpose "children's shelters" are now the predominant detention model in the U.S., housing only children who are in federal custody for immigration violations. Of the three countries studied, Australian policy— at least until June 2005—was situated at the most punitive end of the spectrum, reflecting the exclusionary nature of the country's migration policy as a whole. Detention of undocumented children, whether asylum seeking or not, was the norm, not the exception, and no statutory time limit on the length of this detention existed.

In all three countries studied, there were two sets of concerns raised about the detention of unaccompanied and separated children. First and foremost was criticism of the injustice and human rights violations associated with the practice. For any asylum seeker escaping situations of trauma, persecution, and violence, detention is a completely inappropriate, authoritarian, and punitive response. For children, especially separated and unaccompanied children known to be particularly susceptible to physical and psychological damage as a result of traumatic experiences, the use of detention is severely harmful and likely to carry with it long-term deleterious consequences. Several interview excerpts testify to the profound impact of detention on child asylum seekers.

A child detained in an Australian immigration detention center noted:

"Sometimes I thought it's as if you are disconnected from all world, you're just inside there and it's as if your life has stopped. You're not doing anything; it's like...I don't know, it's hard to explain—too much disappointing. It's very, very disappointing to be there."

A child detained at the Globe Juvenile Detention Center, a "secure facility" in the U.S., reflected on his first impression of detention:

"My first couple of days there, I didn't like it. I didn't like the food there. I couldn't sleep. At 5 a.m. when they opened the cells for us to take showers, there was a table with clothes assigned to us by name. It didn't take into account our size, so I got shoes that didn't even fit me.... The rights we had in this facility depended on what color our shirt was. After three days, I had a gray shirt and the right to sit and eat with others.

I noticed that the shirt colors were changing, and I asked the other kids and over the weeks, I just adapted. I asked if I could call my family, but they told me not until I had been there for 25 days was I allowed to make a call. I tried to call even after I had the right to call, but I couldn't get through.... Sometimes at night when it became very hot— they left the lights on—we would take off our shirts. We would be yelled at because they wanted us to wear our shirts so they would know what color they were and what privileges we had."[60]

The second, related, concern is that detention does not facilitate the administrative process, except insofar as it prevents disappearance of the detainees. Rather it diminishes the ability of officials to make accurate and safe assessments of asylum claims because detained asylum seekers progressively lose their ability to make cogent claims due to depression, lethargy, disorientation, and even psychotic disturbances. If this applies to adults, it applies with even greater force to children. Moreover, in all three countries studied, detention facilities for asylum-seeking children tended to be situated in remote locations, far from the urban centers where asylum advocates and refugee communities are based. As a result of this isolation, and the severe funding constraints on legal representation (and reimbursement of travel costs and time), access to good advocates and community support was difficult to secure.

■ **The United Kingdom**
In the U.K., despite its clear policy on detention, research for this study revealed that significant numbers of age-disputed unaccompanied or separated children had in fact been detained. This occurred in two sets of circumstances—when children were incorrectly assessed as being 18 years and older, or while their age was being disputed (age-disputed applicants are detained as adults pending

consideration of their asylum applications).[61]

Although relatively few adult asylum seekers are detained at the beginning of the asylum process, U.K. researchers found that a significant minority of age-disputed children are detained at this stage. The chances of being detained seem particularly high, if an age-disputed separated child is a national of a country which is deemed suitable[62] for the Fast Track Process at Oakington Reception Centre in Cambridgeshire, although children have been detained at most immigration removal centers at one time or another. Between February 2004 and September 2004 alone the Refugee Council received 207 referrals from individuals claiming to be children detained in Oakington and elsewhere. Most detailed research has been carried out at Oakington and of those whose age was assessed by Cambridge Social Services Department between November 2003 and September 2004, 47.3% were found to be children. However, in response to complaints about the number of children being detained at that center, Cambridgeshire County Council undertook to provide age assessments on site within seven days when requested to do so (there is no statutory duty to obtain such assessments in disputed cases) and the immigration authorities agreed to delay any decision on the age-disputed child's asylum application during the assessment period. This concession substantially reduced the length of time children were kept in custody.[63] However, there is no statutory duty to obtain age assessments and practice is being developed in a piecemeal fashion.

"I was crying. This man came up to me because I was sitting down and crying. He asked me where I was from and he was [from the same country]. He asked me about my solicitor. I had his card. He called him and asked him why he had told me not to correct my date of birth. The solicitor put down the phone. After a few days he came with a letter saying he couldn't continue my case. I would find another solicitor. I was just confused. I didn't know what to do. The man said that the solicitor was a wicked man and that I should not have been there. He said I should not cry. He gave me the telephone number for BID [Bail for Immigration Detainees] and said I should tell them what happened."[64] [BID referred him to the Refugee Council's Children's Panel and it arranged an age assessment and he was released.]

If it is accepted that the individual in question is a child, he or she becomes entitled to support under section 20 of the Children Act 1989 (U.K.). To distribute responsibility for such children beyond the few social services departments in whose areas children are detained, the Association of Directors of Social Service have agreed to a protocol which allocates responsibility for children who have been wrongfully detained.[65] Despite this protocol, U.K. local authorities, as their U.S. counterparts, continue to dispute responsibility for these children which can prolong their detention.[66]

■ The United States
In the U.S., researchers found that the transfer of care and custody of unaccompanied and separated children from the INS to ORR has lead to a steady reduction in the use of secure detention for unaccompanied and separated children: since the ORR takeover, the percentage of children placed in secure detention facilities commingling unaccompanied and separated children with juvenile offenders has decreased significantly, from over 30% of apprehended children when the INS was responsible to less than 3% since the transfer of responsibility.[67] According to ORR, child placements have ceased at more than 28 juvenile detention centers previously used by INS, with ORR using only four secure detention facilities in the fiscal year 2005.[68] Nonetheless,

U.S. researchers still found that some children were held in secure or semi-secure facilities, sometimes by default where alternative accommodation was not available and sometimes due to placements by government agencies other than ORR.[69]

A 19 year old interviewed by U.S. researchers attested to the harsh impact of being incarcerated in a "secure facility" and his testimony illustrates the sort of regime that children placed in these facilities were subjected to.

"They let me out for only 15 minutes a day. The rules were very strict. We had to keep our hands behind our backs. I didn't know what was going on. I was sick. There was a button that I could push to get medical attention, but no one ever came. I asked the man who would bring me my meals if he would get me medical assistance, but still no one ever came."[70]

The overall reduction in the use of secure detention marks an important improvement in the care of unaccompanied and separated children, a change that has also resulted in a reduction in the use of physical restraints with children.[71] The employment of restraints such as shackles, handcuffs, and leg

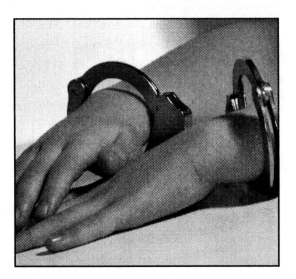

irons has been one of the most egregious human rights violations against unaccompanied and separated child asylum seekers, rightly criticized by Amnesty International.[72]

Attorneys interviewed by the U.S. researchers reported that children detained in secure facilities were more likely to abandon their asylum claim because of the stresses they were experiencing. One legal advocate gave as an example a child with a strong asylum claim who was held for four months in a secure detention facility because of "behavioral concerns."

"In an attempt to get him transferred, I looked at his behavioral records.... He was written up for incidents such as throwing a basketball too hard, failure to stay in a straight line when they were walking to a different building. I went to visit him and to begin preparing his asylum case.... While asking him questions related to his asylum case, all he could ask about was whether or not he would be transferred. At his Master [Calendar hearing], I came ready to file his application; however, he requested an order of deportation. He couldn't take being detained any longer.... He was only able to think about his immediate need, which was to get out of detention."[73]

If secure detention, particularly in juvenile correctional institutions, appears to negatively impact a child's ability to pursue asylum, children held in quality non-secure facilities for prolonged periods were also found to be inclined to forsake valid applications for asylum. One Guatemalan orphan, who was interviewed while being held at a shelter facility in Florida, told researchers:

"I get really sad sometimes because I think about being stuck inside here and I want a mom and a dad and a family."[74]

Another spoke of his anxiety at seeing younger children detained at the facility:

"...it's hard to see little children all alone in detention. Kids who are like five years old. Sometimes they separate them and deport their mommies. I know, I have seen it."[75]

As detention conditions for unaccompanied and separated children in the U.S. have improved, alongside a more child-welfare-oriented approach to their care, concerns about custody conditions have become more nuanced. The heavy reliance on institutional care rather than home-based or community care continues to prompt serious concerns about the impact of this form of care, the time limits on the use of institutional care, and the availability of alternatives. The U.S. system of care for unaccompanied and separated children has improved, but the continued reliance on institutional care diverges from current child-welfare practice with other populations and warrants further examination.

Another important issue regarding unaccompanied and separated children detained in the U.S. is the speed with which their cases proceed: the court calendar for these cases is known colloquially as the "rocket docket." U.S. researchers found that this well-motivated policy had the potential to impact negatively on the children's asylum claims.

"For kids in detention, their cases are fast-tracked. It takes them a while to trust an attorney. Kids almost never come with documents, whereas adults are more likely to come with something or more likely to have success in getting documents."[76]

Clearly the time frame for optimal decision making depends on what is being decided—different considerations apply. In the case of release from detention, speed is essential and expedited decision making

a sign of good practice. But for resolution of the asylum claim as a whole, a shortened time frame is likely to be an obstacle to careful preparation, hindering evidence collection and instruction taking. Instead, best practice requires granting an adequate time for submission of the claim, particularly in the case of unaccompanied and separated children where supporting evidence is likely to take longer to gather than in adult cases.

▪ Australia

Australia stands out among the countries studied as the jurisdiction that has had the most rigid and unsuitable detention policy for unaccompanied and separated children seeking asylum. In spite of the long-standing statutory discretion to allow children arriving without visas to be released into the community, the general practice was to treat detention as mandatory for all undocumented arrivals. Australian researchers found that every unaccompanied and separated child who arrived in Australia between 1999 and 2003 without a visa was taken immediately into detention. After a brief stay in transit at either Darwin or Christmas Island, most were transported to remote immigration detention centers (IDCs). The children were spread between Curtin and Port Hedland IDCs in Western Australia, and Woomera and Baxter IDCs in South Australia, with some spending time also in Sydney's Villawood IDC and in the center at Perth airport. Among the 85 cases studied for the Australian report, the shortest period of time spent in detention was six weeks, and the longest over four years. A number of the young people held for extensive periods were ultimately released into foster care in the community. One of the young people interviewed was released into "community detention" after developing symptoms of acute mental illness.

The Australian researchers found that many of the negative aspects of the young asylum seekers'

experiences of Australian bureaucracy had their roots in Australia's mandatory detention policy. Even though the children were fed, clothed, and housed, they suffered multiple emotional and physical deprivations. Two of the case files examined by researchers contained daily 'incident' reports or other records obtained under the Freedom of Information provisions and kept by the detention authorities detailing the special surveillance measures put in place to ensure that the child being observed did not commit suicide or engage in acts of self harm.

Within the detention centers on mainland Australia, the prevailing practice was to expedite "screening" interviews and asylum processing for unaccompanied or separated children and then to separate the "screened in" children from the detained population as a whole. The Australian researchers found that this regime had several shortcomings. The most obvious was that the "special" treatment only applied if the unaccompanied or separated child passed the first "screening in" hurdle. One of the young people interviewed did not succeed in this regard, with the result that she and her 10-year-old brother spent eight months in mixed detention accommodation with men and women of varying ages and ethnicities. This situation is particularly traumatic for unaccompanied female children.

Extremely fearful of the other detainees, the young Afghan girl spoke of being afraid to go to the toilets at night: "I lived with lots of single men and they are very bad man.... They are shouting... use bad words."[77]

Another shortcoming of the policy governing the treatment of unaccompanied and separated children was that as soon as they reached the age of 18, the young people would be removed from their peer group and become ineligible for special treatment. For example, when the situation in one IDC became particularly volatile, a number of the separated children were transferred into community care. One young man studied, who had just turned 18, was not transferred. According to subsequent psychological reports, this event was a contributing factor to his development of acute mental illness.

The period during which most of the unaccompanied and separated children studied were in detention was highly volatile. There were riots and hunger strikes and repeated incidents where asylum seekers harmed themselves. In some IDCs the children would be taken to another part of the center and separated from adults when there were riots but this did not necessarily stop them being affected. Many engaged in acts of self-harm. One young man stated that he had friends who had drunk shampoo and others who had sewn their lips together.

"People sewing their lips together was common. That used to happen every day. My friends did that. It's just very common. The thing is, you think what is your fault. Leaving your country because it was war-torn, people had been dying—what's your crime? 'Cause you came here to save your life and to seek like a better life?"[78]

A number of the young people interviewed spoke of spending long hours lying on their beds in their sleeping quarters. Nightmares and sleeping problems appear to have been common, a fact confirmed by the medical reports placed on some of the participants' case files. One of the young people interviewed, although an adult by the time he left detention, was diagnosed with severe post traumatic stress disorder with disassociative episodes and had to be repeatedly hospitalized. He made a number of attempts on his life before being released into community detention.

There was a high level of distrust in the IDCs, including distrust of the interpreters, the Department for Immigration, and other detainees. One boy interviewed by Australian researchers believed that DIMIA had recruited other detainees to inform on the detention population. As a consequence he said he was afraid to leave his room in case other people read his documents. He was 15 years old.

Lawyers interviewed by the Australian researchers echo the findings of the U.S. researchers on the detrimental impact of detention on the ability of unaccompanied and separated children to obtain adequate representation:

"What tends to happen with unaccompanied minors or very young people in detention is that they don't tend to get legal representation. This tends to happen a lot more with Afghans than almost any other nationality that are in detention…a lot of the unaccompanied minors have virtually never been outside their village and have no concept of anything beyond that world…. It's not only heart-wrenching, but it's an appalling lack of justice."[79]

Another legal advocate explained how the age of the children made them particularly vulnerable to the abuses that would occur in the detention context:

Not only are they young, they're uneducated and scared…. They don't know anyone else in the detention

center. *A detention center replicates society in many ways…. So they were persecuted depending on which group they were kept in or which compound they were kept in and the younger ones were much more vulnerable to that sort of bullying by the hierarchy…*[80]

While the experiences of the participants were not uniformly traumatic, the context for the vast majority was one of fear and frustration. In its seminal report into children in immigration detention, the Human Rights and Equal Opportunity Commission (HREOC) argued strongly that Australia's immigration detention regime has been very damaging to children.[81] There was nothing in the Australian research to contradict the Commission's findings. In the words of lawyer Abby Hamden:

From what I've seen so far, they are so damaged. They have arrived as young minors who are sensitive and perceive things differently. Even though they come out, are young, and learn English quickly, they are damaged by their experience in the detention center. The fact they were alone, they are alone, and have no support affects them so much. Yesterday I saw the third one who was released recently. He told me that when he sees forms he has panic attacks because it reminds him of having to fill them out in the detention center. When he sees an old woman or man he has a panic attack because he remembers being in a room next to two couples. He is still very damaged.[82]

4.6 Conclusion

Both common humanity and international law demand that children separated from their family and fleeing trauma or violence be the recipients of special care and protection. By contrast evidence presented in the above chapter suggests that in the three countries studied, protective and caring policies, insofar as they exist at all, are frequently overshadowed by official approaches that are negligent at best but all too often deeply punitive and utterly unsuitable for this especially vulnerable population. The failure to appoint effective and independent guardians to act in *loco parentis* from the time of arrival till the time a child is placed in a suitably permanent and caring environment characterizes all three countries. Egregious policies suited to criminal law enforcement, such as prolonged detention, the use of handcuffs, or shackles also feature in some of the environments studied, though fortunately vociferous public opposition to these practices has radically reduced their currency.

The failure to institute acceptable policies in the states studied is not a consequence of lack of information or public recommendations about suitable practice. In all three countries public inquiries, academic studies, and official guidelines have established beyond dispute that certain procedures—for example, the appointment of effective guardians, access to adequate care and nurturing—are essential, and that other procedures—for example, detention, punitive restraining measures, lack of stimulation—are profoundly deleterious. What is lacking therefore is not information or expertise but political will. The evidence presented above suggests that such public commitment is profoundly urgent.

■ Recommendations

We cannot improve upon the clear and cogent recommendations recently set out by the Committee on the Rights of the Child:

Unaccompanied or separated children are children temporarily or permanently deprived of their family environment....

[T]he particular vulnerabilities of such a child, not only having lost connection with his or her family

environment, but further finding him or herself outside of his or her country of origin, as well as the child's age and gender, should be taken into account. In particular, due regard ought to be taken of the desirability of continuity in a child's upbringing and to the ethnic, religious, cultural and linguistic background as assessed in the identification, registration and documentation process. Such care and accommodation arrangements should comply with the following parameters:

- *Children should not, as a general rule, be deprived of liberty.*

- *In order to ensure continuity of care and considering the best interests of the child, changes in residence for unaccompanied and separated children should be limited to instances where such change is in the best interests of the child.*

- *In accordance with the principle of family unity, siblings should be kept together.*

- *A child who has adult relatives arriving with him or her or already living in the country of asylum should be allowed to stay with them unless such action would be contrary to the best interests of the child. Given the particular vulnerabilities of the child, regular assessments should be conducted by social welfare personnel.*

- *Irrespective of the care arrangements made for unaccompanied or separated children, regular supervision and assessment ought to be maintained by qualified persons in order to ensure the child's physical and psychosocial health, protection against domestic violence or exploitation, and access to educational and vocational skills and opportunities.*

- *States and other organizations must take measures to ensure the effective protection of the rights of separated or unaccompanied children living in child-headed households.*

- *In large scale emergencies, interim care must be provided for the shortest time appropriate for unaccompanied children. This interim care provides for their security and physical and emotional care in a setting that encourages their general development.*

- *Children must be kept informed of the care arrangements being made for them, and their opinions must be taken into consideration.*[83]

Endnotes

1 Bhabha, Jacqueline and Schmidt, Susan. *Seeking Asylum Alone, United States.* Cambridge, MA: Bhabha and Schmidt, 2006. (U.S. Report.) 5.1; Crock, Mary. *Seeking Asylum Alone, Australia.* Sydney: Themis Press, 2006. (Australian Report.) Chapter 13.

2 In the U.K., researchers were informed by the Home Office that no data was collected which would identify whether unaccompanied or separated children were being turned back.

3 Sixteen-year-old boy from Albania. Bhabha, Jacqueline and Finch, Nadine. *Seeking Asylum Alone, United Kingdom.* Cambridge, MA: Finch, 2006. (U.K. Report.) 9.1.

4 Fourteen-year-old boy from Ethiopia quoted in Kidane, Selam. *I did not choose to come here : Listening to Refugee Children.* BAAF, 2001. See U.K. Report, Ibid, Endnote 3, 9.1.

5 Boy from Chad, interviewed for this study, age disputed at time of interview but subsequently found to be a child and granted refugee status. See U.K. Report, Ibid, Endnote 3, 9.2.

6 Interview with Chantal Camilien, asylum officer on Supervisory APSO Duty at Krome Detention Center. Miami, Florida. 15 July 2004.

7 Personal communication with Martha Rickey, Children's Attorney, Florence Immigrant and Refugee Rights Project. 1 December 2005.

8 Personal communication with Susan Krehbiel, Director for Children's Services, Lutheran Immigration and Refugee Service. 1 December 2005.

9 Interview with a 17-year-old girl from Guatemala. Interview by Joanne Kelsey. 4 May 2005. She was 15 when she entered the U.S. She was granted asylum by a judge but the government appealed the decision, which was still pending at time of interview.

10 Ibid, Endnote 7.

11 For more on the Visa Waiver Program, see INA §217.

12 DHS, Office of Inspector General. "A Review of DHS' Responsibilities for Juvenile Aliens." OIG-05-45. September 2005. 16–17.

13 Ibid, Endnote 12, 18.

14 Ibid, Endnote 12, 15–16.

15 Personal communication with Lisa Frydman, Staff Attorney at Legal Services for Children, San Francisco, California. 1 December 2005.

16 For example, where the child's visa is found not to be valid.

17 *Paladin Child: The Safeguarding Children Strand of Maxim funded by Reflex : A Partnership Study of Child Migration to the U.K. via London Heathrow.* Reflex, Metropolitan Police, the U.K. Immigration Service,

Association of Directors of Social Services, NSPCC, London Borough of Hillingdon. 2004.

18 Migration Act 1958, s91R.

19 Interview with Steve Evans, Assistant Chief, Office of Border Patrol Headquarters, Washington, D.C. 16 September 2004.

20 Australian researchers came across one example of this with a young Afghan man who had deliberately inflated his age so as not to be associated with his young peers: see Australian Report, Ibid, Endnote 1, 3.2.

21 White Paper *Secure Borders, Safe Haven : Integration with Diversity in Modern Britain* CM 5387, February 2002. Para. 4.55.

22 Ibid, Endnote 21, Para. 4.56.

23 For example Bill Davies, the Head of the Asylum Support Team at Manchester City Council, reported an incidence of a 20 year old being placed with children. See also the statistics, para. 84.

24 The NASS provides accommodation and financial support to adult asylum seekers and their dependants, often on run-down estates on the edges of towns and far from London and the South East where the bulk of recent migrants live.

25 Figures provided by the Refugee Council's Children's Panel (2004), on file with authors.

26 One migration agent interviewed stated that she had pressed the authorities to record birthdays as 31 December rather than 1 January so as to maximize the time accorded to the child as a minor. In one instance the researchers encountered a young person with a date of birth recorded as 0/0/(given year). This designation caused considerable troubles for the young person as the social services computers require the specification of day and month as well as year.

27 A number of the young people interviewed suggested that interpreters were asked for their opinion on matters relevant to their identification both in terms of age and ethnic background.

28 Interview with Shereen Faraj, Division of Unaccompanied Children's Services, Office of Refugee Resettlement, Administration for Children and Families, Department of Health and Human Services. 30 July 2004.

29 Interview with a 17-year-old boy from Haiti. Interview by Wendy Young and Joanne Kelsey, interpreted by Kathie Klarreich. 23 July 2004.

30 *The Health of Refugee Children : Guidelines for Paediactricians.* November 1999. Para. 5.6.3.

31 Ibid, Endnote 30. Para. 5.6.2.

32 This document is now widely used by local authorities throughout England and is relied on in court proceedings. The Home Office has sent it to some local authorities but it has yet to be officially published by the Association of Directors of Social Services or the Home Office.

33 *The Queen on the Application of C v. London Borough of Enfield* [2004] EWHC 2297 (Admin) where an age assessment which failed to take into account the fact that the child in question had been found to be unfit to give evidence and to be suffering from post traumatic stress disorder was found to be unlawful.

34 *R on the application of "I" and R on the application of "O" and Secretary of State for the Home Department* [2005] EWHC 1025 (Admin).

35 UNHCR. *Policies and Procedures in Dealing with Unaccompanied Children Seeking Asylum.* UNHCR, February 1997. 8.

36 This approach is endorsed by the recent General Comment of the Committee on the Rights of the Child; see Committee on the Rights of the Child. General Comment No. 6: Treatment of separated and unaccompanied children outside their country of origin. UN, 2005. CRC/GC/2005/6.

37 These officers who are employed by individual colleges may have funds they can use to assist students who cannot afford to travel to the college or pay for books or other materials. Some have also taken on a more supportive role in relation to unaccompanied children.

38 There is a national scheme of Connexions Partnerships which provide a Personal Adviser to 13 to 19 year olds who need advice about education, career, housing, money, health, and relationships.

39 Commercial companies who enter into contracts with local authorities to provide accommodation for unaccompanied children.

40 Conclusions which are based on a large number of cases involving unaccompanied and former unaccompanied children undertaken by Hereward & Foster, a solicitors firm in London (2005).

41 Information provided by another adjudicator (2004).

42 Information provided by immigration barrister (2004).

43 In civil proceedings in domestic law, minors are required to have an adult Litigation Friend when bringing or defending any action. In the family jurisdiction in a public law case a Children's Guardian will be appointed to represent the child and advise the court as to how his or her best interests can be met.

44 Interview with Shiu-Ming Cheer, former Attorney, Florence Immigrant and Refugee Rights Project. Florence, Arizona. 3 May 2004.

45 Interview with Ivonne Velasquez, MSW, CISW, Executive Regional Director (Southwest), Southwest Key Program, Inc. Phoenix, Arizona. 3 May 2004.

46 Fantz, Ashley and Wee, Gillian. "Chinese Teen Can Leave World of Abuse." The Miami Herald. 12 August 2004. Available at http://www.miami.com/mld/miamiherald/news/breaking_news/9377253.htm.

47 Interview with Julianne Duncan, Ph.D., Assistant Director, Children's Services, Migration and Refugee Services, United States Conference of Catholic Bishops. Washington, D.C. 15 September 2004.

48 Personal correspondence with Maria Woltjen, Project Director. 22 September 2004.

49 Department of Homeland Security, Office of Inspector General. "A Review of DHS' Responsibilities for Juvenile Aliens." OIG–05–45. September 2005. 12.

50 X and Y v. MIMA (1999) 92 FCR 524; Odhiambo and Martizi v. MIMA (2002) 122 FCR 29; Jaffari v. MIMA (2001) 113 FCR 10.

51 X and Y v. MIMA (1999) 92 FCR 524.

52 See P1/2003 v. MIMIA [2003] FCA 1370; and Jaffari v. MIMA (2001) 113 FCR 10. These matters are discussed further in chapter 6.

53 Ibid, Endnote 36, V(b).

54 U.K. Green Paper. Every Child Matters. Cmnd 5860. September 2003. U.K. Report, Ibid, Endnote 3, 8.2.

55 European Union Directive laying down minimum standards for the reception of asylum seekers, Article 19.

56 Figures provided by the Refugee Council from its own records.

57 Interview with Helen Johnson, Manager of the Refugee Council's Children's Panel. 2004.

58 CRC, Article 22.

59 Interview by Mary Crock. Brisbane. 20 April 2005. See Australian Report, Ibid, Endnote 1, 7.2.

60 Interview with youth from El Salvador. Interview by Joanne Kelsey, interpreted by Andrea Pantor. 7 November 2004. He was denied asylum by a judge and was appealing the decision.

61 Under paragraph 16 of Schedule 2 to the Immigration Act 1971 if he or she fell within a category of person deemed to be suitable for detention.

62 In November 2004 the Fast Track Suitability List included a number of major refugee producing countries, including Afghanistan, Bangladesh, Central African Republic, Chad, China, Congo (Brazzaville), Pakistan, Somaliland (but not Somalia), South Africa, Sri Lanka, Uganda, and Zambia. Note, however, that women from Afghanistan, women with one child

policy claims from China, women with claims based on FGM from Ghana, Kenya and Nigeria, and some Turkish claims were excluded from the process.

63 Age assessments at other removal centers are undertaken by the social services department for the area in which the center is located. It appears as if good relationships are being developed between some of these centers and their local social services departments and when these have been developed age assessments are requested promptly. Information provided by Jane Dykins, Head of Children's Section at the Refugee Council (2005).

64 Comments from Bem at page 63 of *No Place for a Child —Children in U.K. Immigration Detention—Impacts, alternatives and safeguards.* Save the Children, 2005.

65 If a child had previously been the responsibility of another local authority, it will resume responsibility for that child. If no local authority has been involved, the local authority undertaking the age assessment will assume responsibility.

66 Information provided by Adrian Matthews, Children's Legal Centre. 2004.

67 Interview with Maureen Dunn, Shereen Faraj, Jed Haven and Tsegaye Wolde, Division of Unaccompanied Children's Services, Office of Refugee Resettlement. 6 October 2005.

68 Ibid, Endnote 67; and personal correspondence with Maureen Dunn. 26 November 2004.

69 See Teichroeb, Ruth. "Jail Alternative Safeguards Teen Aliens: 3,000-Mile Trip from El Salvador Ends in Fife Facility." *Seattle Post-Intelligencer.* 2 December 2004.

70 Interview with a Honduran youth who was 16 at the time he entered the U.S. Interview by Joanne Kelsey, interpreted by Judith Wing from Holland and Knight. 12 July 2004. He was held in secure detention for 10 days before transfer to a shelter facility.

71 One exception to this trend may be in some border control operations, with one shelter care provider claiming that "most children do arrive shackled from Border Patrol." Interview with Ivonne Velasquez, MSW, CISW, Executive Regional Director (Southwest), Southwest Key Program, Inc. Phoenix, Arizona. 3 May 2004. The Chief Border Patrol Agent, El Paso Sector, Chief Luis Barker, interviewed 20 April 2004, denied ever using shackles on unaccompanied children "except in cases where they resist or we think they are engaged in criminal activity."

72 Amnesty International. *Unaccompanied Children in Immigration Detention.* New York: Amnesty International, 2003. 34–38.

73 Personal correspondence from Anita Ortiz, Equal Justice Works Attorney, Children and Family Justice Center, Northwestern University School of Law, Chicago Illinois. 3 February 2005.

74 Interview with an orphaned 16-year-old boy from Guatemala. Interview by Joanne Kelsey, interpreted by Anne Janet DeAses. 21 July 2004. His SIJS application was pending.

75 Interview with mentally handicapped Guinean youth who was 16 when he entered the U.S., was detained as an adult due to an age dispute and remained in detention for nearly three years while seeking asylum. Interview by Joanne Kelsey. 6 July 2004.

76 Interview with Lisa Frydman, former Attorney, Florida Immigrant Advocacy Center, Miami, Florida. 15 June 2004.

77 Quoting Halimi, Australian Report, Ibid, Endnote 1, 7.3.

78 Quoting Homer, Australian Report, Ibid, Endnote 1, 7.3.

79 Interview with Desley Billich, Solicitor, Refugee Advocacy Service South Australia. 4 January 2005. Transcript on file with authors.

80 Ibid, Endnote 79.

81 Human Rights and Equal Opportunity Commission. *A Last Resort? National Inquiry into Children in Immigration Detention.* 2004. Available at http://www.hreoc .gov.au/human_rights/children_detention_report/ report/pdf.htm.

82 Interview with Abby Hamden, Solicitor, Adelaide. 5 January 2005. Transcript on file with authors.

83 CRC General Comment, V(c).

CHAPTER 5

Unaccompanied and Separated Children and Asylum Processes

"I think I am totally broken and I'll be in this cage forever."[1]

Once an unaccompanied or separated child has managed to flee danger at home and reach the territory of a safe state, he or she faces other daunting journeys—less arduous in terms of geographical distance, but complex, tortuous, and often dangerous, both physically and emotionally.

In this chapter we examine the operation in practice of the asylum processes in the three countries studied as these impact unaccompanied and separated children. The procedures in the U.S. and Australia begin with a form of screening process that determines whether or not a child is considered at all as a refugee, while the screening interview conducted in the U.K. is designed to ascertain the unaccompanied or separated child's identity and whether his or her application for asylum should be determined by a safe third country and not the U.K. After considering this threshold stage, we examine the processes for making a formal asylum claim, including access given to legal assistance. Part 3 of the chapter is devoted to initial refugee status determinations. We look at matters such as the training given to decision makers handling cases involving children; how interviews are conducted; and the supervision (if any) of these decision makers. There follows a section devoted to the appellate processes in each country. Here, we examine matters such as the nature of the appeals; the skills and training of decision makers; the provision made for the representation of children;

how appeal hearings are conducted; and how refugee claims are assessed in general terms. The chapter concludes with some short reflections on how the processes for the judicial review of asylum can affect children seeking asylum alone.

5.1 Gaining Admission to the Asylum Process— "Screening In"

After arriving, the most significant hurdle facing the child is to make sure he or she is considered an asylum applicant: someone who is eligible for long-term protection as a refugee. Though this may seem straightforward in theory, securing access to the refugee determination process in practice is anything but straightforward. Many children are simply never identified as asylum seekers; others are excluded in the course of routine border procedures or during preliminary screening processes; yet others battle their way through protracted, often incomprehensible procedures only to find themselves granted a temporary status that leaves them insecure about the long-term future or, still worse, rejected at the end of the legal process and thus forced to confront an entirely new set of anxieties about their prospects for safety.

In practical terms, to gain protection as a refugee, a child needs to enter the asylum determination procedure at the earliest opportunity. Asylum processes offer immediate protection from removal from the country and often represent the most secure long-term solution for the child.[2] The testimony of the children interviewed for this project in the U.K., the U.S., and Australia suggests that most children traveling alone find this first step a real challenge.

Though many of the children interviewed did seem to understand that they were seeking protection, freedom, and a better future, a recurring theme was that they knew nothing of "refugee law" or of the central concept of "asylum." This was true even for those children who said they had been advised about what to say when interviewed by the authorities by agents, parents, or other travel intermediaries. The vast majority approached the legal process with great trepidation.

"They just told me I needed to tell my story and I would be safe. I didn't know what asylum itself was or that what I was doing was called asylum."[3]

Across the three countries studied, "screening" procedures have been developed to identify refugee claims in unaccompanied and separated children brought to the attention of the immigration authorities.[4] A spectrum of approaches exists, from the U.K. approach which is the most child-friendly to the Australian which ranges from demanding to punitive.

■ The United Kingdom

In the U.K., the screening process has two primary functions: to identify children who are unaccompanied or separated, and to establish whether the child thus identified is the responsibility of the U.K. or of some other member state of the European Union under *Dublin II*.[5] The member state responsible for examining the application is the one where an unaccompanied or separated child's father, mother, or legal guardian is legally present, provided that this is in his or her best interests. Where there is no such family member or it is not in his or her best interest, the responsible member state is the one in which the application for asylum is lodged. The U.K. also considers that it has no responsibility where unaccompanied or separated children have previously claimed asylum in Iceland or Norway.[6] One other feature that sets this process apart from equivalent practices in either the U.S. or Australia is that advocates know fairly precisely the type of questions that will be asked. The Level 1[7] Screening Form which is used during the process is identical to the one used for an adult and is largely concerned with the child's identity and family, his or her journey to the U.K., education, and immigration history. Where it emerges that the child has been a victim of trafficking the immigration officer will refer the matter to child protection officers employed by the police and the local social services department.[8] Where an unaccompanied or separated child is deemed to be the responsibility of another EU or non-EU state he or she will be accommodated by a local authority social services department until arrangements can be made to return them to that safe third country. All other children however are "screened in" to the asylum process.

Unaccompanied and separated children seeking asylum are required to complete a 27-page Statement of Evidence Form (SEF) within 28 days of arrival. They are entitled to free legal assistance to complete this form. Details of the procedure are described in 5.2 below.

■ The United States

In the U.S., children do not meet with such child-sensitive responses from the administration. There is no presumption that minority alone will mean that protection obligations of some kind are engaged. Most children seeking asylum alone within the U.S. system lack adequate support and advice. As a result the process of seeking asylum is mysterious at best, often provoking deep anxiety and trauma. The following responses from youth seeking or granted asylum in the U.S. confirm this assessment:

I don't know why I go [to court]. I don't know what asylum means. I don't know that word. I don't want to go back to Haiti. I am afraid to go back to Haiti. The judge doesn't talk to me. I don't know his name.[9]

I think that political asylum is something that helps someone. They help someone to move forward to have money or to be documented. I don't know exactly. Something that helps you.[10]

For me [asylum] is something very important. Now it's legal. I don't know. You come from another country and can't go back to your country, so you ask for asylum.[11]

I understand asylum to be when someone has a problem in their home country and are afraid and can be helped in this country.[12]

Call me what you want. I get to stay. I just get to stay. It means you are afraid to go back to your country because of religious, political, racial, or a few others.... It would be better if the judge was less formal and came here [to the shelter]. It feels like I did something wrong when I am in court. The judge chats with other people in the courtroom, but not us. It would help if the immigration judge talked to us beforehand to explain things.[13]

The wide range of entry methods used by unaccompanied and separated children seeking asylum in the U.S. is reflected in the variety of procedures used to assess eligibility for access to asylum processes. For children interdicted at sea, two serious problems exist. First, there is no clear procedure for distinguishing unaccompanied and separated children from other populations. Second, pre-screening procedures are followed at sea from which the same children would be exempt if on-land. In response to questions raised for this study, the responsible agency, the U.S. Coast Guard, informed the U.S. researchers that any unaccompanied or separated children identified at sea would be reported to the Department of State or the Department of Homeland Security (DHS) so that "those entities may take appropriate measures for when they arrive in-port."[14] They added:

The Coast Guard is sensitive to the issue of unaccompanied minors within a migrant population and takes the appropriate steps to identify and care for them while they are onboard a cutter.[15]

No more specific information about what constitutes "appropriate steps" in practice was provided. Without intentional measures to identify children separated from parents, it is likely that only children who are picked up alone will be identified as unaccompanied and separated children, while children accompanied by non-parental adults—whether relatives, friends, kind strangers, or traffickers—are at risk of being overlooked. Equally troubling is the double standard in practice, that unaccompanied children on-land may largely bypass pre-screening procedures, while those at sea are afforded no such exemption: see further chapter 6 below.

Where children first come into contact with the U.S. authorities at the border rather than at sea, there are clearer procedures. The field manual for the Border Patrol encourages officers to extend special treatment towards unaccompanied minors by "granting a waiver, deferring inspection, or employing other discretionary means such as withdrawal of an application for admission." These are all ways of ensuring that there is no lasting negative impact on the child's immigration record, which is a positive step. In deciding how to proceed with these cases, Border Patrol officers are required to take "every precaution…to ensure the minor's safety and wellbeing." When deciding whether to permit the minor to withdraw an application for admission, (so as to agree to being sent back) the policy requires that children be given an opportunity to present their asylum claim to a judge rather than be sent back home.[16]

Expedited removal, the practice of returning asylum seekers at the border if they fail to satisfy preliminary screening requirements, applies to unaccompanied or separated children only when they have previously been deported or they have been involved in, or accused of, some criminal activity. As discussed earlier in chapter 4, children who enter as stowaways or through the Visa Waiver Program may also be subject to similar pre-screening procedures. It is commendable that the majority of unaccompanied and separated children are exempt from these procedures. However, it remains problematic that these smaller categories of children are still subject to the regime for speedy removal, which may lead to the exclusion of genuine refugees. The U.S. needs to broaden the expedited removal exemption to cover all unaccompanied children in all types of pre-screening procedures. At present, the principle behind the exemption is compromised by the large number of exceptions to the rule.

▪ Australia

The Australian asylum regime, as described in chapter 4, makes no special provision for unaccompanied or separated children at first instance. All asylum seekers without a valid visa must demonstrate that they "engage Australia's protection obligations" before they are allowed to make a formal written application for a protection visa. The decision to allow an asylum seeker to make a formal application for protection is made on the basis of a "screening in" interview. This involves interviewing a prospective claimant alone—with an interpreter if needed—but with no adviser of any kind. Although transcripts of the interviews and even voice recordings are taken, these are not released under Freedom of Information requests. Australian officials did not consent to being interviewed. The only evidence about the workings of this part of the system in practice therefore comes from interviews with the asylum-seeking children themselves.

The "screening in" interviews are carried out at the airport for unauthorized plane arrivals or in immigration detention centers for those arriving by boat without visas. At the height of the boat arrivals in 1999 to 2001, most asylum seekers were sent to centers at Woomera in South Australia or what was originally Curtin Airbase, in the Kimberley region of Western Australia. Before they are "screened in" to the asylum process, detainees in the remote detention centers are held separately and have no access to other detainees. Nor are they allowed to make telephone calls or communicate directly with lawyers, relatives, or voluntary organizations. The justification for this "clean skin" segregation is to prevent new arrivals from being coached by longer-term detainees on how to make an asylum claim.

In most cases, children who arrive within family groups are not subjected to a screening-in interview. Their claims are imputed from the interview with their parents. Unaccompanied and separated children, however, are interviewed alone. Policy guidelines made by the Department of Immigration, Multicultural and Indigenous Affairs (DIMIA) in 2004 suggest that children "of tender age" might be allowed to have another person present when interviewed, but this has not been put into practice.

Although a number of the children interviewed for this study were aged 13 at time of arrival—one had a sibling who was even younger—all but one claimed that they were interviewed without any adult adviser present or prior legal briefing.

This is consistent with findings made also by the Human Rights and Equal Opportunity Commission (HREOC) in its report into children in immigration detention in 2004.[17] In spite of the changes made to other aspects of asylum procedure (and to the detention of children), we found no evidence of any alteration to this aspect of the process in Australia.

Interviews conducted for this study raise concerns about the timing and conduct of "screening" interviews. Several children spoke of being driven to interviews at night. Many were still physically and mentally traumatized by their journeys at the time of their first contact with the administrative process.

A 14-year-old boy was interviewed the morning after his arrival in Australia, while he was still recovering from the traumas of the sea voyage he had endured. Though he had re-hydration drips in both arms on the evening of his arrival at the detention center, he was taken to his first interview the following morning. "I had been very sick, I was dizzy, I was not well. They had just taken the drips out."[18]

A 13-year-old Afghan girl described her screening interview as follows:

"I was scared, confused, and tired. I was cautioned to be very brief with my answers. They did not seem interested in how we [had] suffered."[19]

In detention for more than eight months, this girl spoke later of being questioned on more than 20 occasions. When asked why so many interviews were conducted, she suggested that it was because the officers were bored "so they would interview the children again." In fact, she had initially been screened out of the asylum process and was only re-admitted to the refugee determination procedure after the intervention of an asylum lawyer. However, the complexities of her legal situation remained obscure to her.[20]

■ Recommendations

In our opinion, the U.S. needs to broaden the expedited removal exemption to cover all unaccompanied children in all types of pre-screening procedures. At present, the principle behind the exemption is compromised by the large number of exceptions to the rule.

The Australian experience demonstrates the necessity of ensuring that children seeking asylum alone are allocated an adviser and/or independent and effective guardian so that they are informed about the process they are entering and are in a position to present their story.

The U.K. approach to screening of unaccompanied and separated children seeking asylum provides a useful model which other countries would do well to study and emulate.

5.2 Procedures for Initial or Affirmative Claims

■ Preparation of the Asylum Application: Access to Assistance and Legal Advice

In all three countries studied, the initial determination of refugee status is made on the basis of a written application and, except in the U.K., an interview or hearing of one kind or another. Given that the overwhelming majority of child refugee claimants are not fluent in English, and the forms must be completed in English, the importance of expert assistance with both language and the formulation

of a claim at the earliest possible stage emerged as a universal concern.

Given the common legal standard used to define refugee status, it is not surprising that the three countries studied elicited very similar information through the initial application form, including details of the child's identity, country of origin, past circumstances, and future fears. Ideally an asylum application will supplement this basic personal information with background material documenting country conditions and the threats or incidents alleged in the application. However, the research revealed that children's applications were unlikely to include more than basic biographical information unless prepared with expert assistance. As noted earlier, researchers from all three countries found that children interviewed for the project had a poor grasp of the respective asylum processes beyond the simple understanding that they needed to "tell their story." The recognition of children's difficulties varied significantly between the three countries. Each country included both positive and problematic features.

■ The United Kingdom

In the U.K., as noted earlier, unaccompanied and separated children are granted 28 days to complete a modified Statement of Evidence Form (SEF). This is twice the time afforded adults. All children are entitled to the assistance of a publicly funded legal representative. The form itself is broken down into questions that signpost for both the children and their legal representatives the most important issues to be addressed—a helpful feature. However, in the section relating to persecution on the basis of membership of a particular social group the form does not give examples which would indicate the relevance of child-specific experiences, such as forcible recruitment as a child soldier. This contrasts with other parts of the SEF where a series of more detailed questions are asked in relation to other Convention reasons for being entitled to international protection under the Refugee Convention. Unaccompanied and separated children are provided with the funding to obtain and submit expert and objective material to support their applications. They can also submit a detailed witness statement and supportive witness statements from others with knowledge of the basis of their claims.

■ The United States

The U.S. asylum application form consists of 13 pages of instructions and 11 pages of fill-in-the-blanks text. In contrast with the U.K., no publicly funded legal assistance is available, a very serious deficiency in the U.S. system, though *pro bono* counsel are permitted to attend hearings and to offer assistance throughout the process. If a child or a child's guardian pick up an asylum application from an Asylum Office, they are supposed to receive a list of local non-profit legal assistance agencies. According to Asylum Office headquarters staff, the Asylum Office cannot refer someone to a specific attorney or non-profit agency, nor do they have a formal policy of rescheduling cases of unaccompanied and separated children in order for them to obtain counsel, though such a rescheduling could occur if requested by a child.[21]

As in the U.K., so too in the U.S., unaccompanied and separated children encounter language and legal difficulties completing the form in sufficient detail to spell out an arguable claim. Children in U.S. detention have the greatest difficulties in securing adequate legal assistance and representation. The U.S. researchers found that while it was not impossible for children who did not have legal or other assistance to gain acceptance as refugees, the acceptance rate for those with legal representation was significantly higher. In affirmative asylum cases between 1999 and 2004 where child applicants were represented by an attorney, 48% were granted asylum. In cases without an attorney, only 27% were granted asylum.[22] Clearly legal representation greatly improves a child's chances of being granted asylum.

One former UNHCR legal counselor interviewed by the U.S. researchers recalled visiting a Sudanese child detained in the Liberty County, Texas secure juvenile detention center. He had tried to fill out the application for asylum without the assistance of an attorney or even a translator, but he knew very little English: "All of the sudden these tears were dropping on the table, as he was crying silently. It was very obvious that he had difficulty filling it out."[23]

Fortunately, unaccompanied children have been exempted from the filing deadline of one year from arrival in the U.S. which applies to adult asylum applicants. Instead they are included in the category of persons having a "legal disability."[24] More serious time concerns appear during the defensive, or court-based, asylum process.

■ Australia

The Australian asylum application form is the longest: it consists of four parts and is 39 pages long, including seven pages of instructions. Within the form the central questions are very simple but the form does not explain how an asylum seeker's experiences might relate to the definition of refugee.

A positive feature of the Australian system is that "application assistance" is provided for most unaccompanied and separated children. A federally funded scheme enables non-governmental migration agents (who may or may not be legally trained) to assist applicants to prepare written submissions for the primary asylum application. The representation

of persons in immigration detention is contracted out under this scheme to agents who are paid for the work under a competitive process. One defect of this otherwise positive scheme is that though the migration agents may attend hearings, they do not have a right to participate in the proceedings unless invited by the interview officer. Another problem with the scheme is the difference in quality between migration agents operating within the detention centers, and those operating outside. The research revealed that agents operating within the detention centers were not granted sufficient time to prepare the initial protection applications and were also hampered in taking full instructions from the child applicants by the inaccessible location of the centers and by the intensive "task force" approach adopted.

At the height of the spike in boat arrivals between 1999 and 2002, advisers would travel to the detention centers one week before the arrival of the decision-making departmental officers. The advisers would be given a caseload that would correspond to the interview schedule for the following week and would be expected to complete application forms for all the clients allocated to them.

By contrast the researchers found the legal work carried out by some migration agents operating outside the detention environment to be of outstanding quality. These agents assisted child asylum seekers during the second phase of asylum applications when they were in the process of re-applying for recognition as refugees on the expiry of their temporary protection visas.

In both the U.K. and Australia there was concern among the agents and lawyers interviewed about the time pressure for submitting the initial application. U.K. advocates complained that 28 days was not long enough to elicit a story from unaccompanied and separated children—most particularly in the case of trafficked children who may have a range of reasons for being reluctant to recount their experiences or enunciate their fears, or those who have suffered extreme forms of persecution such as torture or rape.

"Preparing a statement for a separated child can take less time if you ignore what is going on behind your instructions. Most will [give] you a small statement that you can fit on one page…with very vague details. It is your decision if you want to do the job properly. You have to dig deeper to give them any chance of success and if you are concerned about protection issues. I like to see a child for an initial session to take basic details and tell him or her what's going to happen [in the asylum determination process] and what a refugee is. On the next occasion I will begin to take his or her statement very slowly." [25]

The migration agents working at the former Woomera immigration detention center (IDC) in South Australia estimated, when interviewed for this study, that they were expected to spend no more than four hours on each case. As a result the typical length of submissions prepared in the detention context was one to two pages. Some of the files examined by the Australian researchers contained statements that were barely a page in length. It is not surprising, given these constraints, that, from the point of view of the unaccompanied children in detention between 1999 and 2003, this legal assistance process was confused with the government decision-making system. Rather than viewing the agents as their representatives or advocates, the children interviewed for this study all referred to meeting their agents as their "second interview," the first being the initial "screening in" interview. At least two were adamant that they were never allocated an adviser at all (although their case files

showed that they had been allocated a migration agent). This perception did not surprise one of the lawyers involved:

[M]any of the people that we met and assisted had only ever sat across the other side of the desk with a government official [and potential persecutor]…. none of them had any experience at all or any real concept of the role of a lawyer or legal adviser or migration agent…. those sort of foreign concepts were…almost impossible to fully explain in that short space of time. [26]

The agents were funded by the government for one trip only. Unless recalled to take on fresh clients, this was their only opportunity for face-to-face contact with their clients. Although the situation improved slightly as more local lawyers and advocates began regular visits to the detention centers, the intensity of the interview processes was often followed by long delays awaiting a decision.

"Dear Sir,

This is now my sixth month here in detention now, and still there hasn't been any decision made yet. Sir, I can wait longer than this but to be unaware of anything is so much difficult. Sometimes I become very frustrated and I think that I'll be here in this detention forever where no body want to be for a day. Sir, I am an 'UAM'[Unaccompanied Minor] and I am only 15. You can't imagine how a boy in this age feels to be in detention for six months away from his family, even can't sleep properly. My friends have been released or rejected but my case is still unknown. Please Sir don't mind my comments. I think I am totally broken and I'll be in this cage forever. Sir, if you want to say anything please write me quickly as possible.

Thank you very much." [27]

■ Deciding the Child's Legal Status

After the preliminary entry and screening stage, the child is admitted to the formal refugee status determination process for each of the three countries. No child-specific framework of law exists for accepting a child into this system. Instead he or she has to fit into a system geared toward adults, in an adversarial climate designed to deter entry and minimize access to permanent residence. In the U.S. and Australian systems, children are routinely interviewed as part of the decision-making process. In the U.K., apart from the preliminary screening interview, no direct interviewing of children takes place. The U.K. did change its Immigration Rules in 2005 to enable substantive interviews to take place. However, a pilot project identified that it would be difficult to provide children with sufficient time to complete their statement of evidence forms and find a responsible adult to attend any interview, and for the Immigration and Nationality Directorate to still reach an initial decision on their applications within the two-month target imposed by the government. Another pilot is now being planned to seek to resolve this dilemma. Few U.K. legal practitioners favor the introduction of substantive asylum interviews for unaccompanied or separated children. They believe that as the Immigration Service routinely uses asylum interviews with adults as an adversarial opportunity to test their credibility under pressure as opposed to a means of obtaining further information about their claims, such interviews would place children at an unacceptable disadvantage and only serve to re-traumatize them.

As a matter of policy, in the three countries studied, opinions differ on the desirability of child interviews. According to some, the opportunity for a decision maker to come face to face with a child, to listen to his or her story and enter into the life circumstances surrounding the migration, is important and beneficial—it humanizes the process and improves the quality of decision making. For others, operating within a system dominated by suspicion, prejudice, and hostility, interviews simply offer an additional traumatizing experience for the children and an opportunity for decision makers to trick or confuse applicants and uncover inconsistencies in testimony that can lead to refusal of applications.

The evidence from our research suggests that there is no uniformity in the way children are treated; that positive practices are applied in an isolated rather than systematic way; and that external oversight of administrative procedures is very limited. The involvement of both enforcement and service personnel can compromise children's treatment, with enforcement priorities typically encroaching on child welfare concerns. Moreover, data collection is erratic and statistics about the numbers and time frame for handling asylum applications by unaccompanied and separated children are inadequate in Australia and the U.S. As a result, the accountability of the officials involved is limited. Increased reliance in the U.S. and Australia on interdiction and offshore processing even for children's cases demonstrates that these countries are attempting to avoid international and domestic constraints on their conduct, and export protection problems far from their shores in line with the maxim "out of sight, out of mind." Transparency and international oversight of interdiction and external processing operations are thus urgently needed. At present the two international organizations best positioned to take on this oversight function, UNHCR and the International Organization for Migration (IOM), are compromised by their lack of mandate, their funding links to countries involved in violating refugees' rights and even, as in the Australian case, their complicity in the implementation of offshore processes.

The initial identification of children in need of refugee protection is both difficult and deficient. Many children traveling alone in need of protection

will not be in a position to apply for asylum at the border. They may not know that this is the appropriate remedy, they may not be free to apply because they are in the custody of an adult who conducts the interactions at the border on their behalf, or they may not pass through official border control. As a result of these problems many children slip through undetected and end up outside the refugee determination system. In each of the states studied, the age of majority for migration purposes is set at 18, meaning that children are defined as persons aged 17 years or less.

Even where children are identified at the point of entry, securing a satisfactory legal status is not assured. In Australia, an unaccompanied or separated child seeking asylum cannot be granted, or even considered eligible for, permanent refugee protection on arrival. At best he or she will receive a temporary protection status, which is renewable or can be changed after a period of three years. In the U.K., by contrast, up until 30 August 2005, children seeking asylum who were recognized as refugees were granted indefinite leave to remain in the U.K. Now they are granted five years discretionary leave to remain which will be reviewable at the end of that period. But in practice in the U.K. only a fraction of asylum-seeking children—in 2004, 2% of

applicants—receive refugee status; the majority of those granted protection receive a lesser, temporary status outside the scope of the Refugee Convention. In the U.S., unaccompanied or separated children may apply for a variety of statuses through complex procedures which can take from a few months to several years. These legal protections can range from full asylum, entitling them to indefinite permanent residence and family reunion rights, to Special Immigrant Juvenile Status, a visa for abused, abandoned, or neglected children needing foster care which affords permanent legal residence while excluding the possibility of ever reuniting with parents. Alternatively they may be considered for protection as trafficked persons and hence eligible for all social supports available to refugees. Or they may fall through the legal cracks entirely, unknown to immigration authorities or undetected after the expiration of temporary legal status, and thus considered illegal or irregular migrants.

"I understand that all countries have rules about immigration and that those rules must be followed.... But I think everyone should get a permanent visa when they're found to be refugee. Australia should listen to the UN."[28]

The UNHCR Handbook, the soft law but authoritative guide referred to earlier, describes the international approach to deciding a child's legal status. There are three key provisions: expert advice on child development, a focus on objective country conditions, and a generous exercise of the benefit of the doubt in favor of children. To what extent does domestic law in the three countries studied match up to this normative framework?

In all three systems, the decision about an unaccompanied child's eligibility for asylum depends on information derived from documentary evidence, objective information about his or her country of origin, and witness statements and/or interviews. But there is considerable cross-country variation in the procedure for eliciting this information, ranging from detailed attention to child-specific needs, to complete disregard for any such specificity. Of the countries in this study, the U.K. undoubtedly provides the best model, having adopted much of the reasoning contained in the Handbook, so we describe the procedure in some detail.

As noted earlier, unaccompanied and separated children seeking asylum are required to complete a 27-page Statement of Evidence Form within 28 days of arrival. They are entitled to free legal assistance to complete this form. In addition to completing the SEF, the child's legal representative should take a full statement about the nature of the persecution experienced in the past and the persecution the child may fear in the future. The representative should also obtain any relevant country information and if necessary instruct experts on the child's behalf. This system seems commendable and an appropriate model for others to follow: it leads to a situation in which these particularly vulnerable children are allowed to articulate their views and fears in the relatively secure and non-adversarial setting of their lawyer's office. This approach encourages confidence and disclosure, reduces the risk of retraumatization at the point of application (a known side effect of aggressive and adversarial interviewing). The U.K. procedure also reflects the competing requirements of the Convention on the Rights of the Child, balancing best interest considerations with attention to the child's expression of his or her opinion.

The U.K. Immigration Rules state that account must be taken of a child's maturity in assessing the asylum claim and that more weight should be given to objective indications of risk than to the child's state of mind and understanding. They also state that a child's claim should not be refused simply

because he or she is too young to understand his or her situation or have a well-formed fear of persecution. The Asylum Policy Instructions on Children provided to Immigration and Nationality Directorate case workers also state that children are not to be expected to provide evidence with the same degree of precision as adults and may often manifest their fears differently from adults. Another positive feature of the U.K. system is that all applications by unaccompanied or separated children are allocated to specially trained case workers in child-specific teams.

However, the positive nature of this advice is frequently undermined by practice. It is not just that section 8 of the Asylum and Immigration (Treatment of Claimants etc) Act 2004 (U.K.) now requires decision makers "when deciding whether to believe a statement [by an adult or a minor], to take into account anything which is potentially damaging to…credibility including any use of deception to gain access to or failure to apply for asylum on the journey."[29] Of much broader relevance to children's claims is the regrettable but pervasive culture of disbelief and even distrust within the Immigration and Nationality Directorate, not only regarding the claims from unaccompanied or separated children but even regarding the reliability of expert reports.

In Australia, by contrast, all separated and unaccompanied children in need of protection are adversarially interviewed. Three officials are involved in the child's asylum determination process. They are the migration adviser who is available to advise and assist the child asylum seeker about the application, the government interpreter who translates during the child's interview, and the officer from the Department of Immigration (known as the DIMIA official) charged with making the decision. Although policy guidelines have been formulated that encourage the sympathetic treatment of children, no evidence was found that child-specific expertise is required of any of the three officials.

In the U.S., there are two routes to asylum already described—the affirmative process, which child asylum applicants initiate by proactively presenting themselves to the immigration authorities and requesting asylum, and the defensive process which applies to children apprehended or arrested for immigration violations, whether at a port of entry or within the U.S., as well as to those who have been denied asylum in the affirmative process. In the former case, applicants are given an appointment for an individual interview with a trained asylum officer. Legal representatives are allowed to attend, although their services are neither provided for nor arranged by the government, and their level of participation is determined by the asylum officer. The absence of government funding for legal representation of unaccompanied and separated child asylum seekers is an egregious defect in the U.S. system. Interpreters are only paid for by federal funds if the child is in "defensive" proceedings. Entrance seekers in the defensive process are automatically placed into "removal proceedings" in the Immigration Court, where they may seek deportation relief, such as asylum, before a judge. Whereas affirmative asylum applications are initiated by an interview with an asylum officer, defensive applications take

place through a series of adversarial court hearings before immigration judges. By contrast, children being screened for eligibility for Special Immigrant Juvenile Status (SIJS) are questioned by immigration officers. The interviewing style of many of these officers, facing child victims of abuse, neglect, or abandonment, was sharply criticized by respondents to our study. One attorney in private practice in Arizona, who has handled about 40 SIJS cases, was moved to tears when recounting how children have been treated by local immigration officers.

District adjudicating officers are just awful in terms of how they conduct interviews with children. Here, there is this one officer who is just mean…and she uses a very high Spanish. She uses completely inappropriate vocabulary, and the kids just don't understand her. She'll ask things like, "Are you a dependant ward of the juvenile court?" and try to trip the child up when they don't understand her question. One client I just had recently, the way she treated him was just horrible. And when the child gets upset, she'll say things like, "Well, Ms Flanagan, do you want to terminate this interview?" It makes me feel incompetent, but I know it's not just me. I've heard she does the same thing with other people. She treats the children like they are adults. They really need someone decent to interview children…. The questioning is like an interrogation. You'd think the officer was a prosecutor. They are very adversarial, they ask questions designed to trip you up, to show the child in the worst possible light. They keep doubling back and confusing the kid. And the kid's not trying to deceive.[30]

As stated earlier, unaccompanied and separated child asylum seekers are largely exempt from expedited removal proceedings which are a device to screen out apparently unmeritorious claims and thus constitute a preliminary obstacle to adult claimants. However, children convicted of criminal offences, or removed previously from the country are, like adults, subjected to expedited removal procedures and must go through an interview to establish their level of fear if returned to their country of origin.[31] Cases such as the one which follows suggest that, in some cases, the actions which lead to a child being treated as an adult may in fact be indicators of their need for protection as a child. That is, repeated attempts to enter the U.S., or resorting to criminal acts in order to survive, may indicate a child's need for protection from the U.S., rather than indicating that the U.S. needs protection from them.

A 16-year-old Honduran youth was removed from the U.S. twice before entering a third time, at which point he was detained by the Immigration and Naturalization Service (INS). Instead of analyzing the reasons behind his desperation to enter the U.S.—in this case the child was homeless—the authorities viewed his multiple entries as evidence of criminal intent. Many such repeat border crossers are labeled "alien smugglers." Because the child had been removed previously, the INS Office of Juvenile Affairs insisted that he go through a preliminary "reasonable fear" interview. The child was initially held at the Boystown shelter facility in Miami, Florida before being transferred to the Krome Service Processing Center's mental health unit. Here he was kept in isolation because he was a minor in an adult secure detention facility. During this time, the youth became a client of Florida Immigrant Advocacy Center (FIAC), a local legal services agency. Based on psychological evaluations which found, among other things, that the youth suffered from paranoid schizophrenia, the FIAC attorneys did not think that the youth was mentally competent to go through a reasonable fear interview. Nonetheless, the INS insisted. After several months of arguing over the case, the INS scheduled an inter-

view date. By this point, the youth merely wanted to get out of detention and, during the reasonable fear interview, he repeatedly asked to be sent back to Honduras. Based on the objective evidence presented by the attorneys, including psychological evaluations and an affidavit from his mother in Honduras, the officer ultimately agreed that the youth had a reasonable fear of persecution.[32]

This case exemplifies both good and bad practice: expert advice was accepted, objective evidence was considered, and the child was given the benefit of the doubt, as the UNHCR Guidelines for child asylum seekers recommend. However, the child should never have been required to undergo the preliminary screening in the first place, nor should he have been subjected to the protracted asylum proceedings which he faced after this preliminary ordeal was over.

5.3 The Asylum Interview

Once the written submissions have been prepared, the next step in the U.S. and Australia is the formal interview and this forms a critical part of the evidence on which the decision about asylum is based. In any process involving individuals from cultural backgrounds that differ greatly from that of the interviewer, basic training is essential if the interviewer is to understand the story that the asylum seeker is trying to tell. Where the individual is an unaccompanied or separated child, an interviewer needs to be sensitive not only to cultural difference, but also to the developmental factors that will influence the child's ability to communicate. The research revealed that the way all three countries have responded to this real or potential challenge varies considerably.

■ The United Kingdom
The U.K. does not as a matter of practice presently interview the unaccompanied or separated child asylum seekers. The initial administrative decision is based on his or her SEF, witnesses statements drafted on his or her behalf by a legal representative, and any expert or objective material submitted on his or her behalf. The only unaccompanied or separated children who have been interviewed were a very small sample of 120 who took part in an interviewing pilot from October to December 2003. The pilot identified the fact that introducing an interview stage would prevent the Immigration and Nationality Directorate from meeting its target of making an initial determination on asylum applications within two months. A further pilot study is now being planned. A number of unaccompanied or separated children who were wrongfully age disputed will also have been interviewed before being able to establish that they were children. In such cases, where asylum has been refused it is possible to apply

for the record of the interview to be excluded at any subsequent asylum appeal if it is thought that the interview has led to the unaccompanied or separated child's credibility being placed in doubt.

■ Australia and The United States
Although, in theory, Australian case officers may make asylum decisions on the papers, in practice asylum seekers held in detention are usually interviewed.[33] This early interview is crucial to the success of an applicant's claim:

**"Everything is pinned [on this first interview].
If they get it wrong…they are absolutely behind
the eight-ball the whole way through."**[34]

According to DIMA, refugee determination interviews are conducted in a non-adversarial environment, using interpreters and "drawing on all available and relevant information concerning the human rights situation in the applicant's home country."[35] The "relevant information" refers to data provided through the Department's Country Information Service. Similarly, the U.S. "affirmative" asylum process,[36] where applicants inside the country initiate an asylum application, is also characterized by non-adversarial procedures. Officials are required to take an active part in proceedings, asking questions and seeking information rather than adopting a passive adjudicative role.

In Australia, child asylum seekers are not entitled to be legally represented at these interviews, although they are permitted to have an agent and/or support person attend with them. In the normal course, agents do not participate in proceedings. Interjections are generally not welcomed. The U.S. experience is similar. Children have no entitlement to representation; legal representatives are allowed to attend, although their services are neither provided for nor arranged by the government, and their level of

participation is determined by the asylum officer conducting the interview.

Common issues have arisen about the conduct and efficiencies of the interview process. Research in both countries suggests that interpreting services available for child applicants and for decision makers have been seriously inadequate. In the U.S., where children frequently attend interviews without lawyers or their own interpreters because of the absence of federal funding for these services, decision making is severely compromised.

Between 1999 and 2003, only 32% of affirmative applications by children were represented. These figures can vary by nationality and location; for example, only 10% of child asylum applicants in Miami, Florida were represented, while 47% of child applicants in the Washington, D.C. area were represented; only 6% of Haitian child asylum applicants were represented, while 30% of Somali and 71% of Chinese child applicants were represented.[37]

The potential for inadequate or non-existent interpreting services to jeopardize the fact-finding processes at the heart of asylum interviews is obvious. For children seeking asylum alone, access to both lawyers and interpreters significantly impacts asylum success.

In Australia, the adequacy of interpreting services was a concern because of the scarcity of available

translators and because of the ethnic and cultural backgrounds of those who were available. A great number of the unaccompanied children who came to Australia between 1999 and 2003 were ethnic Hazara from Afghanistan who claimed that they were facing persecution at the hands of Taliban forces which were dominated by Pashtu and Tajik clans.

"Our religion was one of the reasons we were persecuted so when we explain our point of view we think that actually [the Tajik] interpreter gets angry at that moment and he thinks we are stupid that we are saying, like, we are saying our point of view that our enemy is sitting on the next seat with us and he's listening to us and when we leave the room he says 'oh he's just bullshitting,' he's just [sorry for the language] but he thinks that we are just lying."[38]

A number of the young people interviewed in Australia blamed bad experiences at their primary status determination interview on the interpreter. Others, however, claimed that their interpreter was very supportive: one stated that his interpreter starting crying during the hearing in response to the boy's own grief and traumatic story. Of great concern in the Australian context were reports that interpreters were being used to do more than interpret: that officers were asking them for opinions about the accents and ethnic origins of the young claimants. Australian researchers were also told of instances in which it was alleged that interpreters told children what they could or could not say.[39]

■ Training and Experience of Decision Makers

One of the rationales given for the absence of representation throughout Australia's status determination procedures is that applicants need not concern themselves with anything other than "telling their story." The task of seeing whether the story fits within the legal definition of a refugee belongs to the decision makers. To be sure, an asylum applicant's account of his or her experiences is at the heart of every asylum process. But the burden of proof ultimately lies with the person making the asylum application. This is true even though the UNHCR Handbook[40] states that the duty to ascertain and evaluate all the evidence is shared between an asylum seeker and the state in which he or she is applying for asylum.

Where the applicant is an unaccompanied or separated child, the question of equality of access to knowledge is also crucial. Without understanding of laws and policies, an individual may fail to disclose material critical to the success of their claim. This is far more likely to be the case when the applicant is a child. In addition, asylum seekers, including mature adults, regularly conceal evidence of physical or sexual torture, out of shame, embarrassment or because they do not realize that it could be germane to their legal case. It is probably unrealistic to expect a decision maker operating in the context of a formal interview, as in Australia and the U.S., to elicit from a child everything potentially relevant to that child's asylum claim. At a minimum for such a system to be effective, decision makers have to be trained in and familiar with the specialist requirements of eliciting information from traumatized and frightened children. The U.K. provides a useful model. Here even the immigration officers conducting screening interviews will generally have received specific training. The Immigration Rules require the interviewer to have particular regard to the possibility that an unaccompanied or separated child may feel inhibited or alarmed by the interview. The Immigration Service also accepts that it owes an unaccompanied or separated child a *de facto* duty of care during that interview.[41] No unaccompanied or separated child is interviewed unless there is an adult present who for the time being at least takes responsibility for him or her. The person who takes the role of this "responsible adult" may be a social worker, foster carer, doctor, priest, vicar, charity worker, relative, or Refugee Council Panel Advisor, but cannot be an immigration or police officer or anyone working for the Home Office. The unaccompanied or separated child is also entitled to represented at any interview by his or her own publicly funded legal representative and his or her own publicly funded interpreter to ensure that the interpreter being used by the Immigration Service or the Immigration and Nationality Directorate is fully understanding and accurately interpreting what he or she wishes to say.

Decisions on claims from unaccompanied or separated children are now made by specially trained case workers in the Immigration and Nationality Directorate (IND). The UNHCR in London have been providing training to the case workers considering applications from unaccompanied or separated children. The training has dealt with child-specific forms of persecution and also looked at the more general Convention reasons and the definition of persecution in relation to unaccompanied or separated children. The IND is also planning training for all its case workers in relation to its Asylum Policy Instruction on Children which is now being distributed. The UNHCR will also be involved in delivering this training. In addition, before the interviewing pilot took place in 2003, the case workers selected to interview unaccompanied or separated children received a two-day training course. The training included the legislative and policy framework underpinning the proposed interviews and advice on developing effective techniques for interviewing unaccompanied or separated children. There were guest speakers from the UNHCR and the London Borough of Croydon's social services department.

In the U.S., all asylum officers are required to attend two five- to six-week training courses on asylum law and procedures. These introductory training courses include a two-hour session devoted to children's issues, focusing particularly on the INS "Guidelines for Children's Asylum Claims." The Guidelines require each Asylum Office to "initiate a minimum of 4 hours of in-service training designed to help Officers to use this guidance, and reinforce their awareness of and sensitivity to children's and cross-cultural issues."[42] The INS Guidelines go on to discuss monitoring and accountability:

Asylum Officer interviewing and decision making should be monitored systematically by Asylum Office Directors and Supervisory Asylum Officers. The latter will be held accountable for ensuring that Asylum Officers fully implement this guidance.[43]

Another example of excellent practice is the development, by the training arm of the Asylum Office, of an entire "Lesson Plan" focused on the Guidelines for Children's Asylum Claims. This plan covers topics such as international guidance, child development, interview considerations, and the legal analysis of claims.[44] The training program includes a documentary film related to refugee children, role-play, and instruction by officers who have conducted interviews with children themselves.[45] The department's policy is not to develop specialist units to deal with asylum cases involving unaccompanied and separated children but to train all officers. Cases are assigned randomly, although there is a special oversight process for claims lodged by unaccompanied children.

In Australia, prior to 2003, no special training to deal with children's claims appears to have been given to case managers. According to several immigration agents interviewed for this study, the DIMA officers involved in children's cases during this period appeared to be visibly uncomfortable with the roles they were asked to perform.[46] The researchers formed the view that the interview process for children in the detention centers between 1999 and 2002 was intimidating and, on occasion, deeply flawed. Policy guidelines addressing the particularities of children's applications were introduced in late August 2003. These recommend that children should be interviewed by experienced, trained case managers.[47] However, according to the HREOC report into children in immigration detention, there was still "no evidence that child-friendly processes are generally adhered to or mandated" in Australia's detention centers in later 2004.[48]

▪ Child-Friendly Interviewing: Concessions for Age, Development, and Trauma

The training received by officers engaged in determining children's cases is reflected in the actual procedures followed during the interviews. Children in the U.S. affirmative process can call witnesses to speak on their behalf, whereas children in Australia cannot. A U.S. asylum officer cannot refuse anyone's testimony, although the scope and length of the witness's statement can be restricted: a written statement may be requested from the witness.[49] Such measures address children's difficulties in providing a coherent and complete account of their situation.

Both parents of a 10-year-old girl were assassinated because the father was privy to compromising information about his employer, a corrupt politician. During her asylum interview, the orphaned daughter focused primarily on the computer her father would bring home from work, unaware of the broader political realm inhabited by her parents. The girl's asylum claim was accepted in large measure because adult witnesses were able to adduce newspaper accounts of the events in question.[50]

The contrast provided by the Australian system could not be more stark. The Australian researchers were able to access tape recordings and transcriptions of interviews conducted within the detention centers between 1999 and 2003. The tapes show decision makers opening children's interviews with unaccompanied children with formulaic and prolix statements about refugee law and Australian procedures. The approach taken could not be described as remotely sensitive, and was quite unsuited to the situation of foreign, traumatized children.

One tape recorded the following exchange (through an interpreter) during a 13-year-old child's interview: [51]

Interviewer: "Do you understand what I said?"

Participant: "Yes."

Interviewer: "Can you please explain to me in your own words what I said previously—to me? What you understand it to mean?"

Participant: "Ah…I mean…my…own birth country…the village where my mum and dad was born…and then shifted somewhere else… with my parent…later."

Interviewer: "It's…ah…what I said previously… is…ah…what I want you to understand is that it is important that you don't lie to me, that you tell the truth during this interview and that you don't mislead me about anything that I ask you."

— No response.

Interviewer: "Can you give me your full name?"

The same interviewer showed no understanding of the emotional impact of the questioning process. When the Afghan child explained that his father had been taken by the Taliban, the interviewer asked him: "Was your mother happy about it?" The boy was asked repeatedly how he felt when his father was taken away by the Taliban; whether he was "happy" that his father had left; how he felt about it now; and how he felt "inside" about what happened to his father. The final exchanges represent a particularly egregious example of poor interviewing technique in the context of an unaccompanied child:

Interviewer: "Do you know the names of any of these [name deleted] men?

Participant: "No."

Interviewer: "Do you know anywhere that you went in Pakistan?"

Participant: "No."

Interviewer: "What do you think of Australia?"

Participant: "Nothing."

Interviewer: "Do you miss your mum?"

— No response.

Despite the different trainings, some common criticisms emerged of the interview techniques used in the U.S. and Australia. All the researchers noted the common perception of aggression from decision makers and children's tendency to take it personally—a perception that probing questions meant decision makers "do not like me."[52] In these circumstances children withdraw into themselves, becoming more reluctant to tell their story. U.S. researchers reported a perceived bias against 17-year-old boys, noting that decision makers were frequently "particularly tough" on children who stand on the cusp of adulthood, with adult appearance but child-like behavior and reactions.

■ Oversight of the Administrative Process

Another common complaint relates to the slow pace of the administrative decision-making processes. In the U.S., all cases decided by an asylum officer are in turn reviewed by a supervisory asylum officer. In situations where these two officers disagree, the case then goes to the director or deputy director for review, and thence to the Headquarters Quality Assurance Branch, if desired.[53] All cases where a child has filed for asylum without parental permission are forwarded to the national Asylum Office Headquarters for review. While a national oversight process could be advantageous in theory, in practice it has had two defects: it has delayed decision making in unaccompanied children's cases, and the policy about which types of cases are to be reviewed has been unclear.[54] This has lead to questions about the ultimate purpose and benefit of the review process.

■ Recommendations

The experiences of children interviewed in both the U.S. and in Australia underscore the necessity that decision makers have training in basic child psychology, cross-cultural understandings, and in interviewing techniques appropriate to children.

5.4 Appeal Processes

■ Rights of Appeal

All three systems provide some form of appeal to unaccompanied or separated children who have been refused refugee status. In practice, however, the right to appeal depends on how a child is categorized, on whether the child is made aware of the appellate rights that exist, and on the availability of competent legal representation. Appeal systems varied considerably in the three countries studied. In the U.S. and to a very limited extent in the U.K., interviews were conducted with court or tribunal members charged with hearing appeals. In Australia, tribunal members declined the invitation to be interviewed and conclusions are based on written answers to questions we posed. In the U.K. the analysis of the appeal process was largely based on consideration of all the written determinations of appeals brought by unaccompanied or separated children in three sample months in 2003 and 2004.

■ The United Kingdom

In the U.K., only a very small percentage of children's refugee claims succeed at first instance (2% in 2004). Most applicants' cases are resolved by the grant of "discretionary leave to remain," a status awarded on the basis of the child's minority alone. Unaccompanied or separated children, who are refused asylum, will generally be granted leave for three years or until they become 18, whichever is the shorter period of time. However, unaccompanied or separated children from Albania, Bolivia, Brazil, Bulgaria, Ecuador, Jamaica, Macedonia, Moldova, Romania, Serbia and Montenegro (which includes Kosovo), South Africa, Sri Lanka, and Ukraine (or other countries which may be added to a list of countries whose nationals are not automatically provided with a right to appeal against a decision to refuse them asylum whilst they are still in the U.K.) will only be granted leave for one year or to their 18th birthday, whichever is the shorter period of time. Unaccompanied or separated children can only appeal against a refusal of asylum if as an alternative they are granted discretionary leave to remain for more than one year. This means that unaccompanied or separated children who are granted discretionary leave when they are 17 or who are from one of the 13 countries named above do not have a right to appeal against a refusal to grant them asylum. A right to appeal will only be revived if they are subsequently granted a further period of discretionary leave which means that in aggregate they have been granted more than one year's leave. The result is that a significant number of unaccompanied or separated children will only be able to rely on the Refugee Convention if they subsequently have to appeal against a decision to remove them to their country of origin.

Access to free legal representation at any appeal hearing was previously not automatic. Representation under the Controlled Legal Representation scheme was only available where an unaccompanied or separated child could show that is was more likely than not that he or she would be able to establish there

was a serious possibility that he or she would be persecuted for a Refugee Convention reason if returned to his or her country of origin. According to data collected by the Legal Services Commission, between 1 January 2005 and 25 April 2005, 13.2% of 17 year olds, 6% of 16 year olds and 10.3% of children under 16 were refused legal representation because they failed to comply with this requirement. The Legal Services Commission has now changed its policy and makes funding available if the account given by an unaccompanied or separated child is capable of attracting protection under the Refugee Convention if it is believed. Few unaccompanied or separated children will fail to pass the means test for free representation as they are by their very nature without family support and dependent on support from the U.K. government.

In a sample period between October 2003 and November 2004, 2,145 unaccompanied or separated children appealed against a refusal to grant asylum. According to Home Office statistics, 3,305 unaccompanied or separated children were refused asylum in 2003 and 3,365 were refused asylum in 2004. Available evidence suggests that quite a number of unaccompanied or separated children do not appeal. Our research revealed a number of reasons for this. Some children did not appeal because their legal advisers, foster carers, or social workers did not appreciate that a grant of discretionary leave (which is temporary) did not give them the same protection as a grant of refugee status (which was at that time indefinite). Others were advised not to appeal because there were concerns that the appeal process would be traumatic or that if they were not believed this would have an adverse effect on any future application to extend their discretionary leave to remain. In further cases, their legal representatives did not recognize the merit of appealing because they did not identify evidence of child-specific persecution potentially leading to appeal success.

Of those who did appeal only about 12% succeeded on asylum grounds and a further 3% succeeded on the basis of a breach of the European Convention on Human Rights. It is difficult to compare this very accurately to the success rate for adults, as the Home Office only publishes figures for all appeals and does not distinguish between appeals from adults and appeals from unaccompanied or separated children. However, the overall success rate in 2003 was 20% and in 2004 it was 19%. Therefore it appears that fewer unaccompanied or separated children succeed in their appeals. Qualitative analysis of a sample written determinations revealed that few children were relying on child-specific forms of persecution even where there appeared to be an evidential basis for doing so.

■ The United States

In the U.S., unaccompanied and separated children typically come before an Immigration Court in one of three ways. Children who have been refused asylum during the affirmative process are "referred" to the court by the Asylum Office to be placed in removal proceedings. These children are allowed to remain in the community while their appeals against removal are heard. The second group includes children detained by the federal government for either being in the country or attempting to enter the country without proper documents. These children are issued a "Notice to Appear" in court, during which they may lodge "defensive" asylum applications against removal. The cases of children in detention are prioritized. The third group includes children paroled from federal government custody (usually into the care of relatives) before their hearings are completed, after which their cases resume at the court nearest their new accommodation.

An average of 524 children annually begin their asylum claims in the affirmative process.[55] An even larger number start their asylum experience in the adversarial or defensive process through the Immigration Court system. As explained earlier, the Immigration Court serves an appellate function for children denied asylum following an affirmative application, and a first instance determination function for those apprehended by the government who are forced to apply defensively. One attorney described the formality of the court system as both a blessing and a curse—antagonistic and intimidating on the one hand, formal and procedurally protective on the other.

"In the defensive process, a tape recorder is running, and there's a transcript. It's more intimidating, which makes it difficult for the client to talk, and you have an adversary, you're cross-examined. And the INS [now ICE] goes into the proceedings with the mindset that you should be deported most of the time. So it's intimidating, and [a] more formal process. But I would never give up the court hearing. A lot of cases get turned around in the second instance, because it's more formal, and there's a transcript. If you get a bad asylum officer the first time, you want the formal court hearing."[56]

■ Recommendation

We recommend that the asylum cases of all unaccompanied and separated children be initiated through the affirmative procedure, taking advantage of the well-trained cadre of asylum adjudicators and the non-adversarial setting. The court process should be reserved for cases on appeal.

Those who are denied asylum by the Immigration Court may appeal such denials to the 11-member Board of Immigration Appeals (BIA). Appeals can be based on either procedural issues or the merits of the case. They rarely involve oral argument. Affirmations of a judge's decision require a review by only one BIA member, while reversals of a judge's decision require review by three board members. There are currently no special procedures in cases involving unaccompanied or separated children. The appeals process for children should be improved by developing a designated tracking system in children's cases, and by the regular compilation of statistical data to allow for better analysis and shepherding of children's cases. Board members and board attorneys should be allowed to specialize in children's cases. Most crucially of all, a system should be established to ensure that children have representation for the appeals process. It is not an overstatement to suggest that unrepresented children are effectively denied their due process rights, since it is unrealistic to expect a child to file an appeal (especially in a foreign language) without legal assistance.

■ **Australia**

The right to appeal an adverse refugee status determination in Australia is tightly circumscribed. Claimants are given 28 days to appeal to the Refugee Review Tribunal (RRT), which is an administrative body rather than a court. The tribunal has no discretion to allow claimants to lodge appeals outside of this 28-day period[57] and has no power to decide a case simply on compassionate or humanitarian grounds.[58] Remarkably, the law does not require claimants to have their rights explained to them. On the contrary, the Migration Act 1958 (Australia) stipulates that DIMIA officers are under no obligation to either advise applicants or to provide them with application forms unless specifically requested to do so.[59] Similar rules apply for applications for judicial review of RRT rulings—applications also must be made within a strict 28-day time limit.[60]

The rigidity of the time limits for appealing represents a particular problem for unaccompanied and separated children. Indeed many lose the right to appeal because of ignorance, disorganization, or lassitude induced by depression. Though the guardianship of unaccompanied children is nominally vested in the Minister for Immigration and delegated to detention center managers, this relationship has not been interpreted as implying any obligation on the minister to ensure that the children in care prosecute appeals against adverse decisions.[61]

A 15-year-old Afghan boy lodged an appeal out of time and sought to challenge the refusal to hear his case on the basis that he had never been properly notified of the decision. He gave evidence of being called to the detention center office where he was told verbally that his application had been rejected. He claimed that he was never handed the written reasons for the adverse decision, and that he did not obtain a copy of the relevant document until some weeks later when he asked for it. The center manager disputed this, although it was conceded that the reasons were never translated for the boy. The minister argued that the fact that the boy cried when told of the decision was sufficient evidence that he had been notified of the decision. The High Court disagreed and found in favor of the boy on the basis that the procedure followed was not in accordance with the strict requirements of the legislation as it then stood.[62]

The conduct of appeals differs within the three countries studied. While the U.K. system is judicial and adversarial, the Australian tribunal is administrative and inquisitorial in nature. The U.S. system, represented by the Immigration Court as well as the BIA, straddles the two systems by including elements of both the U.K. and Australian models. Children in the U.K. have a right to be legally represented, give evidence, and call witnesses. If they give evidence themselves they are likely to be cross-examined by a Home Office Presenting Officer representing the Secretary of State for the Home Department. These officers are nearly always direct employees of the Home Office as opposed to independent legal counsel. The Secretary of State for the Home Department usually relies on the relevant Country of Origin Report produced by the IND's Country Information and Policy Unit and recent case law. He or she does not call live witnesses, who can be cross-examined. In Australia claimants have no right to be represented (although an adviser can be in attendance), but must appear and speak for themselves—through an interpreter if necessary. The tribunal member is in control of who appears and what evidence is sought and considered.

U.K. appeals are generally open to the public, although an application can be made for the public to be excluded if the unaccompanied or separated child is very young or the facts of his or her case are particularly traumatic. The fact that these child asylum appeals are public is in keeping with the general practice in the U.K. of legal proceedings taking place in a public and accountable setting. However, it is at odds with practice in other domestic jurisdictions such as family and criminal courts cases, involving children, where proceedings are not open to the general public. Australian hearings are conducted in private, as are U.S. proceedings.

■ Special Skills and Training

The need for sensitivity is just as great at the appeal level as at the stage of primary decision making. All decision makers surveyed for this report acknowledged the serious difficulties and challenges that arise in hearing appeals against refusal of refugee protection involving unaccompanied and separated children. U.S. Judge Richardson, an experienced judge who has particularly concerned himself with the plight of unaccompanied and separated children appearing before him in his Phoenix, Arizona Immigration Court, commented on the responsibility entrusted to him to decide a child's future with seemingly few options available:

"I have very stressful Friday mornings [the day of the children's docket]. It is very stressful working with children. Sometimes I would like to turn this over to somebody else, but so far there [are] no volunteers. There are so many kids. They are so anxious, and so young and innocent. For many of them, they don't have anything. Many of them are escaping poverty and from abusive family situations. You look at their faces, and they try to be cheerful, and you know that most of them are going to go back to deplorable situations."[63]

Clearly decision makers hearing children's cases require specialist training if they are to perform this complex task well. Even though detailed training courses for adjudicators and judges already exist in the U.S., current and former immigration judges interviewed for this study emphasized the need for additional training and/or specialization in children's issues.[64] The RRT in Australia provides training both at the time members are inducted into their position and as part of continuing professional development. The presence of RRT staff and members at public conferences testifies to the tribunal's active interest in research and development in this area. However, despite this, it was not clear to this study's researchers that adequate training in the relevant skills had been offered to decision makers at the height of the influx of unaccompanied and separated children in 1999 to 2002: see further below. Researchers in the U.K. found that up until 2005 adjudicators had not had any specific training in relation to determining appeals by unaccompanied or separated children. Early in 2005 every adjudicator, or immigration judge as they became in April 2005, had to attend a two-day training course. One of the key case studies considered on this course involved an unaccompanied or separated child asylum seeker. Further training is also being planned.

■ The Imperative that Children be Represented

A common concern voiced during the research was the questionable ability of children to negotiate appellate/defensive processes without assistance. In all three countries, it was clear that children found it difficult to secure the services of high quality legal advisers, a particular concern given the complexity of their appeals. Serious shortages existed in the number of competent people available (though in each country the research also uncovered remarkably able and dedicated advocates). The consensus was that children left to run appeals without competent assistance suffer great disadvantage—no matter what the appeal system.[65]

In the U.K., public funding is generally provided for the representation of children in asylum appeal hearings.[66] However, the U.K. research suggested that where unaccompanied or separated children are denied funding there is a much higher tendency for the child (or former child) not to appear at the appeal hearing. U.S. researchers came across two instances where unrepresented children had agreed to be deported, when in fact they had intended to ask for deferment of their hearings. For example, Tayo, age 16 said:

"I got my foot stuck in my mouth. I asked for voluntary departure by mistake"[67]

Apart from the shortages of counsel, U.S. researchers also noted the drastic impact of the absence of government funding on the availability of representation for unaccompanied and separated children. One immigration judge pointed out that his task would be almost impossible if the children appearing before him were not given assistance of some kind:

"Quite frankly, I don't see how I could operate the juvenile docket without counsel. Otherwise, I would walk into a courtroom with X number

of unrepresented children, who know nothing, scared to death, with nobody there to represent them or help them. What would I do? Just call each one and question them, just sort of probe around in the dark. It would be a nightmare"[68]

This judge's concerns about what would happen to these children without legal representation are shared by legal representatives themselves, some of whom fear for the sustainability of the current system.

There is an assumption that there will be people around to represent kids and protect their interests. People don't realize how tenuous that is, particularly the funding. Everyone doing this is on two-year fellowships. There needs to be a stronger infrastructure to keep people around.[69]

In Australia, where the number of unaccompanied and separated children appealing refugee rulings has been very small, an interesting correlation is apparent between representation and success. Between 1999 and 2005, virtually all unrepresented children appearing before the RRT "without effective guardians" lost their appeals, withdrew their appeals, or "departed the country."

■ The Hearings

The conduct of adjudicators hearing asylum appeals of unaccompanied and separated children was found to vary considerably. Examples of both appalling and excellent practice were documented. Advocates interviewed by researchers in the U.K. and Australia provided accounts of adjudicators questioning vulnerable appellants to the point of physical collapse, and persisting with their questioning.[70]

"F" was an 18 year old from Sierra Leone who had initially been given shelter in a UNHCR refugee camp. He had witnessed fellow villagers and his family being massacred when he was 14. One question asked of him during a very aggressive session of cross examination was "And just who exactly did they kill first then? Your brother or your sister?"[71]

In the U.S. children's representatives reported intimidating and insensitive questioning of children by Immigration and Customs Enforcement (ICE) trial attorneys who represent the government's interests in Immigration Court.[72] Trial attorneys appear to receive no training or special instructions for their behavior towards child applicants.[73] In Australia, the incidence of mental illness in asylum seekers held in detention over long periods of time has made the task of tribunal members particularly difficult.[74]

The interview tapes of one young man interviewed by Australian researchers suggested that his hearing before the RRT had degenerated into a nightmare. According to his lawyer, the boy could be heard sobbing and wailing uncontrollably.[75] The tribunal overturned the adverse credibility findings of the DIMIA decision maker, accepting the young man's account of the alleged murder of his parents and five siblings.

However, it proceeded then to deny the asylum claim on the basis that conditions in Afghanistan had changed to the point that it was then safe for the young man to return (his psychotic state of mind notwithstanding).

5.5 Assessing Refugee Claims

Many of the issues surrounding the decision on whether a child meets the definition of "refugee" are the same at both primary determination and appellate levels.[76] When weighing up the evidence, it is generally agreed that the methods and standards used to assess adult claims are inappropriate. As a result, special guidelines for the assessment of claims involving children have, at differing times, been introduced in all three countries studied.

▪ The United Kingdom

In the U.K. immigration judges have been provided with clear guidance for the conduct of appeals by unaccompanied or separated children.[77] The judges are supposed to make appropriate directions at an initial case management hearing where they can decide whether the unaccompanied or separated child should be cross-examined or whether for instance expert evidence should be called. At the substantive hearing, the courtroom is to be arranged in a child-friendly manner and unaccompanied or separated children should be accompanied by an appropriate adult. In practice, the guidance does not appear to be applied consistently; in many cases it is completely ignored. Immigration judges are allowing children as young as 13 to give evidence and be cross-examined and in one case a nine-year-old Somali girl was cross-examined. In another case the immigration judge would not allow the Home Office Presenting Officer to cross-examine a 12-year-old Somali girl, but then proceeded to do so himself. However, there are also cases where the guidelines have been complied with. For example, a 16-year-old Liberian girl who had been trafficked for child prostitution was not required to give evidence and in another case the immigration judge would only allow a 13-year-old Somali girl to give her identity and to confirm that she was happy to rely on her written statement.

Both IND case workers and immigration judges within the Asylum and Immigration Tribunal appear to find it hard to accept that unaccompanied or separated children can have international protection as opposed to child protection needs. As a result, case workers regularly granted discretionary leave to these children on the basis that there were no adequate care or reception arrangements for them in their countries of origin. The statistics underscore this sad irony that the U.K. system appears to take greater account of child welfare concerns (with 72% of unaccompanied or separated children granted discretionary leave to remain in 2003 and 2004 due to child protection concerns), while ignoring international protection concerns (in 2003 only 4% were granted asylum, with only 2% in 2004.)

"I have seen decision letters where a child was penalized for the action of an adult and called upon to explain decisions taken on their behalf. The decisions are culturally ignorant. Children often [genuinely] say, 'Of course I didn't ask my parents what they were doing.'"[78]

Though U.K. government policy, following the advice set out in the UNHCR Handbook,[79] clearly states that an asylum application made on behalf of a child should not be refused solely because the child is too young to understand his situation or to have formed a well-founded fear of persecution,[80] in practice this guidance is undermined by two characteristics of the determination process. The first is the IND's hostility to the type of individualized expert which may be needed when a child is too young to establish his or her own claim. The second is the almost universal culture of disbelief that appears to exist within the IND in relation to asylum applications from unaccompanied or separated children. Even where there is verifiable evidence from the police or social services that a child has been trafficked, his or her application for asylum is usually refused and the child has to relive the trauma by attending and often giving evidence at an appeal hearing.

"There is the same hostility as with adults. I don't think there is any difference. A culture of disbelief exists just as much [with unaccompanied children] as it does in adult cases."[81]

There is a widespread belief that [unaccompanied children] are only here to get a better education or to get them out of the way of difficult situations where their education may otherwise be disrupted.[82]

Unfortunately, even when the IND does rely on objective evidence it will usually restrict itself to its own Country Information and Policy Unit (CIPU) reports. Recent research published by the Home Office's Research and Statistics Unit[83] found that case workers in the IND relied heavily on these reports when reaching an initial decision on asylum applications. However a sample[84] of current CIPU reports[85] analyzed as part of this research revealed that the information provided on child-specific forms of persecution, including child trafficking, domestic slavery, or forcible recruitment of child soldiers, was insufficient to show there was a serious possibility that an individual unaccompanied or separated child would be persecuted for these reasons if returned to the country of origin. Clearly

this restricted information base is very prejudicial to children's asylum applications.[86] Moreover, the Immigration Advisory Service[87] (IAS) has criticized the CIPU reports, noting that on average 60% of each CIPU report was based directly on information contained in U.S. State Department reports.[88] The remaining 40% of the information was based on desk research into reports produced by international human rights organizations or media reports. IAS cast serious doubts on the accuracy of CIPU reports which alleged that countries such as Iran, Angola, Somalia, Iraq, and Serbia were risk free.

The accuracy and impartiality of CIPU reports is of critical importance, not only for IND decision makers but also because the Immigration Appellate Authority (now the Asylum and Immigration Tribunal) places great weight on them. A representative from the Immigration Appeal Tribunal (IAT) commented that he "can not emphasize strongly enough how much the IAT rely upon the CIPU reports and how important it is that they are impartial."[89]

In contrast to this faithful reliance on CIPU reports, Home Office decision makers' views of expert country reports submitted by children's representatives were overwhelmingly negative unless they "trusted" the particular legal representative who had submitted the report.[90] These findings were particularly relevant to applications by unaccompanied or separated children who of necessity may have to rely on expert reports.

■ The United States

In the U.S. researchers found that asylum officers and judges are advised to give special consideration to a child's emotional and developmental capabilities when assessing the authenticity of the child's testimony. Following the UNHCR Handbook referred to in chapter 4, the Executive Office of Immigration Review (EOIR) guidelines devote an important paragraph to the topic "Make proper credibility assessments":

"Judges should recognize that children, especially young children, usually will not be able to present testimony with the same degree of precision as adults. Do not assume that inconsistencies are proof of dishonesty, and recognize that a child's testimony may be limited not only by his or her ability to understand what happened, but also by his or her skill in describing the event in a way that is intelligible to adults."[91]

The discussion of "Credibility Issues" found in the INS children's guidelines develop these themes in greater detail, covering a child's demeanor, the impact of trauma, the role of age and development, ways of assessing gaps and inconsistencies, and ways of dealing with coaching or fabrications encouraged by adults. These issues are also dealt with in the Immigration Officer Academy "Lesson Plan."

This difficult balance between taking consistency into account without giving it too much weight was noted by Phoenix Immigration Judge Richardson:

"I look at the internal consistency, at their demeanor. It is difficult to concoct a major lie and be consistent even in the courtroom…. I don't necessarily fault a child if they are inconsistent, but sometimes they will block things out as a coping mechanism. So it's difficult."[92]

Judge Richardson noted the need to be mindful of culture, customs, a child's life experience, and any past experience of trauma, abuse, or torture. "Was it so awful [that] they're blotting it out?" Misunderstandings based on differing cultural norms are captured well by the experience of one Ugandan boy interviewed for this report:

"I was denied asylum because the immigration judge did not believe my story because I didn't look him in the eye when I was testifying. It is not in my culture to look older people in the eyes. The immigration judge was very strict. He should have understood that I'm from a different culture and I was raised that way."[93]

By contrast, another asylum officer noted that in some ways children's credibility can be easier to determine than adults', because children, particularly young children, are not as adept at fabricating a story. "When they get nervous, they tell what really happened, that's what will be consistent in their minds. They're not as good at lying."[94] On the other hand, researchers also heard complaints that decision makers at both primary and review stage were harsh in their credibility assessments, making unreasonable demands of children in terms of their ability to remember dates and events, given their cultural background.

■ Australia

Australian researchers noted a tendency to link disputes about the age of a young asylum seeker to his or her general credibility. As noted earlier, for individuals coming from a culture where birthdays are not celebrated and where different ways of recording dates and seasons are used, this approach is seriously flawed. The Australian researchers found similar shortcomings in the methods used to identify the ethnicity of child asylum seekers.[95]

For the unaccompanied children of Hazara ethnicity, the determination of identity as *Afghan* Hazara was of paramount importance because of the known persecutory activities perpetrated by the Taliban against that group. In a number of the cases analysed, decision makers were found to be unreasonable in their questioning about geography, culture, and religion. For example, in one DIMIA interview some 150 questions were asked that were focused on establishing where the child was from. He was asked to describe towns in Afghanistan, the landscape, measurements, festivals, his school, and his journey.

"They were asking so many tricky questions from the village. I didn't know where the mountains, where the bazaar, where's the other village where I was going to school."[96]

Many children were asked to identify the position of their village on a map.

One child was asked to draw a map of his voyage. He told researchers that he just stared at the paper in front of him. He explained that he did not even know what a map was.[97]

Another matter of recurring concern voiced to Australian researchers was the use of language analysis to determine the origins of the Afghan children. It became common practice to send a voice sample, taken from one of the interviews conducted at or after arrival, to a language laboratory in Sweden. The results would then be used as evidence that the speaker was from a certain place. The most damaging assessments concluded that "this person comes from/ has spent time in Pakistan." The test results left many of the young people interviewed by the Australian researchers feeling particularly disempowered because the findings of the language scientists were difficult to rebut. Yet their results were often

given undue weight. Many children explained how, having been taught by teachers from a range of countries and regions, their own linguistic practice had a range of different cultural elements and referents. Some children claimed that they were wrongly labeled because they had used certain words to better communicate with interpreters from different ethnic groups. One boy explained, "He would not have understood me if I had not used those words."

5.6 Conclusion

Applying for asylum is a complex and stressful procedure for any refugee, given the legal complexities, the administrative hurdles, and the emotional and material security at stake for the individual applicant. For unaccompanied and separated children this complexity and stress can easily turn into a Kafkaesque nightmare, where the applicant's lack of understanding is compounded by bureaucratic indifference or hostility. To ensure that children are not doubly disadvantaged by their minority and their separation from adult carers it is incumbent on receiving states to provide a supportive and caring environment in which asylum applications can be advanced, and competent and trustworthy adults who can assist and represent the child applicants.

Not only do advocates voice concern about the treatment of children by trial attorneys, but judges do as well. The American Bar Association president, Robert Hirshon, spoke at a 2002 conference for immigration judges, during which judges noted some trial attorneys' troubling treatment of children in immigration courtrooms. In a subsequent letter to the INS, Mr. Hirshon noted:

One of the concerns raised by [EOIR] conference attendees was the hostile treatment of child respondents by some INS trial attorneys. In questions and discussions after my speech, some of the attendees noted that this treatment most often occurs during cross examination of the children.[98]

Our research revealed an inconsistent picture in each of the three countries studied. Some examples of good practice exist, such as the U.K. system of allocating extra time for the submission of children's asylum applications, the creation of child-specific teams within the Immigration and Nationality Directorate, the adoption of a more favorable merits test when considering the grant of publicly funded legal representation, and the production of guidance for immigration judges. These should be adopted elsewhere. So should the specialist training programs instituted within the U.S. system. In addition, the more child-friendly procedures available through the U.S. affirmative asylum system stand out as an obvious alternative for unaccompanied and separated children who currently must initiate their asylum claims in an adversarial court environment. The more formal Immigration Court process could remain as the secondary procedure for children's asylum cases, rather than as the primary adjudicatory function it currently serves.

On the other hand we also encountered several negative practices which urgently need to be addressed. The lack or shortage of adequately

trained and publicly funded legal representation for separated and unaccompanied children at each stage of the asylum process stands out as the most egregious defect of all three systems. In all three countries, better training of decision makers at every level is needed in basic child psychology and child-sensitive cross-cultural understanding.

The absence of guardians to act as trusted advisers and mentors for children navigating the complexities of the asylum process is another obvious problem: see chapter 4 above. Advocates charged with representing the child applicant face intolerable conflicts of interest when they find themselves called upon to choose between making best interest judgments and following the child's instructions. Each country urgently needs to institute a system of guardianship for unaccompanied and separated children, to meet the children's parenting needs and to discharge its *parens patriae* obligations.

Finally, in all three countries studied, we encountered a widespread and disturbing "culture of disbelief" directed at unaccompanied and separated children. Where support and compassion need to complement official interactions, the research often revealed suspicion, hostility, and punitive attitudes instead. This official stance compounds the rights violations from which many of the child asylum applicants have fled. This urgently needs to be addressed and rectified.

Endnotes

1 Fifteen-year-old Afghan boy detained in Woomera, South Australia. See Crock, Mary. *Seeking Asylum Alone, Australia.* Sydney: Themis Press, 2006. (Australian Report.) 8.3.

2 Early admission to the asylum process will also advantage a child from an evidential point of view, as delays can mean change in circumstances in the country of origin and can pose difficulties for the child in terms of memory and the gathering of material to support her or his claim.

3 S was a separated child from the Democratic Republic of Congo who was interviewed in depth for this research. See Bhabha, Jacqueline and Finch, Nadine. *Seeking Asylum Alone, United Kingdom.* Cambridge, MA: Finch, 2006. (U.K. Report.) 9.1.

4 The practice reflects the basic obligation accepted by all three countries that every effort should be made to ensure that no refugee is returned to a country where he or she may face persecution (as defined). See Refugee Convention, Article 33.

5 EU Council Regulation 2003/343/EC and Council Regulation 2003/1560/EC establishing the criteria and mechanisms for determining the member state responsible for examining an asylum application, lodged in one of the member states by a third country national.

6 Asylum and Immigration (Treatment of Claimants etc) Act 2004 (U.K.), Schedule 3, Part 2.

7 Level 2 and 3 Screening Forms are currently rarely used. Level 2 forms were previously used to ascertain whether an adult or age-disputed child had claimed asylum as soon as reasonably practicable for the purposes of s55 of the Nationality, Immigration and Asylum Act 2002 (U.K.). Level 3 forms were used when there was concern about trafficking or other criminality.

8 Letter to the Immigration Law Practitioners Association from the Immigration and Nationality Directorate. 22 December 2003.

9 Interview with a 10-year-old girl from Haiti. Interview by Joanne Kelsey and Wendy Young, interpreted by Stephanie Corcoran. 22 June 2004. Her asylum case was pending.

10 Interview with a 17-year-old girl from Guatemala. Interview by Joanne Kelsey. 4 May 2005. Her asylum grant was on appeal by the government.

11 Interview with an 18-year-old boy from Honduras. Interview by Joanne Kelsey. 3 May 2005. He was granted asylum at age 17.

12 Interview with a youth from El Salvador. Interview by Joanne Kelsey, interpreted by Andrea Pantor. 7 November 2004. He was denied asylum by a judge and was appealing the decision.

13 Interview with a 16-year-old girl from an Eastern European country. Interview by Joanne Kelsey and Wendy Young, interpreted by Stephanie Corcoran. 22 July 2004. Her asylum case was pending.

14 Letter from Kevin J. Puzder, LTJG, Office of Law Enforcement, USCG, dated 7 May 2004.

15 Ibid, Endnote 14.

16 "INSERTS PLUS/Inspectors Field Manual/Chapter 17: Inadmissible Aliens (3 of 4)." From http://onlineplus.ins/graphics/index.htm under "Immigration Laws, Regulations, and Guides; Immigration Handbooks, Manuals and Policy Guidance." Placing a child in removal proceedings affords a child the opportunity to present his or her case before a judge, rather than being instantaneously returned by withdrawing an application for admission.

17 Human Rights and Equal Opportunity Commission. *A Last Resort? National Inquiry into Children in Immigration Detention.* 2004. 239–242. Available at http://www.hreoc.gov.au/human_rights/children_detention_report/report/pdf.htm.

18 See Australian Report, Ibid, Endnote 1, 8.2. Interview with Barry, October 2003.

19 Australian Report, Ibid, Endnote 1, 8.2. Interview with Halimi, March 2004.

20 Australian Report, Ibid, Endnote 1.

21 Interview with Joanna Ruppel, Christine Davidson, John Lafferty, Asylum Division; and Mary Giovagnoli, Office of the Chief Counsel; U.S. Citizenship and Immigration Services. 30 July 2004.

22 Data used to compile this statistic was provided by Christine Davidson, Asylum Office Headquarters, U.S. Citizenship and Immigration Services, DHS. Personal correspondence dated 26 May 2004. Based on affirmative asylum applications between 1999 and 2003 where a child was the principal applicant.

23 Interview with Regina Germain, Visiting Assistant Professor, University of Denver College of Law, Denver, Colorado; and former Senior Legal Counselor, UNHCR, Washington, D.C. 16 November 2004.

24 For more on the one-year filing deadline, see 8 CFR §208.4 (a)(5)(ii).

25 Information provided by Katherine Henderson, Partner at Browell Smith solicitors in Newcastle, 2004.

26 Interview with David Manne, Coordinator of the Refugee and Immigration Law Centre, Melbourne. 3 March 2005.

27 Letter from unaccompanied minor, *Galileo*, to his legal adviser. Document contained in the case file of Galileo. Australian Report, Ibid, Endnote 1, 8.3.

28 Australian Report, Ibid, Endnote 1, 3.3.

29 Asylum and Immigration (Treatment of Claimants etc) Act 2004 s8.

30 Interview with Judy Flanagan, Attorney, Phoenix, Arizona. 3 May 2004.

31 "Reasonable fear" interviews are conducted on individuals who are subject to reinstatement of a removal order, meaning they have reentered the U.S. illegally after a prior removal order, or those who are removed due to aggravated felony convictions. For more on reasonable fear, go to: http://uscis.gov/graphics/services/asylum/fear.htm. For more on credible fear, go to: http://uscis.gov/graphics/services/asylum/paths.htm.

32 Personal communication with Lisa Frydman, former children's attorney, Florida Immigrant Advocacy Center. 9 November 2004.

33 In Australia, this is not necessarily the case where asylum seekers come on valid visas and make their claims from within the community. According to submissions to a Senate inquiry in 2000, as few as 10% of such claimants are interviewed: Senate Committee on Legal and Constitutional Affairs. *A Sanctuary Under Review: An Examination of Australia's Refugee and Humanitarian Determination Processes.* Canberra: AGPS, 2000. 125ff.

34 Interview with Mary-Anne Kenny, Coordinator of Southern Communities Advocacy Legal and Education Service Inc., Perth, Western Australia. 21 November 2004.

35 DIMIA. Fact Sheet 75: Processing Unlawful Boat Arrivals. Available at http://www.immi.gov.au/facts/75processing.htm. Accessed 10 October 2005.

36 See chapter 4 for the distinction between affirmative and defensive asylum applications within the U.S. system.

37 Ibid, Endnote 22.

38 Interview with Galileo. Interview by Mary Crock. 28 August 2003. See Australian Report, Ibid, Endnote 1.

39 Australian Report, Ibid, Endnote 1, 9.2.

40 UNHCR Handbook on Procedures and Criteria for Determining Refugee Status. Para. 196.

41 Paragraph 2.1 Children Arriving in the U.K., U.K. Immigration Service 05.09.2005.

42 Immigration and Naturalization Service, U. S. Department of Justice. "Guidelines for Children's Asylum Claims." 29.

43 Ibid, Endnote 42, 30.

44 Immigration Officer Academy. "Asylum Officer Basic Training Course, Participant Workbook." Draft, 31 August 2001. 4.

45 Interview with Ginette Prophete, Asylum Officer and Acting Supervisory Asylum Officer, Miami Asylum Office. 14 July 2004.

46 See Australian Report, Ibid, Endnote 1, 8.1.

47 DIMIA. Procedures Advice Manual. Part 40, as amended in August 2003.

48 Ibid, Endnote 17, 264.

49 Office of International Affairs, Asylum Division, USCIS/DHS. "Affirmative Asylum Procedures Manual." 19. Available at http://uscis.gov/graphics/lawsregs/handbook/AffrmAsyManFNL.pdf.

50 Interview with Gloria Blasini, Asylum Officer, Miami Asylum Office. 14 July 2004.

51 Material obtained from John A. See Australian Report, Ibid, Endnote 1, 9.3.

52 See, for example, the words of MJ, whose three-year pursuit of asylum through the defensive process has been well-publicized and is ongoing: "Judge X hates me." MJ is a mentally handicapped youth who was 16 when he entered the U.S. He was detained as an adult due to an age dispute and remained in detention for nearly three years while seeking asylum. Interviewed by Joanne Kelsey. 6 July 2004.

53 Ibid, Endnote 52.

54 Interview with Kathleen Wainio and Eudelia Talamantes, Quality Assurance and Training Officers, and Patricia Vasquez, Deputy Director, Miami Asylum Office. 14 July 2004.

55 Ibid, Endnote 22.

56 Interview with Nancy Kelly, Senior Attorney, Greater Boston Legal Services and Clinical Supervisor, Harvard Law School Clinic. 4 August 2004.

57 See *WACB v. MIMA* (2004) 210 ALR 190.

58 See Migration Act 1958, s415.

59 See Migration Act 1958, ss193(2) and 256.

60 See Migration Act 1958, ss477 and 486A.

61 See Crock, Mary. "Lonely Refuge: Judicial Responses to Separated Children Seeking Refugee Protection in Australia." *Law in Context* 22, no. 2 (2005): 120, part 3.5.

62 *Jaffari v. MIMA* (2001) 113 FCR 524; and *WACB v. MIMA* (2004) 210 ALR 190.

63 Interview with John Richardson, immigration judge, EOIR, Phoenix, Arizona. 3 May 2004.

64 Ibid, Endnote 63. Interviews with Joseph P. Vail, former immigration judge, Executive Office for Immigration Review (EOIR), Houston, Texas, currently Professor, University of Houston Law School, 29 March 2004, and Paul Grussendorf, former immigration judge, Executive Office for Immigration Review, San Francisco, California. 24 May 2004. Researchers requested permission to interview other current immigration judges but were only permitted interviews with judges at EOIR Headquarters.

65 Ibid, Endnote 33.

66 This funding is contingent on children meeting a "merit and means" test. The means test is not a hurdle to representation as unaccompanied or separated children accommodated by a local authority or placed with a family member or friend would be assumed to have no funds of their own. The Legal Services Commission has also issued guidance indicating that unaccompanied or separated children should not be expected to meet the merits test normally applied to adults but should be granted public funding as long as their cases taken at their highest would attract the protection of the Refugee Convention or the ECHR.

67 Teichroeb, Ruth. "Jail Alternative Safeguards Teen Aliens: 3,000-Mile Trip from El Salvador Ends in Fife Facility." *Seattle Post-Intelligencer.* 2 December 2004.

68 Ibid, Endnote 62.

69 Interview with Debbie Lee, formerly at CLINIC/Los Angeles on a two-year fellowship program through the Jesuit Refugee Service. 20 July 2004.

70 Interview with Libby Hogarth, Migration Agent,

Adelaide, Australia. December 2005.

71 Observed by Nadine Finch, Coordinator of U.K. research.

72 Asylum hearing transcript for respondent P.-N., held in Miami, Florida, dated 13 June 2003, documents attorney complaints to judge of trial attorney's intimidating questioning and badgering tone (full name and A# of respondent withheld for confidentiality reasons). 109–110.

73 Numerous requests to the Office of the Principal Legal Advisor for information on the handling of children's cases were unanswered.

74 Interview with Libby Hogarth, Migration Agent, Adelaide, Australia. December 2005. See generally, Steel, Zachary and Silove, Derrick. "The mental health implications of detaining asylum seekers." *Medical Journal of Australia* 175 (2001): 596–599.

75 The boy was so ashamed of the tape that he asked the researchers not to listen to it, although he had consented to its transcription at an earlier time. His wishes were respected. Interview with Sam, February 2004. See Australian Report, Ibid, Endnote 1.

76 For this reason comments in this section are taken from the analysis of decision making at both levels.

77 Adjudicator Guidance Note No. 8 "Unaccompanied Children." April 2004.

78 Comment from Liz Barratt, a solicitor at Bindman and Partners in London. 2004.

79 Ibid, Endnote 40, Para. 219.

80 Immigration Rules HC 395, Para. 352.

81 Comment by Adrian Matthews, Children's Legal Centre. 2004.

82 Ibid, Endnote 80.

83 *The role of early legal advice in asylum applications.* Home Office Immigration Research and Statistics Service Online Report 06/05.

84 China, Iran, Nigeria, Serbia and Montenegro, Sierra Leone, Sri Lanka, Sudan, Uganda, and Vietnam.

85 October 2004, issued on 8 November 2004.

86 See Ibid, Endnote 83.

87 A charity partly funded by the Home Office to provide advice and representation to asylum seekers and others.

88 These reports are compiled by "U.S. Embassies through their contacts with human rights organizations, public advocates for victims and others fighting for human freedom" and not through original or field research. Preface to Human Rights Reports for 2003 by Colin Powell, U.S. Department of State. 25 February 2003.

89 Minutes of second meeting of the APCI. 2 March 2004.

90 See Ibid, Endnote 83.

91 Office of the Chief Immigration Judge, Executive Office for Immigration Review, U.S. Department of Justice. "Interim Operating Policies and Procedures Memorandum 04–07: Guidelines for Immigration Court Cases Involving Unaccompanied Alien Children." 7.

92 Ibid, Endnote 62.

93 Interview by Joanne Kelsey and Wendy Young. 18 February 2004.

94 Interview with Rigoberto Zayas, Asylum Officer, Miami Asylum Office. 14 July 2004.

95 See Australian Report, Ibid, Endnote 1, 11.2.

96 Interview with John A. See Australian Report, Ibid, Endnote 1, 9.3.

97 Australian Report, Ibid, Endnote 1, 9.3.

98 Letter from Robert E. Hirshon, then ABA President, to Owen B. Cooper, General Counsel, INS. 11 June 2002.

CHAPTER 6

The Deflection of Child Asylum Seekers:
Non-Entrée, Interdiction, and Offshore Processing

The starting point in all domestic legal provision for unaccompanied children seeking protection across borders is the availability of asylum as a remedy. As we have noted, all three countries studied are bound by the 1951 Convention and 1967 Protocol on the Status of Refugees which prohibits ratifying states from sending refugees back to countries where their lives or freedom would be threatened.

So children, like all other migrants, can apply for asylum in a country without any prior permission or legal processing. While their asylum application is pending removal is prohibited.

To apply for asylum, unaccompanied or separated children—like all other asylum seekers—have to get access to the country in the first place. But, as already noted, all three countries included in this study have adopted legal provisions that complicate this first step.

Far from being automatic as originally envisaged—the Universal Declaration of Human Rights (1948) states that "Everyone shall have the right to seek and to enjoy...asylum from persecution"—access has become a huge challenge. In this chapter we review preemptive exclusionary rules which create barriers for children seeking to access a country where they will be safe.

6.1 Preemptive Measures to Control Irregular Migration

In each of the countries studied, political concern has grown about irregular migration in general and about asylum seekers in particular: the phenomenon of children seeking asylum alone is one part of a broader picture. As noted in chapters 4 and 5, initiatives have been taken to make it more difficult for asylum seekers to reach the territories of each of the three countries. These measures include the tightening of visa requirements and controls on nationals of refugee producing regimes; the imposition of carrier sanctions on airlines and train and shipping companies found to have conveyed undocumented migrants to the country; and the positioning of intelligence and policing.

Visas operate as permission to travel to a country. In all three states researched, complex regulations have been made that make it more difficult for individuals from refugee producing countries to gain admission through temporary entry schemes such as those created for tourists, students, or business purposes. In the U.K. immigration officers now adopt direct measures to stop embarkation of asylum seekers and irregular migrants from certain countries. The legal provisions designed to prevent access to the U.K. include visa requirements which affect most refugee producing countries (no appropriate visa category exists for a refugee, leaving deception or clandestine entry as the only alternatives); pre-clearance schemes for non-visa countries (recently targeted at the Roma community in the Czech Republic); airline liaison officers who check passengers' documentation before they travel to the U.K.; fines on carriers; and immigration officers operating juxtaposed controls in France and Belgium with the power to refuse entry to passengers even before arrival in the U.K.

The U.S. has established similar means of excluding entrance seekers before they are within the country's borders, in addition to interdiction efforts by the U.S. Coast Guard, discussed more below. The U.S. also supports Mexico's efforts to patrol its southern border and deport people from other Latin American countries before they travel farther north.

In Australia, statistical data is collected on overstay rates and the numbers of people seeking to change their immigration status through asylum or other means. This is then used to determine the "risk factor" profile of applicants for student, tourist, or temporary business entry.[1] It has imposed penalties on airlines and shipping companies who carry undocumented migrants into the country since 1979. This scheme encourages cooperation between travel companies and government departments charged with immigration control. Networks have also been established between countries so that international movements of individuals between countries can be the subject of information exchange.[2]

All such schemes obviously make it more difficult for unaccompanied and separated children to gain access to territory.

6.2 Requirements that Refugees Seek Protection Elsewhere:

Safe Country of Origin and Safe Third Country Provisions

Many U.K. exclusion policies incorporate European initiatives to prevent refugees from "forum shopping" by limiting the ability of asylum seekers to move between states after they have left their country of origin.

In the U.K., an unaccompanied or separated child is considered the responsibility of another EU member state if he or she has already made an application for asylum in that state unless the child has a father, mother, or legal guardian who is already legally present in the U.K. and it would be in the child's best interests to live with him or her, in which case the U.K. will retain responsibility for him or her.[3] If there is no such family member, the U.K. can send the asylum seeker back to that EU member state in which he or she initially claimed asylum once suitable arrangements have been made to do so. In 2004, 4% of unaccompanied or separated children were refused asylum without any substantive consideration of their application on this basis. This was an increase from a rate of 1% in 2003.

The U.S. and Canada established similar "safe third country" agreements in 2004; no special exceptions were made for unaccompanied or separated minors, other than to reiterate that they would be placed into expedited removal proceedings "only under limited circumstances."[4]

Australia has adopted all of the restrictive measures developed in both Europe and the U.S. Its laws now include provisions that bar applications from individuals traveling from certain countries.[5] Broad ranging provisions also limit Australia's "protection obligations" in respect of any person who spends seven days or more in a country where he

or she could have sought protection from either the state or from the offices of UNHCR. These constraints apply to both onshore asylum applicants and to persons seeking admission overseas through Australia's offshore humanitarian programs.[6]

6.3 Interdiction Programs

Safe third country rules are not the only bars to asylum access for unaccompanied or separated children. The countries studied have also engaged in direct action to prevent the movement of asylum seekers both in the countries from which the people are traveling and at strategic points in their migratory journey. Evidence has emerged that initiatives were taken in Indonesia to sabotage boats that were to carry asylum seekers to Australia, forcing them to abort the illicit journey. Although not proven, some have claimed that such actions either caused or contributed to at least one major maritime disaster in which 353 asylum seekers drowned in the seas off the southern coast of Indonesia in October 2001.[7] As detailed below, serious concerns have been raised also by direct action taken to intercept and return asylum seekers and irregular migrants to the countries from which they have fled.

In this chapter consideration is given to a particularly controversial interception measure widely used by both the U.S. and Australia: the interdiction of migrants, including asylum seekers, at sea and the institution of offshore centers for processing their asylum applications. Asylum seekers interdicted prior to gaining entry into a country of refuge have their journeys interrupted and deflected; the vessels they travel in may be turned back, impounded, or destroyed. A description of the policies and practices in force in the U.S. and Australia is particularly significant because of the active consideration that many countries are giving to the establishment of similar offshore centers. In 2005, Italy set in motion plans to institute a center for the processing of intercepted asylum seekers in Libya.[8] The U.K. has also entertained the idea of establishing camps in foreign countries to "warehouse" asylum seekers awaiting the outcome of protection applications.[9]

The Committee on the Rights of the Child, the treaty body that monitors implementation of the Convention on the Rights of the Child (CRC), has made it clear in its General Comment on unaccompanied and separated children that legal maneuvers to artificially exclude some parts of a territory from the reach of domestic law violate states' international obligations: "State obligations under the Convention apply to each child within the state's territory and to all children subject to its jurisdiction (Article 2). These state obligations cannot be arbitrarily and unilaterally curtailed either by excluding zones or areas from a state's territory or by defining particular zones or areas as not, or only partly, under the jurisdiction of the state. Moreover, state obligations under the Convention apply within the borders of a state, including with respect to those children who come under the state's jurisdiction while attempting to enter the country's territory."[10]

■ The United States

In the U.S., especially restrictive measures have been introduced to deal with those who come across the seas, though a far greater number of irregular migrants enter the country by crossing over land borders. U.S. Coast Guard cutters are deployed to physically intercept and arrest undocumented migrants suspected of seeking to enter U.S. territory irregularly. According to the U.S. Coast Guard maritime interdiction statistics, a total of 6,068 migrants were interdicted during the fiscal

year (FY) 2003, an increase compared to the 4,104 interdicted in FY 2002 and 3,948 in FY 2001. In all three years the overwhelming majority of interdicted migrants were Haitians, with Dominicans and Cubans respectively the second and third most numerous groups. No statistics are available for unaccompanied or separated children interdicted by the U.S. authorities.[11]

The Coast Guard describes interception as having both a humanitarian and an immigration enforcement purpose. In practice, however, only a tiny minority of intercepted migrants escape return to their country of origin.[12] These "boat people" are taken on board the cutters from whence they are either returned to their port of embarkation or sent to Guantanamo Bay, in Cuba, for refugee processing and (if successful), resettlement in a third country. Interdicted asylum seekers are rarely granted asylum within the U.S. There would seem to be little doubt that unaccompanied and separated children are caught up in these processes. . In response to the U.S. researchers' request for information for this report, the Coast Guard cited its guidance on unaccompanied minors from the *Coast Guard Maritime Counterdrug and Alien Migrant Interdiction Operation Manual*:

"Unaccompanied Children—Provide special attention and care to children who are not in the custody of a parent or relative. Solicit among the migrant families and single women for a sponsor to look after each child. If no sponsors are found, make special berthing and meal arrangements to ensure the safety and security of unaccompanied children.[13]

According to a detailed study of U.S. interdiction practice conducted between 2002 and 2004 by Yale Law School, it is unclear what steps if any have been taken to ensure the safety or security of unaccompanied or separated children at any stage of the interdiction process. It is not clear, for example, that children who are intercepted are afforded any opportunity to express fears of return.[14] This is of particular concern given that interdicted migrants as a whole are not generally informed of their right to claim asylum. Unaccompanied children are therefore particularly unlikely to feel able to make a claim. Yet according to UNHCR, considerable numbers of unaccompanied children are to be found on intercepted vessels, often forcibly and unwillingly placed there by their parents. They may have strong asylum claims, not only because of country conditions, but also because of their susceptibility, as unaccompanied children, to being trafficked.

The Coast Guard reported to the Yale researchers that it "may segregate migrants, placing small children with adult females unless doing so will disrupt a family unit."[15] According to the study: "It is unclear at what age a person is interdicted by the U.S. authorities, or how a migrant's age is determined." A DHS official informed the Yale researchers that the agency has special guidelines for dealing with interdicted unaccompanied children[16] (though no written guidelines have ever been provided despite requests) and that the majority is aged between 15 and 18 years of age. The Yale study reports that:

"According to the U.S. Coast Guard, interdicted unaccompanied children receive special handling, though it is unclear what sort, other than that they are not repatriated to their country of origin unaccompanied.... children are reported to be interviewed individually unless they refuse. Reports suggest that child-specific procedures may vary depending on the child's nationality."

The Yale study attempted to probe the treatment of particular nationalities of interdicted unaccompanied or separated children. According to their government informants, "though Chinese teenagers are common,

American officials may treat teenagers as adults rather than children." In the case of Cuban children, guidelines for the Cuban Interdiction Program provide that "special measures will be adopted to meet the needs of vulnerable groups, including unaccompanied minors." However, according to the Yale interdiction study, no copy of these guidelines has ever been produced, despite requests, and no clarification has been provided about the meaning of "special measures." Rather "officers are directed to contact immigration headquarters if they encounter an unaccompanied minor.... A special alert is sent to Cuban authorities about having received unaccompanied children. The U.S. makes arrangements with the Cuban government to return unaccompanied children who do not express a need for protection to their adult guardian in Cuba." In the case of Haitians, the former chief deportation officer of the Immigration and Naturalization Service (INS) informed the Yale researchers that "unaccompanied children are sometimes present on Haitian vessels" and that "the INS was considering modifications to procedures concerning Haitian children that would not encourage more Haitian children to go to sea." In a response to an earlier draft of this report, the INS claimed that any modifications regarding child migrants "will affect all unaccompanied minors who might be interdicted at sea, not just Haitians."[17] At the time of this writing, however, no such policies have been disclosed.

■ Australia

Australia has closely followed the U.S.'s interdiction and offshore processing programs. Although there have been accounts of Australian officials taking direct action to deflect asylum seekers during the exodus of boat people from Vietnam after the fall of Saigon in 1976,[18] it was not until the 1990s that the most serious and sustained interdiction program was instituted. The impetus for change was the sudden spike in the number of asylum seekers arriving by boat from Afghanistan, Iran, and the Middle East, transiting through Indonesia to Australia's north. Indonesia became a country of particular significance to Australia because of its geographic proximity to two Australian territories used as a delivery point for asylum seekers: Christmas Island (approximately 211 miles, or 340 kilometers, from the Indonesian Island of Java) and Ashmore Reef (approximately 93 miles, or 150 kilometers, from the Indonesian Island of Roti). Australia responded by entering into a "regional cooperation arrangement" with Indonesia in 2000 pursuant to which Indonesia is paid to intercept asylum seekers before they can travel to Australia. The International Organization for Migration (IOM) has been funded to interview the people taken into custody and inform them of their options.

The agreement with Indonesia also allows Australia to intercept boats and force them to return to Indonesia. Should asylum seekers in Indonesia wish to return voluntarily to their home countries, Australia pays IOM for the cost of voluntary removal. Those who wish to make a refugee claim are referred to UNHCR for assessment and resettlement. Australia bears the cost of UNHCR's assessment and processing and the cost of detaining asylum seekers in Indonesia. Asylum seekers who are recognized as refugees by UNHCR must wait in Indonesia until a signatory country to the Refugee Convention accepts them for resettlement. As with the U.S. procedures,

the initial idea was that no intercepted asylum seekers would be granted asylum in Australia.[19]

It is not known how many separated and unaccompanied children have been caught up in the ongoing "disruption" activities in Indonesia. However, when the Australian government took dramatic action in 2001 to stop the flow of refugee boats to Australia, such children were certainly affected.

The continuing arrival of boats carrying increasingly large numbers of asylum seekers became a major political issue, with Prime Minister Howard intervening personally in August 2001 to halt the developing trend. He ordered that Australia's island territories should be closed to asylum seekers and that any boats should be forcibly returned to Indonesia.

The immediate impetus for the government's action was the discovery on 26 August of a boat carrying 433 asylum seekers. The ship was in distress

and apparently on the verge of sinking in the ocean 86 miles, or 140 kilometers, north of Australia's Christmas Island. At the request of the Australian search and rescue authorities, the asylum seekers were taken aboard by a 49,000-ton Norwegian container ship named the *MV Tampa*. The captain, Arne Rinnan, moved initially to return the rescuees to Indonesia, but set a course for Australia's Christmas Island when the rescuees objected. The Australian government then formally requested Captain Rinnan to take his human cargo to Indonesia, and ordered the ship to remain outside of Australian territorial waters. The captain refused—citing the medical condition of some of the rescuees and his inability to feed and care for 433 people on a vessel equipped to house 30 people and licensed to carry no more than 50 people. (The rescuees included three pregnant women and one person with a broken leg. Early reports suggested that many of the fugitives were dehydrated and that some were unconscious.) When the ship came within four nautical miles of Christmas Island (just outside the three nautical mile territorial zone), the Australian government sent 45 Special Air Service (SAS) troops to board and take control of the *Tampa*, preventing any of the occupants from disembarking. The island's port was closed, with barriers erected to prevent the ship from docking.

The affair became a major international incident and spawned public interest litigation in Australia in which an (ultimately unsuccessful) attempt was made to force the government to take in the asylum seekers. It was only resolved when the tiny Pacific Island nation of Nauru agreed to take the asylum seekers and UNHCR and IOM agreed to assist Australia in determining the people's status as refugees. The program was later extended to include other boats intercepted en route to Australia and agreements were reached with Papua New Guinea to set up another processing center.

The drama of the *Tampa* Affair was followed by a full-blown interdiction and deflection operation that was code-named "Operation Relex." Boats carrying asylum seekers bound for Australia were intercepted by Australian naval and customs vessels. Those deemed seaworthy were towed or accompanied back into Indonesian waters. Together with the "rescuees" from the *Tampa*, asylum seekers who could not be returned to Indonesia were sent to two islands in the Pacific: Nauru and Manus Island in Papua New Guinea. Under what became known first as "the Pacific Solution" and later the "Pacific Strategy," IOM and UNHCR agreed to assist Australian officials in the assessment of refugee claims made by the interdicted asylum seekers. In the face of Australian insistence that it would take no refugees from the interdicted boats, UNHCR agreed to resettle any asylum seekers found to be refugees through its global resettlement program. In the event, Australia's neighbor, New Zealand, immediately agreed to take 131 separated children and families from among those rescued by the *Tampa*. According to statistics collected by IOM, as of December 2005 Australia eventually agreed to take 616 people recognized after processing as refugees out of a total of 1,731 asylum seekers.[20]

According to press reports, there were 37 separated and unaccompanied children taken on board the *Tampa* who were resettled in New Zealand in January 2002. Data supplied by IOM suggest that a further 55 unaccompanied children were eventually sent to Nauru for refugee status processing.[21]

Obtaining information about the Australian government's reception and processing of the asylum seekers sent to Nauru and Manus Island has been just as challenging as the extraction of information about interdiction from the U.S. authorities. In both cases the arrangements regarding unaccompanied and separated children are particularly inaccessible to public scrutiny. These constraints, however, did not prevent advocates from making clandestine contact with individual detainees,[22] both by correspondence and in one instance by gaining admission to the camps.[23] While the Human Rights and Equal Opportunity Commission (HREOC) was undertaking its inquiry into children in detention, the Department of Immigration, Multicultural and Indigenous Affairs (DIMIA) denied them access to Nauru and would not provide any statistics on children detained there.[24] The cooperation of IOM in providing statistical information has been a very recent development.

Australian researchers interviewed two of the unaccompanied children who were processed and accepted as refugees on Nauru. Both had been processed by the Australian authorities and admitted to Australia on temporary protection visas. Interviews were also conducted with Democrat Senator Andrew Bartlett who visited Nauru on two occasions; and written questions were submitted to UNHCR and IOM in Australia.

From these sources, it would appear that, as in the U.S. interdiction program, little or no special arrangements were made for unaccompanied and separated children on Nauru, either in their accommodation and care or in the processing of their asylum claims.

Although promised access to lawyers and a speedy resolution of their cases, both of the children interviewed stated that they were not given any assistance in preparing their asylum claims. Both were interviewed by officials from the Australian government and initially refused refugee status on the basis that conditions in Afghanistan made it safe to return. Neither could be returned to that country, however, because agreement to facilitate this could not be reached with the (interim) Afghan government. After more than three years on Nauru, the boys' cases were re-opened and their claims were accepted. Australia eventually agreed to allow the two to enter the country in spite of its earlier insistence that it would not make this concession. There was no appreciable difference in the time taken to process the refugee claims of the two boys in comparison with the time taken to assess the claims of adult asylum seekers.

There is every indication that the measures to deflect asylum seekers to Nauru and Papua New Guinea were taken as a short-term response to the panic surrounding the Tampa Affair and its aftermath. The IOM and UNHCR pointedly declined to take on the processing of any more boat people apprehended in the Pacific region en route for Australia after the interception of the Tampa and of a second boat, the Aceng. Other Pacific Islands refused to take on processing for Australia.[25] Until May 2006, it looked as though the future of the Pacific Strategy lay in the detention facility being built on Christmas Island. However, whether the new facilities will be made operational remains a moot question. This is because the government moved in May 2006 to revive and extend the Pacific Strategy. A Bill was introduced to ensure that *all* persons arriving or seeking to enter Australia "unauthorized" by boat would be processed offshore (on Nauru). The legislation would apply to both persons intercepted en route to Australia and persons who managed to reach mainland Australia,[26] making the measure unique in world border control measures. The highly controversial legislation was introduced in response to Indonesian outrage at Australia's decision to grant refugee status (and temporary protection visas) to a group of 42 West Papuan asylum seekers. In late June 2006, passage of the Bill was stalled by opposition from parliamentarians within the government.[27] It remains to be seen how the government will proceed. However, the potential is there to entrench modified asylum procedures for boat arrivals (either on Nauru or Christmas Island) similar to those employed on Nauru at the height of the Tampa Affair and at Guantanamo Bay in Cuba. As detailed in the Australian report, the form of modified processing envisaged can have a devastating impact on vulnerable asylum seekers because of the failure to provide any form of application assistance or right to independent review.

Both of the young people interviewed by the Australian researchers had been detained after being caught up in one of the most dramatic incidents to occur in the course of Operation Relex. Shakespeare and Sylvester were two of some 60 asylum seekers rescued from an Indonesian vessel that caught fire and sank near Ashmore Reef in November 2001 just two days before the federal election in that year. The incident is described in detail by David Marr and Marianne Wilkinson in their book *Dark Victory*.[28] Extraordinarily, Sylvester claimed that his boat had made the last part of the voyage to the reef without a ship's captain, the captain having made his escape back to Indonesia so as to avoid apprehension by the Australian authorities. The fire on the boat was catastrophic in its intensity and impact, forcing all those aboard to abandon ship. Two women—a mother in her 50s and a young woman in her 20s—lost their lives. Another

young unaccompanied Afghan boy was later to be awarded a bravery medal for his efforts in trying to keep the older of the women afloat.

At 14 years of age Shakespeare was singled out as one of the youngest asylum seekers on his boat. When taken on board an Australian customs boat, cold and wet, the young boy stated that he was taken to an upper deck, away from his fellow asylum seekers. His most potent memory was of being given chocolate, and of being asked many questions about where the boat had come from and who had been in charge. He said he could not be very helpful. He was shown a map of the Indonesian area, but could not make any sense of it because he had never seen a map before and had no idea of how the picture related to where he was or where he had been.

In litigation instituted when the three boys (Shakespeare, Sylvester, and their friend) were brought to Perth for an inquiry by the coroner into the death of the two women, a freedom of information request by solicitors uncovered an extraordinary Operational Planning Minute to the Minister for Immigration dating from December 2001. The document states at paragraph 16 that there were "31 male unaccompanied minors on Christmas Island in the two detention facilities; twenty one 16 and 17 year olds. All claim to be Afghan." What follows suggests that the decision to move the young asylum seekers to Nauru may have been a deliberate attempt to shut out HREOC, which was then well into its inquiry into children in immigration detention. Justice French wrote as follows, beginning first with the relevant passage from the memorandum to the minister:

"As you know HREOC is currently investigating all minors in Detention. There is going to be a particular focus on the discharge of your responsibilities under

the IGOC Act. We are currently obtaining legal advice as to the implications of transferring unaccompanied minors in your care to another country. Nevertheless, you would have to make a decision as their guardian to relocate the 30 unaccompanied and unattached minors from Christmas Island to Nauru."

The "IGOC" Act is a reference to the Immigration (Guardianship of Children) Act 1946. Under the heading "MINISTER'S ACTION" there was an entry which read; "UAMS TO GO/UAMS TO REMAIN ON CI." That is a reference to unaccompanied minors. Neither option was crossed out but in handwriting there are words below which appear to read "as logistically required." The handwriting is difficult to read. The Minister's signature follows."[29]

As noted earlier, the ramifications of being sent to Nauru instead of to mainland Australia were very serious. Again, statistics supplied by IOM suggest that of 55 children sent to Nauru for processing, 32 young Afghans were returned to war-torn Afghanistan in 2002–2003. Over the same period, no child was returned to that country from mainland Australia. The divergent statistics underscore the inferior nature of both the processing and protection available in the offshore centers.

6.4 Conclusion

Non entrée and interdiction policies militate against the rights of all asylum seekers to access protection from persecution; they are particularly devastating for unaccompanied or separated children without resources to demand a hearing, to make safe arrangements, or to provide evidence in support of their claim for protection. The policies described above violate international law in fundamental respects—denying child asylum seekers the right to seek asylum and protection from *refoulement* to their countries; compromising their rights to liberty, security, and protection of their best interests; and violating their basic claims to humanitarian care. The fact that none of the three countries studied have child-specific policies for these particularly troubling procedures (which carry the significant risk of *refouling* children) is of great concern and urgently requires rectification.

Endnotes

1   See DIMIA. "Fact Sheet 86: Overstayers and People in Breach of Visa Conditions." Available at http://www.immi.gov.au/facts/86overstayers_1.htm. Accessed 10 October 2005.

2   In Australia, see for example DIMIA. "Fact Sheet 77: The Movement Alert List." Available at http://www.immi.gov.au/facts/77mal.htm; and "Border Control." Available at http://www.immi.gov.au/illegals/border.htm. Accessed 10 October 2005.

3   See Article 6 of the Council Regulation (EC) No. 343/2003 establishing the criteria and mechanisms for determining the member state responsible for examining an asylum application lodged in one of the member states by a third country national.

4   See DHS. "Implementation of the Agreement Between the Government of the United States of America and the Government of Canada Regarding Asylum Claims Made in Transit and at Land Border Ports-of-Entry." *Federal Register* 69, no. 45 (8 March 2004): 10623. Available at http://www.lexisnexis.com/practiceareas/immigration/pdfs/695137p74.pdf.

5   See Migration Act 1958, s91Aff.

6   See Crock, Mary. *Seeking Asylum Alone, Australia.* Sydney: Themis Press, 2006. (Australian Report.) 5.2; and Crock, Mary. "Echoes of the Old Countries or Brave New Worlds: Legal Responses To Refugees And Asylum Seekers In Australia And New Zealand." *Revue Québécoise de Droit International* 14, no. 1 (2001).

7   Kevin, Tony. *A certain maritime incident: the sinking*

of SIEV X. Melbourne: Scribe Publications, 2004; and Marr, David and Wilkinson, Marianne. Dark Victory. Sydney: Allen & Unwin, 2003.

8   See Amnesty International. Public statement, "Italy: Government must ensure access to asylum for those in need of protection." Available at http://web.amnesty .org/library/Index/ENGEUR300012004?open&of= ENG-ITA.

9   See Ford, Richard. "Second Asylum Plan Scrapped." *The Times*. 17 June 2005. Available at http://www.timesonline .co.uk/article/0,,2-1657794,00.html. Accessed 31 January 2006.

10 Committee on the Rights of the Child. General Comment No. 6: Treatment of separated and unaccompanied children outside their country of origin. UN, 2005. CRC/GC/2005/6.3.

11 U.S. Coast Guard Maritime Interdiction Statistics. Available at http://www.uscg.mil/hq/g-o/g-opl/AMIO/ FlowStats/FY.htm. Accessed 10 February 2004.

12 U.S.C.G. "Alien Migrant Interdiction, Overview." Available at http://www.uscg.mil/hq/g-o/g-opl/AMIO/ AMIO.htm.

13 Personal correspondence from Kevin J. Puzder, LTJG, Office of Law Enforcement, USCG, dated 7 May 2004.

14 Freiman, Jonathan M. "Migrant Interdiction: Law and Practice." Allard K. Lowenstein International Human Rights Clinic, Yale Law School. 24–25, 42–44. Unpublished paper on file with the author.24–25, 42–44.

15 Ibid, Endnote 14, 25.

16 We note here that no written guidelines have been provided to U.S. researchers in this project, in spite of requests.

17 Ibid, Endnote 14, 44.

18 See *Admission Impossible*, Film Australia, aired by Australian Broadcasting Corporation, *True Stories*, 31 March 1992, where a former immigration officer claimed to have boarded refugee boats in the waters off Indonesia and Malaysia so as to drill holes in the boats, forcing the occupants to seek refuge in the adjoining countries.

19 In practice, Australia has relented so as to allow some refugees to be reunited with family members in Australia.

20 Statistics provided by Keiko Forster (IOM). Letter to Mary Crock dated 15 December 2005. On file with authors.

21 Ibid, Endnote 20. See further chapter 2 above.

22 Detainees were eventually given access to computers and to the internet and so established email contact with advocates in Australia. See Gordon, Michael. *Freeing Ali: The Human Face of the Pacific Solution.* Sydney: University of New South Wales Press, 2005.

23 BBC, Sarah McDonald. "Australia's Pacific Solution." Aired 29 September 2002 on BBC Two at 1845 BST. Transcript of program available at http://news.bbc .co.uk/hi/english/static/audio_video/programmes/ correspondent/transcripts/2279330.txt.

24 HREOC. *A Last Resort? National Inquiry into Children in Immigration Detention*. 2004. Para. 3.1.9. Available at http://www.hreoc.gov.au/human_rights/children_ detention_report/report/pdf.htm.

25 A variety of Pacific Island states were approached by Australia in 2001, among them Tuvalu and Kiribati. See "Adrift in the Pacific: The Implications of Australia's Pacific Refugee Solution." Oxfam, March 2002. Appendix One. Available at http://www.caa.org.au/ campaigns/submissions/pacificsolution.

26 See Migration Amendment (Designated Unauthorised Arrivals) Bill 2006 (Austl).

27 See Senate Legal and Constitutional Legislation Committee. *Provisions of the Migration Amendment (Designated Unauthorised Arrivals) Bill 2006* (Canberra: June 2006) where the government controlled committee advised against the passage of the Bill. See http://www.aph.gov.au/senate/committee/legcon_ctte/ migration_unauthorised_arrivals/index.htm.

28 See Ibid, Endnote 7, Marr and Wilkinson chapter 20.

29 See *WAJC v. MIMIA* [2002] FCA 1631 at [4].

CHAPTER 7

Children and Refugee Status:
Who Gains Recognition as a Refugee?

7.1 The Importance of Asylum

The grant of asylum or permanent protection under the Refugee Convention represents the most protective state response for someone fleeing persecution, in terms of long-term security, family reunion rights, and access to state benefits.

This is not surprising. It reflects enduring international recognition of the legitimacy of refugees' claims for protection, and of the obligations of states to respond to the tragedies and hardships that lead people to flee their homes. It is our view that refugee protection is the most appropriate status for unaccompanied and separated children fleeing persecution on the Convention grounds of race, nationality, religion, or political opinion; but also for those fleeing trafficking for sexual exploitation; escape from the prospect of bonded labor or other forms of contemporary slavery; persecution arising out of membership of marginalized and disenfranchised social groups such as street children,

orphans, the disabled, beggars, victims of domestic abuse; or harmful traditional cultural practices. All these categories of persecution are capable of falling within the protective mantel of refugee protection. And they should, we argue, be considered in this light, rather than under a bewildering array of less protective and less inclusive categories: see further chapter 8 below.

This is not to argue that all the ills facing unaccompanied and separated children who cross international borders should fall within and should be solved through the refugee system. Nor should states adopt forthwith open-ended child protection measures which signal an abandonment of migration management policies.

Quite the contrary. Most contemporary social and political crises facing children should be addressed at source, if necessary with the subsidiary assistance of international aid or intervention.

However, a small proportion of disadvantaged children have a disproportionate claim on our attention and our responsiveness because they lack adult protection at a critical juncture in their lives. As the case studies in this report demonstrate, many of the child migrants involved in seeking asylum alone have deeply traumatic backgrounds. Our argument is that these migrants should be given a fair chance to prove their entitlement to the expansive protections that the international community as a whole, and the three countries studied in particular, have long considered appropriate. They should be received, assisted, and represented in a timely manner. If their cases are proved they should be given full protection as asylees or refugees. If their cases are not proved, they should be returned home unless human rights reasons prevent this or no appropriate family reception circumstances exist. Ours is not a call for open borders, for expansion of

refugee protection, or for a ban on return of unsuccessful child asylum applications. Rather it is a call for non-discrimination and consistency with the legal and moral principles established over half a century ago by the countries studied.

Our research reveals that in global terms, only a minority of unaccompanied and separated children in need of international protection are recognized as refugees. Given the vulnerability of children and their strong claim to precisely the international compassion that inspired the establishment of the refugee regime in the first place, current state reluctance to grant asylum to unaccompanied and separated children is a remarkable and depressing commentary on our times. We have shown that there are significant procedural reasons why these children continue to fall through the cracks of the refugee protection system.

In this chapter we examine how the legal standards for the grant of refugee status have been interpreted in each of the countries studied. We begin by examining the type of fear that must be demonstrated under the Refugee Convention before turning to the question of what constitutes "persecution" for refugee purposes. The discussion of persecution begins by setting out the key interpretative principles that have been accepted in international jurisprudence. There follows a more detailed examination of how the concept needs to be interpreted to account for the experiences and particular vulnerability of children. In this context we examine in turn persecution that is not specific to children; persecution that is particular to children, and behaviors that become persecutory because of the minority of the individual being targeted. Thereafter we provide an overview of domestic case law on the five grounds on which persecution must be based under the Refugee Convention. The chapter concludes with a review of cases involving vulnerable children in a variety of quite different situations.

7.2 Defining Persecution

To qualify for asylum, a child, like any other applicant, must demonstrate a "well-founded fear of persecution." This phrase is drawn from the 1951 UN Refugee Convention, the international law instrument that establishes the legal parameters within which asylum applications must be judged in any given domestic context. The Convention has been incorporated into the domestic law of all three of the countries studied. The key term, in this definition, is the word "persecution," a term that is not defined in international law. This open-endedness is not a coincidence—the terms "torture" or "cruel, inhuman, or degrading treatment or punishment" which feature prominently in international human rights law could have been used instead if the goal was to reference a clearly circumscribed domain of behavior. Instead the term "persecution" was chosen precisely in order to accommodate a wide range of situations and to encompass new developments threatening human dignity as they evolved and were brought to international attention.

Despite this open-endedness, certain principles are clearly established. A threat to life or freedom, arising out of a failure of state protection and based on civil or political discrimination, always constitutes persecution. So, an unprotected child whose flight is motivated by such a threat, because he or she is an indigenous person, or a member of a vulnerable minority group, should fall within the definition. Similarly, other serious but non-life-threatening violations of human rights for the same reasons—such as torture—would also qualify. A child fleeing torture specifically targeted at street children or at children of dissidents would thus also be covered. It matters not whether the state is directly responsible for instigating the torture (an act of commission) or whether the state is indirectly responsible for knowingly failing to prevent the torture (an act of

omission). But, and this is the third principle, the protection to be afforded asylum seekers is broader, and tracks developments in human rights law more generally. Thus, for example, the Basic Law Manual, which governs U.S. asylum procedure, explicitly recognizes this importance of international standards, in framing decision making in this area. The instruction to asylum officers states: "One must determine whether the conduct alleged to be persecution violates a basic human right, protected under international law."[1] The U.K. and Australia have also recognized the importance of general human rights principles in construing the scope of asylum protection. In the U.K. the Asylum Policy Instruction on Children, which is issued to all Immigration and Nationality Directorate (IND) case workers, addresses this question. The U.K. has ratified the UN Convention on the Rights of the Child but applied a reservation in relation to the right to enter and remain in the U.K. The policy states:

"[I]t is, however, IND's policy to seek to adhere to the principles contained in the Convention where possible subject to the need to maintain an effective immigration control. In particular case workers should bear in mind the core principles of best interests, the right of participation and non-discrimination."

The Australian courts have also favored a broad interpretation of persecution, which is reflected in turn in the broad definition of "persecution" incorporated into the Migration Act 1958 (Australia).[2] In *Applicant S v. MIMIA*, the Australian High Court confirmed that the characterization of persecutory behavior is to be determined by the standards of human rights law and by the extent to which an individual is subjected to discriminatory treatment.[3] This in turn has given rise to questions about when (if ever), validly enacted state laws will or could amount to persecution. In the same case, the court noted that the more "*ad hoc and random*" the infliction of harm, the more likely it is that an individual is being subjected to persecution rather than a "law of general application."[4] The test is whether a general law has a legitimate objective and uses means proportionate to the objects desired. In *Chen Shi Hai v. MIMA*, the High Court stated:

Whether the different treatment of different individuals or groups is appropriate and adapted to achieving some legitimate government objective depends on the different treatment involved and, ultimately, whether it offends the standards of civil societies which seek to meet the calls of common humanity.[5] (Emphasis added.)

For unaccompanied and separated children seeking asylum alone, this approach has the benefit of expanding the categories of persecutory behavior to include actions that might be taken in line with either broad scale policies or with the tolerance of the authorities. The relevant standard to be applied is that of the "civilized and organized society."

The expansive and inclusive conception implicit in this approach is important, since human rights violations that affect child asylum seekers may well fall outside the range of domestic experience and be unfamiliar to domestic fact finders and decision

makers. For example, in the U.K. immigration judges may be unfamiliar with the child soldier recruitment practices of the Ugandan Lord's Resistance Army, just as Australian decision makers may be unaware of the Taliban's targeting of children from particular minorities in Afghanistan.

Moreover, it is not just spectacular individual acts that constitute persecution. Lesser measures that do not individually amount to persecution, can nevertheless cumulatively constitute persecution, where they operate incrementally and in aggregate. This principle is well established in both international and domestic law. So, whereas one act of beating a street child for sleeping in a public place may not constitute persecution, a pattern of such conduct over time certainly could. Indeed discriminatory acts which are not even particularly serious taken singly can, where they constitute a persistent pattern, rise to the level of persecution. Taunting, baiting, and excluding "second children" from government services, in an area where a governmental "one-child" birth policy is strictly enforced, exemplifies how this principle might impinge on a child asylum seeker in practice. So, too, does the forced recruitment of first born sons into a guerilla force.

Finally, although lawful punishment cannot generally constitute persecution—as the UNHCR Handbook puts it, "a refugee is a victim…of injustice, not a fugitive from justice"[6]—the distinction between punishment and persecution can become complicated. Thus, excessive punishment (for example, the death penalty for a small drugs-possession charge) or discriminatory punishment (for example, imprisonment for pursuing "illegal" religious education) may constitute persecution, and decision makers must be open to looking behind the formal claim that harsh behavior constitutes mere punishment. This may be particularly pertinent in the case of politically active adolescents, where the line between punishing insubordination and pro-

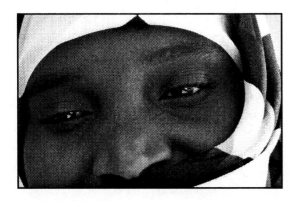

hibiting expression of legitimate political expression may be wrongly drawn. Police brutality towards street children caught thieving or begging, or towards adolescent activists on the streets of Baghdad or Port au Prince, are examples. Whether or not other conduct can be considered "persecution" depends on the circumstances of each case. Individual situations have to be evaluated separately and in detail. Blanket decision making, for example that all Mexican children arriving unaccompanied across the southern U.S. border or that all Nigerian children trafficked into the U.K. are not eligible for asylum, would violate this requirement.

The UN Refugee Convention and its attendant Protocol combine to define a refugee as any person who:

owing to well-founded fear of being persecuted for reasons of race, religion, nationality or membership of a particular social group or political opinion, is outside the country of his nationality and is unable or, owing to such fear, is unwilling to avail himself of the protection of that country.

■ Establishing a "Well-Founded Fear": Subjective and Objective Tests

All refugee determination systems based on the Refugee Convention require the individual applicant to prove that he or she has a "well-founded fear" of persecution. In general the applicant must

both show a subjective fear of persecution upon return to his or her country of origin *and* demonstrate from an objective viewpoint that the fear is "well-founded."

Unaccompanied and separated children may have greater difficulty than their adult counterparts satisfying the subjective part of this test. The child's capacity for subjective fear may be marred by his or her experiences and stage of development. In many of the cases reviewed for this study, the decision to flee was made by parents, guardians, or other adults conscious of a threat to the minor rather than by the child him or herself. In some cases, children interviewed for this study actively resisted suggestions that the flight might have involved fear on their part, and instead expressed resentment about the decision that they flee.[7]

Recommendations and policy guidelines issued by UNHCR and by the three countries studied recognize that children may have difficulty satisfying the subjective requirement of the Convention definition of "refugee." Accordingly decision makers are advised to give more weight to the objective elements of a child's claims. The UNHCR Guidelines also state that if there is reason to believe that the parents or guardian of an unaccompanied or separated child have a well-founded fear for the persecution of their child, then the child may be imputed to have such a fear.

The particular vulnerability of children who are alone or separated from their families should increase the likelihood of a finding of persecution. However, in practice this has been difficult to ensure because of the absence of a rigorous or authoritative account of what constitutes persecution from a child's perspective or because of the difficulty in accessing the asylum determination system. As a result, the grant of asylum under the Refugee Convention to separated or unaccompanied child applicants represents the exception rather than the rule in two of the three countries studied, despite compelling and convincing evidence of persecution. In the U.K., in 2004, only 2% of asylum applications by unaccompanied children were successful. This increased marginally to 5% in 2005 and the first quarter of 2006, but was still a lower percentage than that for adults. In the U.S., figures are only available for children applying through the affirmative asylum process at Asylum Offices, a group which constitutes less than one-tenth of the population of children in federal government custody who will go before the Immigration Court. Within this population, the rate of success in asylum applications is similar to the adult rate—between 30% and 40% between 2001 and 2003—however, the grant rate for child applicants has dropped more precipitously than for applicants overall—from 63% of children granted in 1999 to only 31% granted in 2003, compared to 38% of all applicants granted in 1999 to only 29% granted in 2003.[8] In Australia, the very limited number of unaccompanied and separated children makes it difficult to gauge overall trends: between 1999 and 2003 the acceptance rates for children seeking asylum alone were broadly similar to that of adult asylum seekers, although children unrepresented at appellate level generally fared very poorly.[9]

As earlier chapters report, children interviewed about their asylum claims are not prompted with questions about child-specific persecution. In the U.K., where unaccompanied and separated children are not interviewed but are required to respond to a Children's Statement of Evidence Form, no questions explicitly elicit information about child-specific persecution. In Australia, children receive no legal advice or representation at all prior to their first, critical screening interview, although they are assisted if they can overcome this hurdle. In the U.S., legally represented children have a far better success rate in asylum applications than those who are unrepresented.[10]

7.3 What is Child Persecution?

It is helpful to identify three distinct but general categories of what may constitute "child persecution." First, there are situations which constitute persecution for both adult and child asylum seekers. Second, there are situations of child-specific persecution, where the fact that the applicant is a child is central to the harm inflicted or feared. Finally, there are forms of harm that become persecution when (and only when) the victim of the harm is a child. In this section we examine each of these categories in turn. Even in countries like the U.S. and Australia, where children seem to be gaining recognition as refugees at a similar rate to adults, there are aspects in both law and practice that are of concern. For example, Australian researchers found many cases where (accompanied) children were included in the asylum applications of their parents instead of being the subject of separate submissions made on their behalf.

■ Mainstream Cases

In all three countries studied, the asylum cases where children were registered as primary applicants most commonly involved allegations of persecution that were not peculiar to minority status. These include cases where children, like their adult counterparts, flee their countries to escape from politically, ethnically, or religiously motivated persecution. Examples include: Tamil children fleeing attacks by the Sinhalese army; Somali children fleeing vendettas by opposing clans; Guatemalan children escaping from targeted state violence against indigenous groups; Afghan Hazara children fleeing Taliban recruiters; Haitian children fleeing violence at the hands of government thugs. In these instances, even when children are unaccompanied or separated from their families, the child persecution alleged may not need to include reference to any child-specific

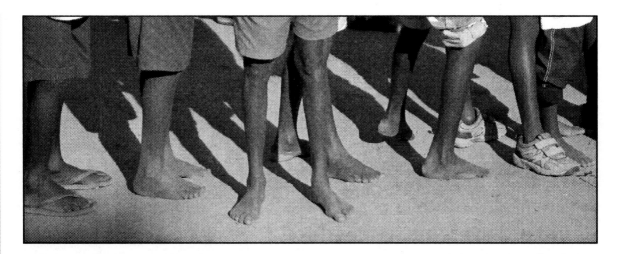

features. Though the separated status of the children may give rise to special procedural problems, it does not necessarily constitute an issue for the substantive adjudication of the asylum claim. No special account of child persecution is therefore required.

However, even in these mainstream cases, child-specific issues may arise and be neglected. For example, a child may be persecuted as part of an oppressed minority group in order to increase pressure on politically prominent or targeted parents. Asylum officers and judges who ignore child-specific factors may miss such a dynamic and overlook the particular risks facing such a child.

■ Persecution that Only Applies to Children

The fact that the asylum applicant is a child may be a central factor in the harm inflicted or feared. Only children can be conscripted as child soldiers; subjected to child abuse; recruited into gangs of street children; threatened with infanticide or pre-puberty female circumcision; subjected to child sale or marriage; or made to suffer persistent discrimination as "second children."

A 13-year-old girl from India was granted asylum in the U.S. due to suspicion that the girl had been brought to the U.S. for an arranged marriage.[11]

In these cases, an understanding of child-specific persecution, and an acknowledgment of its impact, is critical to adjudication of the asylum claim. It is here that the expansive and evolving notion of what constitutes persecution must be applied to correct adult-centered and static conceptions of the role of asylum. Until recently, many of the categories of child-specific persecution listed above were not considered to fall within the asylum rubric at all. This is not because the behavior concerned did not have the hallmarks of serious harm or threat to life and freedom, but because a traditional conception of the limits of persecution hampered both advocates and decision makers in advancing and pursuing such claims. Given the rapidly expanding scope of human rights norms, and of global knowledge of rights violations inflicted on children, it is critical that the concept of persecution central to the adjudication of asylum claims keep in step.

The development of a body of jurisprudence within the U.S. on the validity of asylum claims by Central American street children illustrates the proactive and child-centered use of refugee protection that we consider both appropriate within refugee law and necessary as a child protection measure. The following case of a Honduran street child is an example in point.

Children and Refugee Status | Eldin's Story

Eldin never met his father and was abandoned by his mother as an infant. He lived with his maternal grandparents, relatives, and others in a two-room house. He recalls that there often was not enough food for everyone. Sometimes he would not eat for a whole day. The two-room house had no bathroom, lights, heat, or beds; the people living there—up to 20 or 25—would sleep on the floor on torn blankets.

In addition to hunger, if he took "too long" to fetch wood or water, Eldin suffered severe physical abuse at the hands of his grandfather and uncles.... He was beaten, sometimes across the face, with belts, ropes, cables until he bled.... He lived in fear of his grandfather and eventually ran away.... By the age of nine, Eldin was living on the streets, trying to feed himself by selling fruit or clothing, earning tips for helping people onto and off of buses, shining shoes.... He would sleep in different places at night: sometimes in the gutters, on the sidewalk at a bus stop, curled up hidden under a car, or in cardboard cartons. He had no shoes, and he would wear the same clothes for weeks.... Eldin was afraid of gangs. The gangs carried weapons, including guns and knives. They often beat him up, leaving him unconscious once, and someone even attacked him while he was sleeping. The gangs threw rocks at him, wounding his head, arm, and legs and leaving scars.... A doctor's examination confirmed injuries compatible with this account, including five scars on his extremities and reduced hearing in one ear. Gang members would sometimes steal his money and even threaten to kill him. Eldin also saw gang members beat up, threaten, and kill street children. They would tell him to rob and steal, threatening him with retaliation if he refused. On many occasions he was asked to join the gangs. Eldin refused but could not gain any protection from

the police. Indeed, certain members of the police told him to rob and steal on their behalf. After one occasion in which gang members threatened to kill Eldin for not joining them, he fled Honduras in fear and went to Mexico, with the help of a bus driver. After living on the streets in Mexico, Eldin managed to contact his mother, legally resident in California. She drove across the border, picked him up in Tijuana and crossed back with him: he was 13 years old. When arrested and placed in removal proceedings, he testified before the immigration judge about his fears of returning to Honduras, where he has no place to go, will be forced back on the streets, and risks being killed or tortured. Much of Eldin's testimony was confirmed in court by Bruce Harris, Executive Director for Latin American Programs for Casa Alianza, a non-governmental organization (NGO) that provides support services for street children in Latin America.[12]

SEEKING ASYLUM ALONE | A COMPARATIVE STUDY

In Australia, the recognition as refugees of children born in contravention of China's "one child" policy is another example of good practice.[13] So is the U.K. grant of asylum to trafficked children.

■ Behavior Which Constitutes Persecution for a Child but Not an Adult

Finally, there are situations where the behavior complained of should be considered persecution when inflicted on or threatened against a child, even though the same behavior may not rise to the level of persecution in the case of an adult.

As the U.S. 7th Circuit Court of Appeal has stated, "There may be situations where children should be considered victims of persecution though they have suffered less harm than would be required for an adult."[14]

This category epitomizes the relativism inherent in the concept of persecution. It is also the one which is most likely to present adjudicatory difficulties for child advocates and decision makers concerned with children's cases, since similarly placed adults would not succeed in obtaining asylum. There are two reasons why conduct that might be considered mere harassment or interference when directed at an adult could rise to the level of persecution for a child. First, a child's heightened sensitivity might influence the emotional response to the conduct. This dynamic is commonly witnessed in adversarial situations (including courtrooms) and should be fairly uncontroversial. Aggressive questioning, restraints on freedom such as handcuffs or shackles, detention, rough handling such as slapping, shouting, threats, can produce high levels of terror, anxiety, and distress in children where these behaviors may not rise to the level of "serious harm" for adults.[15] These experiences may result in temporary or permanent trauma to a child. A child-centered perspective would identify such behavior as persecution, whereas an approach lacking this might miss the significance of the experience and trivialize its impact on the applicant. For example, overnight incarceration of street children may instill utter terror or despair for a child, as might a bullying and aggressive rebuke, threat, or admonishment from a uniformed state agent carrying out a house search. It is not only conduct directed at the child that can elicit this heightened response. Behavior that targets close relatives, such as parents or siblings, may also terrorize and traumatize a child so as to constitute persecution, in circumstances where an adult would not be so affected.

Second, conduct may rise to the level of persecution for a child where it would not for an adult because of children's heightened dependence. Children's vulnerability in the face of separation or loss of family is widely acknowledged. Forced separation from parents, as where the latter are detained or where children are abandoned or neglected, may in some circumstances constitute persecution for a child where similar separation for an adult could not be so considered. The same argument may apply to children who become homeless as a result of domestic abuse or family destitution, and who are, as a result, deprived of basic social and economic rights such as access to schooling, housing, and basic health care.[16] They are not just clear candidates for welfare protection or foster care, as a matter of immediate social provision. Where such domestic protection is unavailable, these children may validly claim to face persecution.

"I didn't really think about getting to the U.S. or what would happen to me there because I was so worried about what I would eat and about not arriving at all…. The hardest part of this whole thing was making the decision to come because everyone would keep telling you that you are

going to die." [Child who came to the U.S. to seek safety from the extreme physical and emotional abuse inflicted by his mother in Honduras.][17]

In the U.S., it is not only the threat of future persecution that provides the basis for an asylum claim. Past persecution can constitute an independent ground of eligibility if it is serious enough to justify protection, irrespective of future harm. This is particularly important in the case of children, where the trauma of terrifying situations may linger on in nightmares or enuresis, maladaptive behavior, psychological ill health including depression and suicidal thoughts. In Australia, children who present with horrific accounts of trauma suffered in their country of origin are usually able to show that their trauma was due to matters that render them vulnerable to future harm on refugee grounds. In the U.K. a child fleeing exceptionally traumatic circumstances might be granted discretionary leave to remain even if no well-founded fear of (future) persecution could be demonstrated.

Children and Refugee Status | *Sam's Story*

"Sam" was born to a wealthy and politically influential Hazara family in Afghanistan. His father was a regional commander with two wives and many children. Sam's older brothers were established businessmen. From the age of eight or nine, Sam had lived with his large family in an Hazara stronghold, until the city fell to the Taliban in a dramatic firefight in 1999, on a day Sam will never forget.

Aged fourteen, he had been sent with friends of his father's to represent the family at a funeral. When the Taliban attacked, he was forced to flee with his father's friends, joining a convoy of displaced people that snaked its way irregularly across the Afghan countryside. Sam was told that his father had been killed by the Taliban in an assault on their house. He later met one of his father's bodyguards who confirmed the news. The rest of his family had disappeared. Two brothers were missing in one part of the country; every indication pointed to his mother, sister, and little brother having been killed along with his father. The Taliban victory in Sam's home town had seen 11,000 people, mainly Hazaras, lose their lives.

Over the following days, Sam saw many atrocities: he stumbled over dead bodies, saw people around him dying of disease, hunger, and injury. His father's friends delivered him to a mosque, where he was given sanctuary for eight months. Eventually he made his way south to the province where he was born, seeking out an aunt who lived on a farm. His aunt took the boy in and hid him among the household for the best part of two years. In his 16th year, Sam was told that his extended family could no longer live with the risk he posed—and that the boy himself must find a viable life. His uncle made arrangements with the people smugglers and he was sent on his way to Australia…[18]

7.4 The Five Grounds and Children's Claims

Proving persecution is not sufficient of itself to ground an asylum claim. Many people who experience persecution are not considered to be refugees. For example, if someone is persecuted as a result of a personal vendetta (for example, a love feud) or a perpetrator's mental disorder (for example, the object of a paranoid fantasy), he or she will not be eligible for refugee protection. This is so, even though the persecution alleged is real and serious. To qualify as a Convention refugee, an applicant must prove that he or she faces persecution on the basis of civil or political discrimination (as defined). Technically, this translates into a requirement to prove that the alleged persecution is based on one of the five grounds listed in the definition of "refugee" in the Refugee Convention. Like adults, children will only be considered to be refugees if they can demonstrate that they may face persecution on one of these grounds. In all three countries studied, the response of decision makers has been very mixed, with examples of both good and bad jurisprudence from the perspective of the refugee child.

▪ Religion

A child's religious beliefs or behavior, or refusal to hold religious beliefs, may put the child at risk of persecution. In Australia, young Afghan asylum seekers of Shiite religion and Hazara ethnicity have been granted refugee status on grounds of both religion and ethnicity. As in other countries, successful claims in these cases have not always required applicants to show that they were active practitioners: it is enough that a person is *perceived* to belong to a particular sect or religion and is liable to be persecuted for this reason.

U.S. legal representatives have successfully advanced religion-based asylum claims on behalf of a former gang member who had a religious conversion and on behalf of children persecuted for being members of minority religious sects in India, Pakistan, and China. In the U.K. a number of unaccompanied or separated children from Eritrea have had their asylum appeals allowed on the basis that they would face persecution as Jehovah's Witnesses if returned. Some unaccompanied or separated children have also had their appeals allowed on the basis of the persecution they would face from the Mugiki Sect if returned to Kenya.

▪ Nationality

A child may, like an adult, face persecution because of his or her nationality. There may even be an aged-based element, as where a child faces legal disqualification or exclusion amounting to persecution for being born stateless. For example, a child might be denied all form of schooling because of his or her nationality; or the child might face deportation to a dangerous location, from the only country he or she has known as home, because of immigration rules excluding the child and/or the family. One example might be a Hmong child fearing return to Burma. In the past in the U.K., a number of unaccompanied or separated children born in Ethiopia have had their appeals allowed on the basis that they had a parent who was deemed to be Eritrean. This parentage meant that the children would face discrimination and even expulsion from Ethiopia if returned there.

As the U.S. 7th Circuit Court of Appeal has noted, denial of access to education on the basis of ethnicity can amount to persecution: "If Romania denied its Ukrainian citizens the right to higher education enjoyed by ethnic Romanians, this would be, we imagine, a form of persecution."[19]

There are also cases where children from minority nationalities are forced to receive their state education in the majority language. Such practices can result in denial of cultural and linguistic rights and in exclusion from access to work and other key social structures. This could rise to the level of child-specific persecution on the basis of nationality. In Australia, children faced with such discrimination would be accepted as refugees only if the discrimination feared met the description of serious harm in section 91R of the Migration Act 1958 (Australia).[20]

There have been other instances of foreign children suffering discrimination on the basis of nationality. Children can be stateless by virtue of being born abroad to non-citizens whose home country does not recognize children born to its nationals either out of wedlock or on foreign soil. Unfortunately, such children are rarely recognized as refugees, even if they have no state prepared to admit them. In Australia, this situation led to the incarceration for three years of a child born in immigration detention to a Malaysian mother arrested as an unlawful non-citizen.

■ Political Opinion

Decision makers and advocates frequently make two false assumptions about the relationship between childhood and political activity or belief. The first is the widespread notion that children are incapable of holding political opinions; that they are insufficiently mature or experienced to have an understanding of political issues and differences. As many notable counter-examples demonstrate, this may be a radical misperception, particularly in highly politicized and polarized societies. Whether a child is capable of (or indeed does) hold a political opinion is a question of fact. This can be determined by assessing the child's maturity, intelligence, and ability to articulate thoughts. There is no standard distribution of such capacity. It is worth noting,

however, that in polarized and politically unstable societies, children and youth are often extremely engaged in political struggles and frequently occupy leadership positions. The role of Soweto school children in tire burnings and more generalized political opposition to the apartheid regime in South Africa is one example. The engagement of Palestinian children in the first and second Intifadas and the (disturbing) presence of children among the population of "enemy combatants" detained by the U.S. in Guantanamo Bay are other examples. In such circumstances children should not, but may in practice, have difficulty claiming that the persecution they face is on the grounds of political opinion. Successful child asylum claims based on political opinion have been made in the U.S., for example, for Chinese Falun Gong members. In the U.K. Kurdish unaccompanied or separated children have had appeals allowed on the basis of their own and their families' involvement in political opposition to the Turkish government. In another case, a very young boy sent out of Afghanistan by his uncle had his appeal allowed on the basis of a fear of persecution based on his father's activities within the security services under the Dr. Najibullah government some years before. In this case, the boy had no knowledge at all of his father's politics or the exact nature of his employment but the immigration judge accepted his identity on the basis of the oral evidence of another uncle who was settled in the U.K. and the likelihood of future persecution on the basis of expert evidence.

A second assumption that impacts on children's ability to claim asylum on the basis of political opinion is the view that persecutors would not target children for political reasons, because children are considered too insignificant as opponents or too ignorant as adversaries to hold political positions.

One U.S. immigration judge made this observation in the case of a 15-year-old Haitian who fled

because her pro-opposition statements resulted in her being targeted by government militias: "It is almost inconceivable to believe that the Ton Ton Macoutes could be fearful of the conversations of 15-year-old children."[21]

Such skepticism or downright incredulity is misplaced and often demonstrates poor cross-cultural understandings of particular societies and of the place of children within them. In practice, children in many countries decide to immerse themselves in the political battles of their kin. They are often—as the escalation in recruitment of child soldiers brutally demonstrates—on the front lines of confrontation and risk. Their political involvement can lead to targeting for persecution by government or hostile forces. Moreover, even if they are not directly involved in politics, children can be associated with the political activities or opinions of their parents or other relatives. As a consequence they may have political opinions attributed or imputed to them, and this may also lead to persecution. Attorneys, asylum officers, and adjudicators need to be alert to these political realities to avoid projecting inaccurate stereotypes about childhood innocence or naïveté onto politicized children.

In these cases, there seems to be a marked divergence in the approaches taken by U.S. and Australian decision makers. As the following example demonstrates, U.S. officials have been prepared to impute political opinion to children. In analogous situations, Australian decision makers would probably only recognize the claimant as a refugee if the child could be seen to belong to a particular social group. In one

Children and Refugee Status | Xue Yun Zhang's Story

Xue Yun Zhang, the oldest of three children, was 14 when she left China for the U.S. Xue's parents had successfully hidden the birth of their youngest child, a son, from the local birth planning bureau for six years, but when their secret became known, bureau officials imposed a substantial fine on the family and forcibly took Xue's father off to be sterilized:

"**My mother was crying**, and our sisters and brothers were crying..." she stated in her affidavit applying for asylum. The operation so affected Mr. Zhang's health that he had to give up work. Mrs. Zhang tried to make up the financial shortfall by working but the family could not pay the fine. As a result officials confiscated some of their possessions, threatened to evict the family from their home, and prohibited the children from attending school until the fine was paid. According to Xue's asylum application: "In light of these problems, my father thought there was no future for me in China, so when he heard of an opportunity to send me [to the U.S.], he did so." She claimed asylum on the basis of the persecution she had experienced as the child of parents who had violated China's family planning policies, and of her future fear of arrest and torture if returned to China. The Court of Appeal concluded that Xue's experience of economic and educational deprivation, together with her father's forcible removal and sterilization, could be considered persecution as a result of a political opinion imputed to her on account of her parents' resistance to China's population control measures.[22]

unsuccessful case in the U.K., a boy feared persecution on the basis that he had been used to distribute leaflets by an opposition party in Togo. A fresh application for asylum was refused despite the existence of expert evidence showing that children were used regularly to distribute propaganda clandestinely due to the brutal and oppressive treatment of known adult political activists.

■ Particular Social Group

The meaning of "membership in a particular social group," the catch-all phrase that appears both in the 1951 Refugee Convention and in domestic legislation, has been a matter of less certainty than the other Convention grounds. However, litigation and scholarly debate[23] have lead gradually to broad consensus about the application of the term. The early jurisprudence in Western countries defined the phrase "particular social group" in terms of "immutable" characteristics and/or association between members of a group. The Canadian Supreme Court in *Canada (Attorney General) v. Ward* (1993) provided three examples of such groupings:

1 *Groups defined by an innate or unchangeable characteristic;*

2 *groups whose members voluntarily associate for reasons so fundamental to their human dignity that they should not be forced to forsake the association; and (3) groups associated by a former voluntary status, unalterable due to its historical permanence.*[24]

The Australian courts expanded these categories by confirming that association between members is not a prerequisite for a "social group": see further below. Because the Convention requirement is that persecution be "by reason of" membership of a social group, it is accepted that the existence or otherwise of a group is less important than the (objective) perception that such a group exists.[25]

So, persecution based on membership in a particular social group is understood to mean persecution directed at an individual because of his or her membership in a group sharing immutable characteristics. This may be so because they cannot be changed (sex, race, family, personal history, or experience). Alternatively, the characteristics may be so fundamental to the group that members should not be required to change (personal belief system, sexual orientation). For children, the most frequent group memberships grounding an asylum claim is likely to be the family or age.

A 14-year-old Honduran boy was granted asylum by an immigration judge in Arlington, Virginia. Though the case essentially concerned forced gang recruitment, the judge found that the boy was persecuted because of his membership in the particular social group of his nuclear family since his father had been targeted by the same gang before his death.[26]

Membership in a group traumatized by witnessing persecution of relatives may also be the basis for a valid asylum claim. On the other hand, so far no court has held that "unaccompanied or separated children" per se constitute a particular social group,[27] even though in practice this status certainly places children at extra risk of harm. In the U.K. case law indicates that the particular social group must not be defined solely by the persecution alleged; rather the group must be characterized independently of the fact of persecution by certain significant social, economic, or political conditions in the country of origin. In the lead case of *Islam v. Secretary of State for the Home Department*, the particular social group was "women in Iran" and was constructed by the fact that women were discriminated against in Sharia law and in social and political life.[28]

This distinction between the persecution alleged

and the identification of a social group is clearly illustrated in a number of first and second instance U.K. decisions which have allowed appeals by girls who had been trafficked to the U.K. for the purposes of child prostitution or domestic slavery. The act of trafficking and the treatment they received on the way to and/or in the U.K. was the persecution relied upon. The particular social group was defined as the socially constructed position of girls in countries of origin such as Nigeria or Albania, where they were discriminated against in terms of the law and social and cultural practices and beliefs.

In some cases, group membership for the child asylum applicant will be constituted through discrimination based on a form of child-specific persecution. This may take one of three forms: the government may participate directly in the abuse—such as by conscripting child soldiers or authorizing shooting at street children; the government may acquiesce or fail to proscribe cultural or social practices which (whatever their intent) are *de facto* persecutory, such as female circumcision; or, despite criminalization of the behavior, the government may in practice fail to protect children being harmed by their carers or other members of their society, as in cases of incest, child abuse, forced or bonded labor, child sale, persecution of disabled or mentally handicapped children.

As noted earlier, while the Taliban were in control in Afghanistan, the vast majority of the young Afghan asylum seekers in Australia had little difficulty in gaining recognition as refugees on the same bases as their adult counterparts. Many were Shiite Hazara—members of a group widely accepted as being at risk of persecution from the predominantly Pashtun Taliban on grounds of both ethnicity and religion. After the fall of the Taliban-controlled government, however, the children lost the comfort of the broad and accepting approach that had been taken to the Afghan asylum seekers.

In Australia, the predominant view in the lower courts was that unaccompanied and separated children cannot be identified as belonging to a "particular social group" in their own right for the purposes of the refugee definition.[29] A subsequent ruling from Australia's High Court suggests that these Federal Court rulings may no longer represent good law in Australia.[30]

The case of *Applicant S* concerned a young Afghan male of Pashtun ethnicity who fled Afghanistan after narrowly avoiding recruitment by the Taliban on two occasions.[31] The Refugee Review Tribunal (RRT) rejected the man's refugee claim on the basis that he was not "targeted to the extent that he was listed or registered for recruitment" by the Taliban. He was merely seen as a young, able-bodied man who was available in a particular area at a particular time. The High Court upheld the first instance ruling by Justice Carr to the effect that this characterization of the applicant's case revealed a failure to consider at all whether the applicant belonged to a "particular social group" for the purposes of the Refugee Convention.[32]

There is one other aspect of the High Court's ruling in *Applicant S* that is likely to benefit children who seek asylum alone in Australia. The court also considered the question of whether laws or policies of general application, or behaviors that are not predicated on "enmity or malignity," can ever constitute persecution for the purposes of the Refugee Convention. In *Applicant S,* the Minister for Immigration argued that young, able-bodied men could not be refugees because the Taliban "merely sought to harness the valued resource of those capable of fighting."[33] The fact that young conscripts might die or suffer harm in the fighting did not mean that the regime was trying to rid itself of the young men. The court rejected this submission in a ruling that provides a welcome indication that legal formalism should not be allowed to override basic notions of ethics and human rights in the interpretation of the Refugee Convention.

Australia is not the only country where use of the "particular social group" ground has offered some hope for unaccompanied and separated children. In a recent ruling, a U.S. appeal court found that disabled children and parents who provide care for them constituted members of a particular social group and that such a family, taken as a whole, had suffered persecution. Interestingly, the court held that the disabled child's asylum claim provided the basis for a derivative claim by his parents, a reversal of the usual situation where adult claims are the basis for protection of dependent children.[34]

One of the principal findings of this study is that advocates and decision makers have failed to advance child asylum claims in appropriate cases because of an adult-centered approach to refugee protection. As the preceding paragraphs indicate, there is a broad spectrum of behavior that properly falls within the scope of the Refugee Convention and that can provide critical protection for unaccompanied and separated children. But until recently little attention or creative legal energy has been dedicated to such cases. As a result children with a claim to international protection have been discriminated against relative to their adult counterparts. This chapter concludes with a survey of some common forms of child-specific persecution, set out not as a comprehensive catalogue of child persecution, but by way of illustration and encouragement to those involved in this area of work.

7.5 Common Forms of Child-Specific Persecution That Give Rise to an Asylum Claim

■ Family Violence

One U.S. attorney estimated that 90% of her child asylum clients had claims based on some type of intra-familial violence.[35] Another noted domestic abuse as the most common type of claim she sees under the "particular social group" category.[36]

In principle, recent developments in both Australia and the U.K. regarding the grant of refugee status to women fleeing domestic violence should be applicable to children who suffer similar violence. So far researchers have not identified any cases in either the U.K. or Australia where such arguments had been raised in cases involving children. However, in the U.K. the fact that a significant number of children have been trafficked by members of their own family may in future give rise to similar arguments.

■ Living as a Street Child

Children from Honduras, Guatemala, and El Salvador made up more than three quarters of the children in the care of the U.S. Office of Refugee Resettlement (ORR) in fiscal year 2004.[37] Many of these children flee not just extreme poverty, but also acutely dangerous social situations capable of rising to the level of persecution and grounding asylum claims. An earlier part of this chapter described the case of Eldin Escobar, whose attorneys have claimed that being a street child constitutes a particular social group under the Refugee Convention. At the time of this writing, other such cases citing street children's vulnerability to sexual exploitation, HIV/AIDS, and physical attack are also pending. If these cases are successful, they will constitute an important milestone in establishing a new aspect of economic and social persecution that is child specific and falls within the "particular social group" ground. Australia has so far shown little enthusiasm for recognizing as refugees children fleeing such circumstances. However, over time this precedent could be as trend setting for the future of children's asylum protection as rape and sexual violence cases were for gender asylum protection a decade ago.

■ Family Status

Some children face persecution because of the status of their family or their status within their family. Orphans, for example, may be objects of severe social stigma:

An American attorney interviewed for this study represented a child from Guatemala who was an orphan and suffered abuse at the hands of other townspeople. When another orphan in the town committed suicide, several townspeople asked her client why he did not commit suicide as well.[38]

Unconventional family patterns may also result in stigmatization of children. This may result from social prejudice towards families who deviate from strictly conformist norms, including children who are born out of wedlock, children conceived from an illegitimate relationship such as incest, or through rape, including rape as an instrument of ethnic cleansing.

Discrimination amounting to persecution against children may be the result of legal norms about family size and pattern. The best known example of this situation is the Chinese "one-child" policy, which may affect "second" or subsequent children born in parts of China where the policy is rigidly enforced. The case of Xue Zhang and of Chen Shi Hai described above illustrates the problems children can face in this situation. The repercussions of exclusion from education can follow a child into adult life, relegating him or her to unemployment and social marginalization. Additional situations under this category might include children of parents with some kind of mixed ancestry who face persecution (such as children of a mixed union across ethnic, clan, or tribal lines; such cases may also be considered examples of race-based discrimination).

■ Gang Violence

Domestic abuse, homelessness, and discrimination based on family status are all factors that contribute to the existence of street gangs. Persecution arising from gangs is a central issue confronting a significant proportion of the Central American population of unaccompanied and separated children in U.S. government custody. Casa Alianza, the Latin American

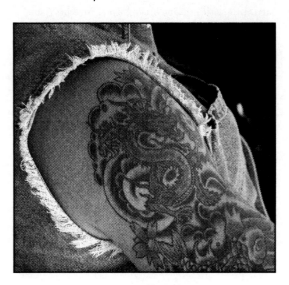

affiliate of the NGO Covenant House which serves homeless and street youth, estimates that there are more than 69,000 gang members in Central America and that more than two thirds of them are between the ages of 12 and 17.[39] With 76% of children in ORR custody having come from Central America, many of them have fled the fear and intimidation of gangs or "maras." Indeed the 2001–2002 update to the "Machel Study," a UN study of the impact of armed conflict on children, noted gang activity as a particular concern for adolescents from Honduras, the largest nationality in ORR care:

"The issues of the maras must be studied carefully due to the fact this social phenomenon may increasingly generate forced displacement of youth, and may become an increasingly common reason for persons to seek asylum abroad."[40]

Though asylum claims in the U.S. based on gang violence are growing, they remain controversial. Some advocates report that immigration judges are apprehensive about granting asylum to youths with gang connections due to a concern that the social group category "was not defined to protect a criminal class."[41] One such attorney noted a case where the immigration judge looked for some alternative reason to grant a child asylum other than fear of gang persecution. The judge ultimately granted the child asylum based on his religion, since he had converted to Christianity while in federal custody and gangs are known to persecute former members who become Christian converts.[42] Attorneys, too, report looking for asylum claims other than gang violence, even when fear of gang persecution is the crux of a child's claim, due to concern that immigration judges will not grant claims based on gang persecution.[43]

Although concerns about past criminal behavior may be justified in the case of adult refugee claimants,

domestic law has always given special consideration to juvenile delinquency. This reflects appreciation of children's immaturity, their limitations in logical reasoning, and their susceptibility to outside influence. As an experienced attorney pointed out to the U.S. researchers: "The options [for most Central American street children] are: try to make it on the streets, or join a gang."[44]

7.6 Conclusion

Advocates and decision makers involved in the asylum applications of unaccompanied and separated children have considerable scope to apply the Refugee Convention definition of refugee to their young clients' circumstances. A central conclusion of this study is that greater use be made of (a) the UNHCR Guidelines on the application of the Refugee Convention to children and (b) the General Comments made by the Committee on the Rights of the Child. The prevailing presumption of ineligibility must be replaced by a more diligent, child-centered focus. This requires intervention on several different dimensions. First, more information must be gathered about the treatment of children in countries from which significant numbers of asylum seekers flee. This requires better human rights reporting of child-specific human rights violations and in the case of the U.K. an improvement in the quality of the Country Information and Policy Unit reports on specific countries produced by the Home Office. Second, advocates and government officials need to engage more assiduously in eliciting the stories of children seeking asylum alone. Better training is required to build up techniques for obtaining evidence from vulnerable and traumatized children. Finally, practitioners concerned with children's rights and the protection of asylum seekers need to work cooperatively to develop and share relevant precedents and insights. The overall objective must be to foster a new, rights based approach to child asylum. As the General Comment of the Committee on the Rights of the Child states:

"[T]he refugee definition of the 1951 Refugee Convention must be interpreted in an age and gender-sensitive manner, taking into account the particular motives for, and forms and manifestations of, persecution experienced by children. Persecution of the kin; under-age recruitment; trafficking of children for prostitution; and sexual exploitation or subjection to female genital mutilation, are some of the child specific forms and manifestations of persecution which may justify the granting of refugee status if such acts are related to one of the 1951 Refugee Convention grounds. States should, therefore, give utmost attention to such child specific forms and manifestations of persecution as well as gender-based violence in national refugee status determination procedures."[45]

Endnotes

1   U.S. Department of Justice Immigration and Naturalization Service. The Basic Law Manual (1994). 24. Cited in Anker, Deborah. *The Law of Asylum in the United States.* 2nd ed. 1999. 174, note 14.

2   In s91R of this Act, persecution is said to constitute *serious harm* defined in turn to *include* (the definition is not exhaustive):
    (a) a threat to the person's life or liberty;
    (b) significant physical harassment of the person;
    (c) significant physical ill-treatment of the person;
    (d) significant economic hardship that threatens the person's capacity to subsist;
    (e) denial of access to basic services, where the denial threatens the person's capacity to subsist;
    (f) denial of capacity to earn a livelihood of any kind, where the denial threatens the person's capacity to subsist. See also *Minister for Immigration and Multicultural Affairs v. Haji Ibrahim* (2000) 204 CLR 1.

3   (2004) 206 ALR 242.

4   See (2003) 217 CLR 387 at [39]–[49], discussing the High Court ruling in *MIMA v. Israelian* (2001) 206 CLR 323.

5   (2000) 201 CLR 293 at 317.

6   UNHCR. Handbook on Procedures and Criteria for Determining Refugee Status. Para. 56.

7   See Crock, Mary. *Seeking Asylum Alone, Australia.* Sydney: Themis Press, 2006 (Australian Report.)

8   See Bhabha, Jacqueline and Schmidt, Susan. *Seeking Asylum Alone, United States.* Cambridge, MA: Bhabha and Schmidt, 2006. (U.S. Report.) 188.

9   See Australian Report, Ibid, Endnote 7.

10 In fact, the rate of success mirrors the access to representation—from a high of 49.4% granted in the Arlington, Virginia Asylum Office where 47% of child asylum seekers are represented, to a low of 23.3% granted in Miami, Florida where only 10% of unaccompanied children are represented. Data used to compile these statistics was provided by Christine Davidson, Asylum Office Headquarters, U.S. Citizenship and Immigration Services, DHS

(personal correspondence dated 26 May 2004). Based on affirmative asylum applications between 1999 and 2003 where a child was the principal applicant.

11 Experience of U.S. researcher Susan Schmidt in working as Director for Children's Services, Lutheran Immigration and Refugee Service.

12 *Eldin Jacobo Escobar v. Ashcroft*, 3rd Cir. No. 04–2999, 2003.

13 *Chen Shi Hai v. MIMA* (2000) 201 CLR 293.

14 *Mei Dan Liu v. Ashcroft*, 380 F.3d 307 (7th Cir. 2004).

15 However, in European Convention on Human Rights law and thus in U.K. law it would—see case of *Selmouni v. France* 25803/94 [1999] ECHR 66.

16 In the U.K. this would only give rise to need for international protection if there was an additional element of discrimination in terms of the child's legal or social rights—see *Islam v. Secretary of State for the Home Department (House of Lords)* [1999] 2 AC 629.

17 Interview with Honduran youth who was 16 at the time he entered the U.S. Interview by Joanne Kelsey, interpreted by Judith Wing from Holland and Knight. 12 July 2004.

18 See *Sam*'s story, Australian Report, Ibid, Endnote 7, 11.4. By the time Sam's asylum claim was determined in Australia, the Taliban had been driven from power by U.S. forces. He was denied refugee status.

19 *Bucur v. INS*, 109 F.3d 399, 403 (7th Cir. 1997).

20 See Marr, David and Wilkinson, Marianne. *Dark Victory*. Sydney: Allen & Unwin, 2003. Chapter 20; and *Chen Shi Hai v. MIMA* (2000) 201 CLR 293.

21 *Lucienne Yvette Civil v. INS* 140 F.3d 52, 55 (1st Cir. 1998).

22 *Xue Yun Zhang v. Gonzalez* May 26, 2005 No. 01–71623 (9th Cir. 2005).

23 See for example, Crawley, *Heaven. Refugees and gender: Law and process*. Bristol: Jordan, 2001; Spijkerboer, Thomas. *Gender and refugee status*. Aldershot: Ashgate, 2000; Dauvergne, Catherine. "The dilemma of rights discourses for refugees." *University of New South Wales Law Journal*. 23, no. 3 (2000).

24 [1993] 2 S.C.R. 689 at 739.

25 In Australia, see *Kuldip Ram v. Minister for Immigration and Ethnic Affairs and RRT* (1995) 130 ALR 314 at 317; *Chen Shi Hai v. MIMA* (2000) 201 CLR 293; *Applicant S v. MIMIA* (2003) 217 CLR 387.

26 Personal correspondence with Christina Wilkes, then Attorney and Equal Justice Works Fellow at Just Neighbors Ministry. 11 September 2005.

27 Two Australian refugee claims involving unaccompanied and separated Afghan children, one of whom claimed to be fleeing forcible conscription by the Taliban, unsuccessfully raised this point in support of their application. As noted below, however, a subsequent ruling by the High Court suggests that the courts may now be open to arguments on this point.

28 [1999] 2 AC 629.

29 See *SHBB v. MIMIA* (2003) 175 FLR 304 and *VFAY v. MIMIA* (2004) 134 FCR 402.

30 In fact, both *SHBB v. MIMIA* and *VFAY v. MIMIA* appealed to the High Court of Australia. After the ruling in *Applicant S v. MIMIA* (2003) 217 CLR 387 their cases were settled by consent before going to hearing.

31 *Applicant S v. MIMIA* (2003) 217 CLR 387. Note that s91X of the Migration Act 1958 prohibits the use of the names of refugee claimants in any proceedings for the judicial review of relevant administrative decisions.

32 *Applicant S v. MIMIA* (2003) 217 CLR 387.

33 Ibid, Endnote 32, [37].

34 *Tchoukhrova v. Gonzales*, 404 F.3d 1181 (9th Cir. 2005).

35 Interview with Vanessa Melendez Lucas, Clinical Assistant Professor, Children and Family Justice Center, Northwestern Law School, Chicago, Illinois. 6 July 2004.

36 Interview with Elissa Steglich, Attorney, Midwest Immigrant and Human Rights Center/Heartland Alliance, Chicago Illinois. 22 April 2004.

37 Statistical data provided by Shereen Faraj on 6 October 2005 for unaccompanied alien children in ORR/DUCS care as of 30 September 2004: 30% Honduran; 20% Guatemalan; 26% Salvadoran.

38 Interview with Lisa Frydman, then Attorney, Florida Immigrant Advocacy Center, Miami, Florida. 14 July 2004.

39 From "The Street or the Gangs: One of the Few Options for Children in Central America." PowerPoint presentation by Bruce Harris, Regional Director for Latin America Programmes, Casa Alianza/Covenant House. August 2004.

40 UNHCR. *Refugee Children Coordination Unit. Summary Update of Machel Study Follow-up Activities in 2001–2002.* 54.

41 Ibid, Endnote 35.

42 Ibid, Endnote 35.

43 Ibid, Endnote 36.

44 Interview with Julia Hernandez, Children's Attorney, ProBAR, Harlingen, Texas. 8 July 2004.

45 Committee on the Rights of the Child. General Comment No. 6: Treatment of separated and unaccompanied children outside their country of origin. UN, 2005. CRC/GC/2005/6. VI(d).

CHAPTER 8

Protection Outcomes

8.1 Protection Options for Unaccompanied and Separated Children

One of the most alarming trends noted in recent years in the three countries studied has been the inclination to restrict protection for unaccompanied and separated immigrant children identified as being at risk.

All three countries have created a range of options for unaccompanied and separated children that afford less permanent and comprehensive protection than full status under the 1951 Refugee Convention. In general these alternative protection outcomes lack one or more of the following key attributes: immediate access to permanent legal residency (and, eventually, citizenship); entitlement to family reunion; and access to welfare and education benefits on an equal footing with citizen children.

In this chapter we consider the outcomes available to unaccompanied and separated children who are identified as being in need of protection of some kind. We begin with a review of the practice of granting protection to children on the basis of their minority and/or their general vulnerability. There follows a comparative analysis of how the three countries treat children who are recognized as refugees. The chapter concludes with a discussion of the protections granted to victims of trafficking.

What emerges from the research is that protection during minority is granted to a significant group of the child applicants. However, long-term legal residency, which guarantees a safe and secure future, is far more elusive.

The availability of short-term protection may act as a distracting palliative, which deflects advocates and policy makers from the more significant challenge of ensuring permanent legal status for unaccompanied and separated children.

8.2 Protecting Immigrant Children on the Basis of Childhood / Vulnerability

In all three countries studied, children traveling alone who are identified as being at risk can be granted immediate protection of some kind. The legal frameworks for making these rulings—and the frequency with which they are used—vary greatly. Of the countries studied, it is the U.K. that stands out for addressing the needs of vulnerable child migrants most comprehensively in the short term. However, this protection is generally confined to a period of one or three years or at best the child's minority. Permanent refugee protection is rarely granted to unaccompanied and separated children. The U.S. system is less consistent in its child-centered focus, with significant procedural limitations; however, a growing body of jurisprudence on child-specific persecution sets an important and useful

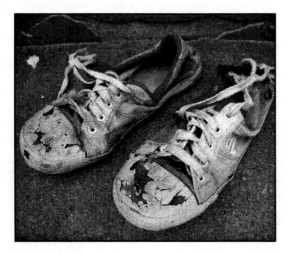

international precedent, and several visas exist for child victims of abuse or crime. In Australia, evidence of minority and vulnerability lead to significant immigration concessions on rare occasions, and then only with the personal intercession of the Immigration Minister. A more systematic consideration of child-specific needs and vulnerabilities is urgently required. Aspects of the systems in each country are considered in turn.

■ The United Kingdom

Until April 2003, where an unaccompanied or separated child was refused asylum, he or she was generally granted exceptional leave to remain until the age of 18. It was never stated explicitly whether this leave was granted in recognition of the risk to the child's human rights were he or she to be returned to his or her country of origin or whether leave was being given on the basis of the child's minority alone. The general assumption was that childhood was the key. In April 2003 exceptional leave to remain was replaced by Humanitarian Protection and discretionary leave.

Humanitarian Protection is granted to an unaccompanied or separated child who is deemed not to be entitled to protection under the Refugee Convention but would face a serious risk to life or safety for a non-Convention reason if returned to his or her country of origin. Such leave would be appropriate if an unaccompanied or separated child would face the death penalty, unlawful killing, or inhuman or degrading treatment or punishment which would arise for non-medical reasons and meets the need for the U.K. to act in compliance with Articles 2 and 3 of the European Convention on Human Rights. Such leave would now be granted for a period of five years and he or she could then apply for indefinite leave to remain in the U.K.

In the alternative, an unaccompanied or separated child may be granted discretionary leave to remain in recognition that any attempt to return him or her to his or her country of origin would result in a breach of another article of the European Convention on Human Rights, such as his or her right under Article 8 to enjoy a family or private life. Discretionary leave will also be granted if his or her return would result in ill health which breached the U.K.'s commitments under Article 3. Such leave would usually be granted for three years and he or she could apply to extend his or her leave shortly before the three-year period came to an end.

Discretionary leave is also granted purely on the basis of the fact that an unaccompanied or separated child is a minor if no adequate care or reception arrangements are in place in his or her country of origin. Such leave will only be available while he or she is under 18 and will be an initial period of one or three years dependent on the child's country of origin. The unaccompanied or separated child can apply to extend his or her leave either as a minor on the basis of age or on human rights grounds if the leave will expire at 18. However, by late 2005, the basis of this leave was in doubt, as the U.K. government began exploring ways to return unaccompanied or separated children to their countries of origin at the point at which they are refused asylum. Such returns will take place even though the child's family cannot be located if adequate care and reception arrangements can be made with a contractor. In early 2006, there were plans to return unaccompanied or separated children to Angola, the Democratic Republic of Congo, and Vietnam despite the fact that these are known to be countries from which children are trafficked. Indeed, many of the children concerned may have been brought to the U.K. originally by child traffickers. Plans to return unaccompanied or separated children to Albania were on hold as a result of a large amount of opposition to the plan from non-governmental organizations and lawyers in both the U.K. and Albania itself.

Discretionary leave to remain may also be granted to an unaccompanied or separated child who has been taken into the care of a local authority as a result of family breakdown or child abuse. Before the April 2003 changes, this meant that a child who was under 14 would usually be granted indefinite leave to remain. However, it would appear that at present the normal outcome is that the child will be granted discretionary leave for either one or three years in line with the general policy referred to above which is to not return minors to their country of origin until adequate care and reception arrangements are in place. An unaccompanied or separated child who is granted discretionary leave does not have a right to be joined by his or her parents or siblings. Neither does an unaccompanied or separated child granted Humanitarian Protection.

■ The United States

The U.S. system is complex and varied. It combines elements of child-specific sensitivity with features that are distinctly at odds with children's needs and interests. Several categories of visas are available to children who are identified as being in need of protection on grounds other than refugee status and trafficking. This section examines in turn the special visas created for separated children who have suffered abuse in their country of origin; concessions made for children who suffer domestic violence or abuse after they enter the U.S.; and various measures aimed at offering temporary protection to immigrant children in times of special need.

The U.S. system has a unique and welcome feature—the creation of a special permanent status that answers to the needs of unaccompanied and separated children in need of protection. Although only a minority of such children applying for asylum in the U.S. receive refugee protection, roughly 500 children each year are accorded Special Immigrant Juvenile Status (SIJS).[1] This status affords permanent settlement and eventually citizenship. The SIJS visa is available for children not cared for by their parents due to "abuse, neglect, or abandonment," for whom it is not in their "best interests" to return to their home country. SIJS was originally created in response to concerns about undocumented children who spent years in state-funded foster care programs facing uncertain futures. It both introduces "best interests" considerations into substantive immigration law and requires collaboration between state child welfare entities and federal immigration authorities.[2]

The SIJS visa is available to foreign-born children who have suffered abuse, neglect, or abandonment, who need long-term foster care, and for whom return is against their best interest.

Children applying for SIJS visas are encouraged to apply for permanent residency simultaneously and the two statuses are usually granted at the same time.

For countries dealing with significant numbers of unaccompanied and separated children, this aspect of the U.S. system is worth considering, even though it has some limitations (see further below).

Eligibility for SIJS depends on an order from a state juvenile court that the children in question are "dependent." In other words, the children must be certified as being in need of state care because of their situation or the abuse they have suffered. The procedure for obtaining SIJS can be tortuous, time consuming, and fraught with considerable procedural difficulty. For children detained by the federal government, the Attorney General (the legal custodian of unaccompanied and separated children in immigration custody) must "consent" to a local juvenile court getting involved in the child's case in the first place. The determination of "consent" is an arbitrary process based on little if any expert child welfare knowledge and a surprising lack of procedural sensitivity. Consent decisions are often based on a telephone interview where the child is questioned about his or her history of abuse or neglect through an interpreter. This procedural hurdle serves to deter detained children from pursuing SIJS relief.

As a result most SIJS applicants are children whose presence was previously unknown to immigration authorities—children who are not detained, but who apply from within the community. The state juvenile court investigates the case to decide whether the child is in fact "dependent" and eligible for long-term foster care. The willingness of juvenile courts to establish dependency for children without immigration status can vary greatly between jurisdictions, and even between judges within the same jurisdiction, indicating a concern that some local jurisdictions are placing local interests over the needs of unaccompanied and separated children.[3]

Once a dependency finding has been made in juvenile court, the child can then apply to the immigration authorities for SIJS. This is an administrative process that requires a federal immigration officer to assess the juvenile court order and supporting evidence. The officer decides whether the eligibility criteria for a grant of SIJS have been met. This process involves interviewing the child again, and advocates report that this can be adversarial and conducted without much sensitivity to the vulnerability of the child. U.S. researchers reported considerable variation between immigration officers.

SIJS applicants face the complication of being engaged simultaneously in two legal systems — the local juvenile court for decisions and oversight regarding dependency and care, and the federal immigration authorities for a determination of their legal status. The two systems do not always complement each other; indeed U.S. researchers found mistrust between the systems, and disagreements over legal and financial responsibility for the children in question.

In addition to these procedural shortcomings, there is one serious substantive defect that creates long-term difficulties for SIJS children. A child recipient of SIJS is forever barred from submitting a family reunification petition. This permanent severance of the parent/child bond is unnecessary and unjust. Although children with SIJS must have lost contact with or been abandoned by their families before their migration to the U.S. to be eligible for the status, circumstances may change over time. Parents, siblings, or other relatives might be legitimate candidates for family reunification at a later date. The enforced and indefinite family separation mandated by SIJS constitutes a violation of the right to respect for family life enshrined in international law. This perpetual ban on family reunion sits uneasily with a central provision of the Convention on the Rights of the Child:

"State parties *shall ensure* that a child *shall not be separated from his or her parents against their will,*

except when…such separation is necessary for the best interests of the child."[4]

Several other forms of immigration protection in the U.S. are available for particular categories of unaccompanied or separated children. In the case of abused children, one example is the concession made for victims of domestic violence. The Violence Against Women Act (VAWA, passed in 1994) provides an avenue to lawful permanent residence for undocumented children who have been abused by a U.S. citizen or permanent resident parent. Children whose presence in the U.S. is unknown to the immigration authorities can lodge a VAWA petition affirmatively. Children who are in removal proceedings can apply, defensively, for VAWA cancellation of removal, provided they have been in the U.S. for at least three years prior to application. VAWA child applicants must demonstrate "good moral character." The past abuse must have constituted battery or "extreme cruelty" (physical or psychological). Applicants must also show that removal would result in extreme hardship to the child, the parent, or the child's child. The standard of evidence for VAWA protection is that of "any credible evidence," a lower and more child-friendly threshold than for asylum. In these cases there is no prohibition on future petitioning for family reunification.

Unaccompanied and separated children in the U.S. are eligible for a protective status similar to a T-Visa (see below), if they have suffered serious mental or physical abuse as a result of certain crimes within the U.S.—including rape, trafficking, incest, domestic abuse, or female genital mutilation. This U-Visa offers three-year temporary protection, followed by the possibility of permanent residence. This status does not cover child victims of crimes occurring in other countries.

In addition to these crime-related protection visas, unaccompanied and separated children may be entitled to a range of other immigration options that can deliver a form of protection. One such measure is cancellation of removal for children who have managed to stay on in the country (whether legally or illegally) for 10 years and who can demonstrate that their removal would cause "extreme and unusual hardship" to a U.S. citizen or permanent resident parent, spouse, or child. This status is unlikely to benefit unaccompanied or separated children, since their chances of having U.S. citizen or permanent resident close relatives who would suffer extreme hardship as a result of their removal, are minimal. The form of this status illustrates well the adult-centered approach of the drafters of immigration legislation, since it is written from the perspective of those who *have* dependants rather than those who *are* dependants.

Another protection option is deferred action, a very limited and entirely discretionary administrative measure, which simply delays removal in compelling cases without any guarantee of permanence. Alternatively, if the child comes from a country which has been designated temporarily unsafe by the authorities, he or she may be eligible for "Temporary Protected Status" (TPS). Children with this status, which as the name suggests does not lead to permanent residence, can get permission to work, and do not have to prove any individualized danger or fear. Children from one country deemed unsafe by the U.S. have a particularly advantageous immigration situation: Cuban children who have entered the U.S. legally can apply for permanent residence once they have been in the country a year. Like recipients of TPS they do not need to demonstrate any individualized need for protection. Finally, unaccompanied and separated children who are "more likely than not" to face torture if returned home may be granted protection under the UN Convention against Torture (CAT). Though this CAT status is not permanent, and does not give rights to welfare benefits, it is available

irrespective of the reasons for the torture, provided the torture would be carried out by or with the consent of a public official.

■ Australia

Before 1989, Australia's Migration Act 1958 contained broad discretionary provisions that allowed for the grant of visas to any person who could demonstrate strong compassionate or humanitarian grounds for the grant. With the shift to a much tighter regulatory framework in that year, the flexibility of the system diminished dramatically: children traveling alone lost an important safety net. Quite apart from the uncompromising procedures confronting children upon arrival in Australia (see chapter 4 above), there are also very few options for regularizing the status of a child traveling without a valid visa. Provision is made for the grant of asylum and for the grant of protection to victims of trafficking. However, there is no general scheme for either the identification or protection of children who are otherwise "at risk."

Separated and unaccompanied children stand in the same position as vulnerable adults in this sense. They may apply for a visa, lodge an appeal, and then lodge a request for the Immigration Minister to exercise her or his personal discretion to intervene so as to grant a visa. The minister's discretion is not one that can be compelled. Nor are decisions to intervene or not to intervene the subject of any form of appeal or judicial review.[5] Guidelines have been produced on the exercise of these powers. They cover near-miss refugee cases and other instances where individuals might fear gross abuse of their human rights if returned to their country of origin. In practice, it is extremely difficult to secure ministerial intervention. For unaccompanied and separated children who arrive without any support from within the Australian community, it is effectively a theoretical option. Australian researchers found that the only children to benefit from ministerial intercession in

their study were those who had been in Australia for long periods of time. All had acquired influential networks of advocates able to offer assistance.

The exercise of ministerial discretion can result in a range of outcomes. This study revealed unaccompanied and separated children denied refugee status who received three-year temporary protection visas; permanent protection visas; and in two instances, international student visas (which were later replaced with protection visas).

In one case, a disabled child who claimed refugee status on the basis that she and her family would face severe discrimination if returned, eventually received permanent residence because her parents were granted discretionary visas on employment grounds. The centrality of the child's circumstances to the exercise of discretion was not acknowledged in the choice of remedy.[6]

The apparently random outcomes of the exercise of discretion do not constitute a satisfactory basis for the grant of official protection.

Two final protection options in Australia mirror U.S. provisions outlined above. One further option is available to immigrant children in Australia who are threatened with domestic violence. Concessions have been built into many of the family migration categories to allow for the grant of permanent residence to sponsored family members who suffer abuse at the hands of their sponsor. The provisions operate as a waiver to the usual requirement that a family relationship survive a two-year probation period before permanent residence can be obtained.[7]

Finally, various concessions are made for children who spend much of their childhood in Australia, even as unlawful non-citizens. Children born on Australian soil to non-citizen parents do not automatically acquire Australian citizenship. However, they may be eligible for the grant of this status if they remain in the country for 10 years.[8] Special visas are also available to children who spend their "formative years" in Australia.[9] The residency criteria for access to these protections will usually preclude unaccompanied or separated children, since they are identified at or soon after entry into Australia.

8.3 Protections Afforded to Children Recognized as Refugees

■ The United Kingdom and the United States
The greatest divergence between the three countries studied lies in the protections afforded to unaccompanied and separated children who succeed in gaining recognition as refugees. Under Australian law, unlike U.S. law, a child accepted as a refugee will only receive permanent status at first instance if he or she entered the country on a valid visa. In all other cases, permanent protection is only available after a period of temporary protection. In the U.K., unaccompanied or separated children granted asylum are in the first instance be granted five years

limited leave to remain and are then able to apply for indefinite leave to remain.

In practice, however, permanent refugee protection is elusive for unaccompanied and separated children in all three countries. In the U.K., the vast majority of children only receive a temporary status in response to their first asylum application—for example, in 2004 only 2% of U.K. child asylum seekers were granted asylum when they first applied to the Immigration and Nationality Directorate. This rose to 5% in 2005 but was still a lower percentage than that for adults granted asylum, which was 7%. The differential widened in the first quarter of 2006 with 5% of unaccompanied or separated children being granted asylum as opposed to 10% of adults. Once recognized as refugees, they remain the responsibility of a local authority until they reach 18, at which point they are entitled to apply for welfare benefits and local authority housing. Social services have to be notified of a successful asylum decision, and the child becomes eligible for the full range of educational grants and loans, on a par with domestic children. Child asylees in the U.S. also become eligible for an array of social services on par with domestic children. This is an example of non-discriminatory practice, which follows both the Refugee Convention and Convention on the Rights of the Child (CRC) requirements.

However, a key area of discrimination remains. In the U.K., unlike their adult counterparts, unaccompanied or separated children granted refugee status cannot exercise family reunion rights, except in "extremely compelling or compassionate circumstances."[10] as the Immigration Rules only permit a refugee to be joined by a spouse or dependant child and not by a parent.

In the U.S., a majority of children are unrepresented and thus disadvantaged in accessing full legal protection in the first place, but those children who are granted asylum may apply to have immediate family members join them. However, as in the U.K. an adult bias is also evident in the definition of immediate family members, identified as spouses and unmarried children. This overlooks a child's most important family members: parents and siblings.

▪ Australia

A defining aspect of Australia's current refugee protection regime is that refugees who enter Australia without permission are granted temporary rather than permanent protection. The subclass 785 visa entitles a holder to three years' temporary residence, while the refugee visas granted to persons under the offshore refugee processing schemes associated with the "Pacific Strategy" (see chapter 6) entitle holders to between three and five years temporary residence.

So, most unaccompanied and separated children arriving without visas will receive a grant of a temporary protection visa upon gaining recognition as a refugee. This may be converted, on application by the child, into a permanent visa after a period of years. As noted earlier, following the terrorist attacks in the U.S. on 11 September 2001, the Migration Act 1958 (Australia) was amended to toughen Australia's "safe third country" rules. The so called "seven day rule" reduces Australia's protection obligations for applicants who have spent seven days or more prior to their arrival in a country where they could have sought refugee protection. The temporary protection visa (TPV) usually confers protection for 36 months. A second application for protection may be considered 30 months after the grant of the first TPV. The TPV represents a reduced form of refugee protection, of limited duration, without the possibility of family reunion and with limited access to government settlement and welfare services. A child who applies for an extension of the TPV status may be granted a permanent protection visa on the second application, or another temporary protection visa. Alternatively he or she may have their refugee status withdrawn and face detention and/or removal.

The introduction of the "seven day rule" in 2001 had the potential of leaving some refugees on perpetual TPVs, requiring them to be re-processed every three or so years. For the unaccompanied and separated children, this process has represented a particular challenge—not least because of the many changes that inevitably occur over a three-year period both to the children themselves and in the country from which they have fled. Where refugee status ceases under Article 1C, a TPV holder will be placed in substantially the same position as that of a first time asylum seeker. He or she will have to go back through the whole process of showing a well-founded fear of persecution on one of the five Convention grounds set out in Article 1A(2). Should Article 1C(5) not apply, however (that is, there has been no substantial change in circumstances), the TPV holder will enter the second visa application process with the presumption that she or he remains a refugee. The onus will then be on the government to demonstrate that the protections that attach to refugee status under the Convention should no longer be given.

In recognition of the need to find a resolution of the corrosive uncertainty of temporary protection, the Australian government moved in 2004 to lift the absolute bars on access to other visas. The changes mean that applications can be made by TPV holders for some non-refugee visas within Australia. These include spouse, student, and business visas. The previous requirement that applicants leave Australia to apply for such visas was dropped. In addition, concessions were made for some visas so as to encourage TPV holders to apply for migrant visas in regional parts of Australia. For unaccompanied and separated children finding it hard to negotiate the re-application process, the changes are particularly helpful.

8.4 Protections Afforded to Victims of Trafficking

Another special group of vulnerable unaccompanied and separated children are those who are victims of human trafficking. This study has argued that these children fall within the refugee definition and therefore should be eligible for asylum. Under international law recruitment of children for sex or labor exploitation is by definition coercive and can thus be considered

persecutory. However, in none of the countries studied is it common for victims of trafficking to be recognized as refugees. Many are simply not identified, and those that are frequently lack the specialist assistance needed to pursue an asylum claim.

Instead of vigorously using asylum to afford protection to trafficked children, the U.K. has tended to ignore this route to protection and at best child victims are granted discretionary leave to remain for a limited period of time as minors. In contrast, both the U.S. and Australia have instituted specific anti-trafficking statuses for victims of trafficking, including children. These measures follow the UN Convention on Transnational Organized Crime and two of its supplementary protocols, the Trafficking Protocol and the Protocol Against the Smuggling of Migrants by Land, Sea and Air. The main purpose of these new international provisions is to criminalize the commercial networks involved and increase effective prosecutions. A secondary goal is to provide protections for victims of trafficking and establish that neither trafficked nor smuggled persons are prosecuted for their irregular entry. These are positive provisions, a welcome departure from earlier punitive approaches to these populations. However, to date, it appears that only very small numbers of children have benefited from these protective statuses.

■ The United Kingdom

The U.K. has taken more steps than Australia and the U.S. to identify child victims of trafficking and such victims in the U.K. will usually be provided with accommodation and support by local authority social services departments. However, no specific immigration status has been created for them to provide more sustainable and international protection.

A minority of unaccompanied or separated children who are trafficked will come to the attention of the Home Office and an even smaller minority will apply for and be granted international protection under either the Refugee Convention as members of a particular social group or under Articles 3 and 4 of the European Convention on Human Rights on the basis that they have been subjected to inhuman and degrading treatment and enslaved.

The U.K. has opted out of the European Union Directive on Short Term Residence Permits offered to Victims of Action to Facilitate Illegal Immigration of Trafficking in Human Beings who Co-operate with the Competent Authorities and has failed to sign the Council of Europe Convention on Trafficking in Human Beings.[11] The U.K. does not at present intend to provide even a temporary period of leave to victims of trafficking while they consider whether to cooperate with any prosecution of their traffickers.

■ The United States

In the U.S., trafficked children may benefit from the Victims of Trafficking Protection Act 2000 (U.S.), which is designed to criminalize those responsible for human trafficking, while protecting the victims. The Act creates the T-Visa, available to victims of "a severe form of trafficking in persons." This includes trafficking to induce a child to perform a sex act as well as to engage in forced labor, debt bondage, and other forms of slavery like work. One serious concern with the implementation of the T-Visa is the tension between protection and enforcement. To qualify for the visa, an applicant must cooperate with the criminal investigation into the trafficker. While children under 18 are technically not required to cooperate, there is in practice a virtual requirement that they do so, since the Office of Refugee Resettlement (ORR) requires a letter from a law enforcement entity before it will certify a child as a trafficking victim and eligible for services. This deters some children, given the serious risks of retaliation by trafficking networks against the children and their families. Furthermore, the burden of proof to qualify for a T-Visa can be high. To qualify for a T-Visa,

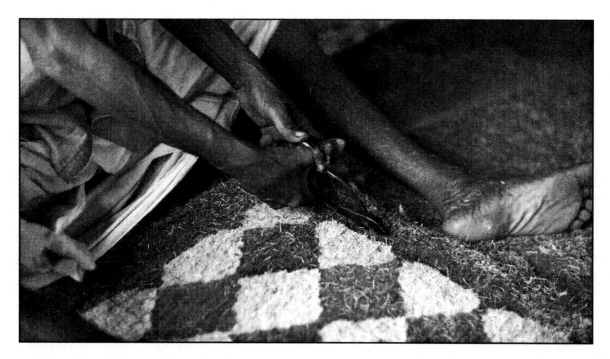

the child must show that he or she would face "extreme hardship involving unusual and severe harm" if removed from the U.S. Given the home circumstances of children vulnerable to trafficking, this requirement presents a virtually insuperable hurdle. However, if a child is successful in securing a T-Visa, the benefits are significant. Child T-Visa recipients (unlike SIJS holders) are entitled to bring their close family members to the U.S. to join them. They are also eligible for the same federal welfare benefits as refugees. In comparison, SIJS children are only entitled to state level benefits for children in care. Three years after obtaining the T-Visa, they can apply for permanent residence. In this respect, the T-Visas are similar to the Australian trafficking visas, where victims of trafficking are granted residence for two years in the first instance (graduating to permanent residence if the need for protection persists). Unlike adult recipients of T-Visas, trafficked children in the U.S. do not need to demonstrate coercion or fraud with respect to the participation in commercial sex. In practice, this form of protection

has yet to deliver significant benefits. In more than three years (between October 2001 and January 2005) only 32 unaccompanied children in the U.S. were certified as victims of trafficking, less than one a month.[12] This contrasts with an official U.S. estimate of 17,500 to 18,500 people trafficked into the U.S. annually.[13]

■ Australia

In Australia, there has been a welcome change in approach so that trafficked persons are now seen as victims rather than just as unlawful non-citizens. However, the protections instituted continue to have a strong law enforcement flavor. Amendments to Australia's Criminal Code Act 1995 created offences relating to slavery, sexual servitude, and misleading recruitment practices for sexual services. In 2002 an aggravated offence of people smuggling was created. This covers cases involving deceptive recruiting, slavery, and sexual servitude. The offence is punishable by up to 20 years imprisonment. These legislative measures were supplemented one year later with a

AUD$20 million package aimed at combating people trafficking. One of the most important elements of the support scheme was the creation of special visa subclasses for trafficked persons—Class UM and Class DH visas. These visas provide in sequence for temporary stay of two years, which can be converted to permanent residence where the need for protection is ongoing. Although a welcome initiative, there is still an unfortunate linkage between protecting trafficked persons and prosecuting their traffickers. Trafficking victims only gain protection if they cooperate in the prosecution of their traffickers. To obtain temporary protection, a person, including a child, must hold a criminal justice stay visa (available for witnesses in a criminal trial). The minister must be "satisfied" that the trafficking victim contributes significantly to, and cooperates closely with, the prosecution case. (In this respect the Australian concessions sit uneasily with the Trafficking Protocol which call on states to put the protection of victims above law enforcement matters.) Permanent protection is only available if the person would also be in danger if returned home.

8.5 Conclusion

All three countries studied have acknowledged the protection needs of a broad class of unaccompanied and separated children whom they do not consider eligible for refugee status. This protection recognition is a positive feature of state policy. However, this study has argued that some of these children, for example

those trafficked or fleeing child abuse, may well fall within the scope of the refugee definition. It is also suggested that advocates and decision makers should review their use of the key concept of "persecution" to ensure that child-specific forms of behavior are not arbitrarily excluded from protection. While trafficking safeguards for children indicate progress, they nonetheless attempt an uneasy, and often uneven, balance between protection and enforcement functions, making refugee recognition preferable to recognition as a trafficking victim.

It remains the case that a significant population of unaccompanied and separated children will need protection even though they do not fall within the refugee definition—children who are victims of abuse in the host state, children who have been abandoned by parents, children who were smuggled into the host state but cannot safely return home. For these children, both international law and common humanity require that host states provide permanent, non-discriminatory protection, approaching this particularly vulnerable population as children first and aliens second, not vice versa. The evidence reviewed in this chapter suggests that the three countries studied have some way to go in reforming their policies before they can be said to comply with this approach.

Endnotes

1   Data provided by Steven Heller, Resident and Status Services, Office of Program and Regulations Development, Citizenship and Immigration Services, U.S. Department of Homeland Security (29 July 2004). Also available under Table 5 of the Yearbooks of Immigration Statistics: http://uscis.gov/graphics/shared/aboutus/statistics/ybpage.htm.

2   Thronson, David B. "Kids Will Be Kids? Reconsidering Conceptions of Children's Rights Underlying Immigration Law." *Ohio State Law Journal* 63, no. 3 (2002): 1005.

3   Personal communication, ISS U.S. Branch, research by Alice Tarpley. 12 May 2005.

4   CRC, Article 9(1).

5   Migration Act 1958, ss 351 or 417, for example. See also *Ozmanian v. Minister for Immigration, Local Government and Ethnic Affairs* (1997) 141 ALR 322.

6   The child had applied for refugee status, which was refused in a case that went to the Federal Court but was discontinued in March 2004: *Applicants A86/2003 v. MIMIA*, Federal Court of Australia. One by-product of the choice of visa in this case was that the family would be denied access to any form of social security support for two years after the grant.

7   Migration Regulations 1994 (Australia), regs 1.21–1.27.

8   See Australian Citizenship Act 1948, s10C.

9   Migration Regulations 1994, Schedule 1, 1115 Special Eligibility (Residence) Class AO; Schedule 2, Subclass 832 Close Ties Visa.

10 Paragraphs 352A–352F provide for the spouse and children of an adult refugee to be granted leave to enter the U.K. to join him or her if they meet certain criteria. There is no equivalent provision for child refugees to be joined by parents or siblings. Discretion can be exercised by the Secretary of State for the Home Department in extremely compelling or compassionate circumstances. This concession was confirmed in paragraph 13 of an Unaccompanied Asylum Seeking Children Information Note, which is no longer relied on by the Immigration and Nationality Directorate but there is no reason to believe that discretion will not continue to be exercised in this way until this policy is expressly withdrawn.

11 CETS No. 197. Adopted by the Council of Ministers on 3 May 2005 and opened for signature on 16 May 2005.

12 Data provided by Margaret MacDonnell, U.S. Conference of Catholic Bishops/Migration and Refugee Services. 14 February 2005.

13 The Human Smuggling and Trafficking Center, U.S. Department of State. Fact Sheet: The Distinctions Between Human Smuggling and Human Trafficking. 1 January 2005. Available at http://www.state.gov/g/tip/rls/fs/2005/57345.htm.

CHAPTER 9

Towards More Comprehensive Protection

for Unaccompanied and Separated Children Traveling Alone

9.1 Outlining the Protection Deficit

There are many reasons why children traveling without their families confront harsh conditions. As described in chapter 2, the very fact of family separation is itself a traumatic reality which entails profound material and psychological deprivation.

Children may be separated from their families by the effects of war (as in Afghanistan, Bosnia, Kosovo, Liberia, Sierra Leone, Somalia, Sri Lanka, Sudan); persecution (China, India, Iran, Iraq); natural disasters (Ethiopia, Honduras); civil, political, and economic upheaval (El Salvador, Guatemala, Haiti, Mexico, Nigeria); or a combination of these. They may be subjected to arduous, terrifying journeys. They may be exposed to starvation, to the rigors of the elements as they cross borders by foot, or to the predatory behavior of smugglers and traffickers for whom human transport is at best a lucrative business and at worst—all too frequently—an occasion for physical and sexual abuse.

Sadly, the arduousness of the children's journeys is often complicated by encounters with untrained state officials, unsuitable policies and procedures, detention practices, and other administrative hurdles which are oppressive and terrifying rather than reassuring and protective. As a result, stories of children in distress, withdrawn into deep depression, or paralyzed by acute anxiety are commonplace.[1]

This report has documented some of these experiences in relation to unaccompanied and separated child migrants in Australia, the U.K., and the U.S. It highlights a disturbing and systematic protection deficit at the heart of the immigration systems of these three developed countries. The deficit is at once surprising and predictable. It is surprising because in all three countries the prevailing political and moral rhetoric is that vulnerable children traveling on their own and far from home should be accorded compassion and special care. Many advocates, scholars, and practitioners working in juvenile justice, child care, or administrative law fields are incredulous when exposed to the case histories contained in this report—some of which suggest callous indifference and even, on occasion, disturbing cruelty. While it is surprising, the protection deficit is also predictable. It results from the political marginality of children, their lack of bargaining power, and their exclusion from decisionmaking processes. Indeed the normal exclusion of children as a voiceless group of citizens is compounded in the case of the population studied in this report by two aggravating circumstances— their non-citizen status, and their lack of access to parental or other protective adult involvement.

The three states studied have all subscribed in one way or other to the major human rights instruments relevant to the treatment of unaccompanied and separated children traveling alone. But, as the research demonstrates, there are significant divergences in implementation and serious protection deficits overall. The tension between migration control, law enforcement, and a child-rights perspective inheres in almost all stages of the asylum-seeking process that children go through in each of the three countries studied. The report has addressed in detail both the shortcomings and the improvements and positive practices that emerged from the research.

This concluding section outlines the major concerns and deficiencies that we have identified in the legal frameworks, procedures, and outcomes at each step of the asylum-seeking process experienced by unaccompanied and separated children in the three states studied.

The report concludes with recommendations for policy makers and advocates responsible for the treatment of unaccompanied and separated child migrants. Though international law has, to some extent, addressed both the substantive and procedural aspects of child migration, translating these international standards into binding policies under domestic law has proved difficult. Both substantive legal and procedural issues regarding children who travel without the protection of a responsible adult urgently require attention. Indeed, in some cases procedural accommodation is particularly important in eliciting the "voice" of the child migrant him or herself. This final chapter also highlights particularly significant examples of good practice, both to give credit where it is due and to encourage wider uptake elsewhere.

9.2 Deficiencies in the Current Systems of the Three States

Data Collection

■ Inadequacy

Data collection is a vital tool for monitoring the status and progress of key social phenomena such as the migration of unaccompanied and separated children. It is also essential for evaluating the efficacy of public intervention and the discharge of official responsibilities. This study revealed sharp differences between the three countries studied. In Australia and the U.S. the statistical record kept by state authorities on unaccompanied and separated children is seriously deficient. Indeed the absence of reliable and professionally produced data would be politically unacceptable in fields of greater public scrutiny or concern, such as infant mortality or the incidence of child abuse. In Australia there is a radical absence of any reliable data, the available statistics

varying widely over time and according to source. In the U.S. there is some partial information collected from a variety of different access points in the immigration system. However it is unsystematic and suffers from the absence of any integrating oversight or systematization. Moreover there are some particular deficiencies within the U.S. system. It is noteworthy, for example, that there is no annual data on how many children go through Immigration Court proceedings. By contrast the U.K. government has dramatically improved its data collection over the past years, responding to earlier criticisms. It now collects clear and useful data on applications made by unaccompanied and separated children, as well as on the initial outcomes of these applications. This system of data collection and dissemination provides an excellent model for replication by other states. The two areas of U.K. practice that should be addressed are the absence of specific official data on the outcome of appeals by unaccompanied or separated children, and the lack of data on the number of unaccompanied or separated children refused entry by immigration officers placed at railway stations and ports in France and Belgium or airports in other countries.

■ Lack of Accountability

The deficiencies in the data collection on children seeking asylum alone raise immediate questions about the attention given to the issue of child migration in the countries studied. The information deficit limits both the accountability of the officials involved and the compatibility between the administrative system in place and the rule of law.

Recommendations and Positive Practice

- The leadership shown by the U.K. in improving data collection is acknowledged and should be emulated.

- If states are going to address their child protection responsibilities seriously, improvement of their record keeping must be an urgent priority. This should include comprehensive statistical profiles of unaccompanied and separated child asylum seekers at all stages of the immigration process, from interception prior to arrival, to the type of status awarded or denied, right through to the outcome of appeals and other forms of judicial review. Gender, age, and country of origin disaggregation (as done in the U.K. statistical record) is desirable.

Deflection of Child Asylum Seekers

■ Wide Use of Interdiction

The widespread use of interdiction and the institution of offshore asylum processing centers to deflect migrants, including child asylum seekers, from access to protection is a clear strategy, adopted by both the U.S. and Australia, to avoid international and domestic constraints on their conduct. Our research showed that both U.S. and Australian interdiction programs provided little or no special arrangements for unaccompanied and separated children dealt with offshore, in terms of accommodation and care or asylum processing. The situation in Australia is of particular concern in light of proposals to extend the "Pacific Strategy" to include all unauthorized boat arrivals—including those who make it to the Australian mainland.

Non-entrée and interdiction policies are particularly devastating for unaccompanied and separated children without resources to demand a hearing, make safe arrangements, or provide evidence in support of their claim for protection. According to the United Nations High Commissioner for Refugees (UNHCR), considerable numbers of unaccompanied and separated children are to be found on intercepted vessels, often forcibly and unwillingly placed there by their parents. They may have strong asylum claims, not only because of country conditions, but also because of their susceptibility, as unaccompanied or separated children, to being trafficked. These practices violate international law in fundamental respects—denying child asylum seekers the right to seek asylum and protection from *refoulement* to their countries, compromising their rights to liberty, security, and protection of their best interests.

■ Safe Third Country—
Preemptive Exclusionary Rules

In the U.K. asylum seekers who arrive via EU states, Norway or Iceland, which are deemed to be "safe third countries," are not permitted to make a claim for asylum in the U.K. but are returned to that safe third country as soon as suitable arrangements can be made for this to happen, without any consideration of the merits of their asylum claim.

The U.S. and Canada established similar "safe third country" agreements in 2004; no special exceptions were made for unaccompanied minors, other than to reiterate that they would be placed into expedited removal proceedings "only under limited circumstances."[2]

Australian law now includes provisions that bar applications from individuals traveling from certain countries. Further provisions also limit Australia's "protection obligations" in respect of any person who spends seven days or more in a country where he or she could have sought protection from either the state or from the offices of UNHCR.

Recommendations and Positive Practice

■ There is an urgent need for more transparency and greater international oversight of interdiction and external processing operations and safe third country policies and procedures. The fact that none of the countries studied have child-specific policies for these particularly rights violative procedures is of great concern and urgently requires rectification. Interdiction is an inhumane and dangerous policy, particularly unsuited to the needs of unaccompanied and separated children. There is a critical need for greater cooperation between the international organizations best positioned to take on an oversight function, UNHCR and the International Organization for Migration (IOM), and the UN Committee on the Rights of the Child.

Identification of Child Asylum Seekers

■ Lack of Well-Articulated Child-Specific Identifying Procedures

In the U.S. and Australia there is a lack of well-articulated, child-specific procedures for distinguishing unaccompanied and separated children from other populations. In the U.S. no clear written rules exist to assist Coast Guard, Border Patrol, and Customs and Border Protection officers in deciding on the *bona fides* of accompanying adults when they interview children. Without clear protocols to assist in identifying children separated from parents, it is likely that only children who are physically completely alone when they come into contact with immigration officials will be identified as unaccompanied and separated children. Children accompanied by non-parental adults—whether relatives, friends, kind strangers, or smugglers and traffickers—are at risk of being overlooked. This lacuna in current practice is considered to be a major reason why such relatively few cases of child trafficking are detected at ports of entry.

■ Age Disputes

Age disputes present challenges for all three countries. Even in the U.K., where commendable and very significant improvements have been made in the development of a holistic rather than a one-dimensional physical test approach to age determination, our research found that many children have their age disputed and thus undergo distressing experiences of mistrust and fear of being rejected for asylum. In the U.S., while a "preponderance of the evidence" test is used in questions of age for children whose application for refugee status is processed abroad,[3] children who enter the U.S. without legal status, typically without documentation, are held to a much more rigid, and medically questionable, standard. Finally, in Australia, confusion about age can

be particularly damaging in the context of initial interviews because of the power of immigration officials to use both general demeanor and/or later contradictions as evidence of adverse credibility.[4] The pervasive climate of official disbelief in respect of this population is highlighted by the fact that children sent for age testing in Australia were also frequently challenged about their stated origins and were referred for expert language testing.

Recommendations and Positive Practice

The U.K. currently has a program for training immigration officials in the identification of children likely to be at risk. It has made extensive efforts to identify children in genuine need at the earliest possible stage and to institute programs to target trafficking in children through training of in-country border officials and the instigation of research.

■ Both the U.S. and Australian governments should institute training and operational programs to assist immigration officials to identify separated children who may be being trafficked or otherwise in an abusive situation.

Establishing someone's precise age in the absence of reliable documentation or contemporaneous evidence of birth is impossible. In the U.S. and Australia, consideration should be given to following the best practice developed in the U.K., where the reductive and widely discredited one-dimensional physical tests approach used in determining a child's age has been replaced by a more holistic approach.

■ Age assessment should be based on the totality of the evidence, taking account of both physical and psychological maturity[5] and including documents, evaluations of healthcare professionals and case workers, information from family members, and any scientific examinations.[6] Where the outcome

of age determination affects decisions about detention or inclusion in fast track removal procedures, additional safeguards—including a rebuttable presumption that the person's claim to be under 18 should be accepted—should be adopted, as has recently been the case in the U.K. This process should be overseen by a panel of independent experts and not left to either central or local governmental bodies which may have vested interests in the outcome of assessment.

- The accurate assessment of age should be viewed as a child welfare issue, rather than an enforcement issue. The assessment should be used to determine the type of care to be given to the child, rather than the credibility of his or her claim to refugee protection.

- In contested cases, the benefit of the doubt should always be given to the minor, given the importance of the "best interests of the child" principle.

Reception of Child Asylum Seekers

■ Pre-Screening Procedures

Both the U.S. and Australian systems present children with significant hurdles in their access to asylum protection at very early stages in the process, when their vulnerability and need for adult guidance are greatest.

In the U.S., double standards appear to apply according to whether children are apprehended before or after making landfall on U.S. territory. Although policies suggest that unaccompanied and separated children should not be subject to "pre-screening" procedures in the U.S., children intercepted at sea and those covered by the Visa Waiver Program are not granted this exemption. The demanding interviews to which this group of children are subjected upon arrival in order to establish their fear and thus eligibility to claim asylum, are inappropriate and clearly against the child's best interests.

In Australia, all unaccompanied and separated children who arrive without a valid visa are subjected to a similar "pre-screening" process. An unaccompanied or separated child who arrives in Australia without a visa or who is otherwise refused "immigration clearance" at point of entry,[7] is taken immediately into what is known as "questioning" and then "separation" detention, without permitting contact with other detainees or anyone who might provide "coaching" on how to get through immigration controls. In order to access Australia's asylum procedures, a child who enters Australia without a valid visa must demonstrate *without legal assistance of any kind* that he or she is a person in respect of whom Australia owes "protection obligations." This is an extraordinarily punitive and challenging approach to protection of asylum-seeking children.

Recommendations and Positive Practice

- In practical terms, to gain protection as a refugee, a child needs to enter the asylum determination procedure at the earliest opportunity. Asylum processes should offer immediate protection from removal from the country and should represent the most secure long-term solution for the child.

- The U.S. should broaden the expedited removal

exemption to cover all unaccompanied children in all types of pre-screening procedures. At present, the principle behind the exemption is compromised by the large number of exceptions to the rule.

■ Australia should abandon its practice of pre-screening all unaccompanied and separated children arriving by irregular means.

■ In both the U.S. and Australia children seeking asylum alone should be allocated an adviser and/or effective and independent guardian so that they are informed about the process and are in a position to present their story.

The U.K. approach to screening of unaccompanied and separated children seeking asylum provides a useful model which other countries would do well to study and emulate. It comes closest to adopting a child-rights perspective in terms of care and protection upon arrival:

■ The screening process is intended as a mechanism for eliciting basic information about a child. It is designed to be child-sensitive rather than demanding and punitive (as is the case in Australia).

■ The interview is conducted on the day of arrival (or shortly thereafter) by a specially trained immigration officer. Both an interpreter and a "responsible non-adversarial adult" accompanying the child are required to be present, though their role is simply one of support and facilitation rather than active intervention in the asylum determination process itself. To effectively meet the child's best interests, he or she should be accompanied at the interview by a trained and suitable guardian.

■ The procedures governing initial government contact with unaccompanied and separated children in Australia and the U.S. urgently require reform. Identification of such children should immediately result in involvement of the welfare agencies of the state in question. Other positive aspects of the U.K. model, such as the entitlement to legal representation, should also be emulated.

■ Children should only be interviewed after being given access to professional or legal advice in the presence of an effective and independent guardian.

Guardianship

An egregious deficit of the current asylum systems in all three jurisdictions is the absence of guardians to act as trusted advisers and mentors for children navigating the complexities of the asylum determination and appeal processes. The lack of effective adult support can have a negative effect on the child's ability to articulate a full story, to comprehend and trust the procedure, and to comply with administrative procedures.

■ Conflicts of Interest

Why are guardians necessary in addition to advocates? Because there is a widespread consensus, across the three countries studied, that the conflict of interest facing child advocates who are charged with representing the child applicant's expressed wishes and at the same time making a best interest judgment (which might conflict with the child's wishes) is intolerable. In Australia, the minister charged with enforcing Australian migration law also has legal guardianship of unaccompanied and separated children. This dual institutional responsibility prevents effective execution of the guardianship role and gives rise to this fundamental conflict of interest. In the past the Minister for Immigration has delegated guardianship to the managers of the privately owned detention centers who have custody of "screened-in" asylum seekers—a profoundly unsatisfactory arrangement. It is only upon release from detention that the minister delegates legal (and effective) guardianship to state welfare authorities which become responsible for the daily care and control of the children. Now that the release of children has become the norm, the delegation of guardianship responsibilities to welfare agencies occurs at an earlier stage. This represents a marked improvement to the Australian system.

■ Problems Resulting from Shared Guardianship

In the U.K., the range of services provided do not in reality represent an effective form of guardianship responsive to the best interests of the child. The multiplicity of supportive personnel can lead to confusion and the absence of any emotional bond with a trusted or caring adult figure in *loco parentis*. As discussed in chapter 4, the plethora of different agencies leads to "buck passing" between them. The same is true for the U.S., where responsibility for dealing with unaccompanied and separated child asylum seekers is shared among a bewildering range of federal agencies.

■ Effect on the Appeal Process

The absence of guardians to act as trusted advisers and mentors for children during the asylum appeals process is a persistent and serious problem. In Australia, though the guardianship role is vested in the Minister for Immigration, this relationship has not been interpreted as implying any obligation on the minister to ensure that the children in care prosecute appeals against adverse decisions. Children in all three states frequently become demoralized by the length and complexity of the process.

Recommendations and Positive Practice

In all three countries studied, the presence of a responsible adult to advocate on behalf of the unaccompanied or separated child vastly improved the child's access to justice and his or her sense of emo-

tional wellbeing. It also enhances the quality of legal representation provided. The findings of this research therefore corroborate the recommendation set out in the General Comment of the Committee on the Rights of the Child:

States should appoint a guardian or adviser as soon as the unaccompanied or separated child is identified and maintain such guardianship arrangements until the child has either reached the age of majority or has permanently left the territory and/or jurisdiction of the state in compliance with the Convention and other international obligations.

The guardian should be consulted and informed regarding all actions taken in relation to the child. The guardian should have the authority to be present in all planning and decision-making processes, including immigration and appeal hearings, care arrangements and all efforts to search for a durable solution.

The guardian or adviser should have the necessary expertise in the field of child care, so as to ensure that the interests of the child are safeguarded and that the child's legal, social, health, psychological, material and educational needs are appropriately covered by, inter alia, *the guardian acting as a link between the child and existing specialist agencies/individuals who provide the continuum of care required by the child.*[8]

■ Each country urgently needs to institute a system of guardianship for unaccompanied and separated children to meet the children's parenting needs and to discharge its *parens patriae* obligations.

Detention

■ Detention as a Common Aspect of State Policy

All three countries studied have a history of subjecting children seeking asylum alone to detention. This punitive and unsuitable measure has been peripheral and occasional in the U.K., a product of contested age determination (so that only children wrongly classified as 18 or over are detained). It has been mandatory, pervasive, indefinite in length, and brutalizing in Australia—at least until late June 2005 when the law was changed so that "community residence" orders for children came to replace immigration detention. The absence of any legal time limits on the length of detention of children has had devastating effects. It has resulted in repeated incidents of self-harm by desperate children.

In the U.S., detention policy has existed somewhere between these two ends of the spectrum. It has been widespread but discretionary, variable in its punitive character (from very harsh jail settings to relatively supportive and nurturing shelters). It has frequently involved separating children from close relatives with whom they may have traveled, thus increasing the trauma of imprisonment. In the absence of criminal charges, detention of unaccompanied or separated children is unjustifiable and constitutes a serious breach of international standards.

■ Diminished Ability to Present Cogent Claims

Detention does not facilitate the administrative process, except insofar as it prevents disappearance of the detainees. Rather it diminishes the ability of officials to make accurate and safe assessments of asylum claims because detained asylum seekers progressively lose their ability to make cogent claims due to depression, lethargy, disorientation, and even psychotic disturbances. These effects are known to apply to adults; they apply with even greater force to children.

■ Isolation and Lack of Access to Asylum Advocates

In all three countries studied, detention facilities for asylum-seeking children tended to be situated in remote locations, far from the urban centers where asylum advocates and refugee communities

are based. Official policy seems to be based on the notion of "out of sight, out of mind." As a result of this isolation, and the severe funding constraints on legal representation (and reimbursement of travel costs and time), access to good advocates and community support is particularly difficult to secure. This appears to be an intentional consequence of official policy. Another problematic aspect of current policy governing the treatment of unaccompanied and separated children in all three countries is that as soon as they reach the age of 18, they are summarily removed from their peer group and become ineligible for special treatment.

■ Use of Handcuffs and Leg Irons

The U.S. authorities continue to use restraints such as shackles, handcuffs, and leg irons when transporting or escorting unaccompanied and separated children outside detention facilities—children who are typically not charged with any criminal offence or suspected of violent behavior. This practice, rightly criticized by Amnesty International[9] but still in use by several government agencies, including Border Patrol officials, has included handcuffing and shackling of children in public places such as courts, airports, and airplanes. Neither of the other countries studied have engaged in these brutal practices.

Both common humanity and international law demand that children separated from their family and fleeing trauma or violence should never be subjected to prolonged or arbitrary detention, or to the use of handcuffs or shackles. It is well-known that detention, punitive restraining measures, and lack of stimulation, are profoundly deleterious to children.

Of the three countries studied, only the U.K. has a longstanding policy that unaccompanied or separated children under 18 should not normally be detained (although children can be detained with their parents). This policy should be adopted by the other countries immediately.

There are some positive developments in this area in both the U.S. and Australia. The overall reduction in the use of secure detention in the U.S. (as a result of the transfer of care and custody of unaccompanied children from the Immigration and Naturalization Service to the Office of Refugee Resettlement) is an important improvement in the care of children seeking asylum alone and needs to be acknowledged, though concerns raised by a reliance upon institutional care must also be addressed. The amendment of Australia's Migration Act 1958 in June 2005 so as to provide that children should not normally be detained is another example in point.

SHOWER SHOES

Instead, children are now made the subject of "residence" orders, allowing them to live in (supervised) communities that are deemed not to constitute immigration detention.

We adopt the recommendations of the Committee on the Rights of the Child, in General Comment V(c):

Unaccompanied or separated children are children temporarily or permanently deprived of their family environment....

[T]he particular vulnerabilities of such a child, not only having lost connection with his or her family environment, but further finding him or herself outside of his or her country of origin, as well as the child's age and gender, should be taken into account. In particular, due regard ought to taken of the desirability of continuity in a child's upbringing and to the ethnic, religious, cultural and linguistic background as assessed in the identification, registration and documentation process. Such care and accommodation arrangements should comply with the following parameters:

- *Children should not, as a general rule, be deprived of liberty.*

- *In order to ensure continuity of care and considering the best interests of the child, changes in residence for unaccompanied and separated children should be limited to instances where such change is in the best interests of the child.*

- *In accordance with the principle of family unity, siblings should be kept together.*

- *A child who has adult relatives arriving with him or her or already living in the country of asylum should be allowed to stay with them unless such action would be contrary to the best interests of the child. Given the particular vulnerabilities of the child, regular assessments should be conducted by social welfare personnel.*

■ *Irrespective of the care arrangements made for unaccompanied or separated children, regular supervision and assessment ought to be maintained by qualified persons in order to ensure the child's physical and psychosocial health, protection against domestic violence or exploitation, and access to educational and vocational skills and opportunities.*

■ *States and other organizations must take measures to ensure the effective protection of the rights of separated or unaccompanied children living in child-headed households.*

■ *In large scale emergencies, interim care must be provided for the shortest time appropriate for unaccompanied children. This interim care provides for their security and physical and emotional care in a setting that encourages their general development.*

■ *Children must be kept informed of the care arrangements being made for them, and their opinions must be taken into consideration.*

Legal Representation

■ Lack of Professional or Legal Support During the Screening Stage

None of the three legal systems studied provide any formal advice or briefings for children entering the asylum system. Children may not know what they are applying for or what process they are entering. As a result the process of seeking asylum is mysterious at best, often provoking deep anxiety and trauma.

In Australia, children have no right to an adviser, "responsible adult," or any other representatives at the initial, screening-in stage, despite the fact that the screening interview is recorded and is critical in establishing whether a full asylum claim can be

made. This practice is profoundly detrimental to children's best interests and urgently needs to be changed.

In the U.S., unaccompanied and separated children are placed in the care of the immigration enforcement authorities without any access to child welfare services, legal advice, or representation for the first 72 hours. The critical importance of effective protection from abuse, blackmail, intimidation, or other forms of coercive pressure during the early phase of detention is widely acknowledged in both international and domestic standards, and builds on well-established evidence of risk during this stage. Access to legal advice is a particularly crucial form of protection. Within these first three days, many children agree to "voluntary return," because they find the prospect of prolonged detention alarming and because they lack legal advice about their options.

■ Lack of Legal Representation During the Asylum Process

Our research revealed that in the U.S. the absence of publicly funded legal assistance and competent legal representation for unaccompanied or separated child asylum seekers at each stage of the asylum process is a serious flaw. The U.S. asylum application form consists of 13 pages of instructions and 11 pages of fill-in-the-blanks text—a virtually insuperable hurdle for a child not assisted by counsel. The situation in Australia is better with the funding of migration agents as advisers. However, in that country too, issues arose about access to good quality legal advice and to advisers given the space and time to advise adequately.

■ Lack of Legal Assistance During Appellate/ Defensive Processes

The ability of children to negotiate appellate/ defensive processes without assistance is a large concern. Unrepresented children are effectively denied their due process rights, since it is unrealistic to expect a child to file an appeal (especially in a foreign language) without legal assistance. In all three countries, it was clear that children found it difficult to secure the services of high quality legal advisers, a particular concern given the complexity of their appeals, and children left to run appeals without competent assistance predictably suffer great disadvantage.

■ Legal Aid Tests

While public funding is provided for the representation of children in asylum appeal hearings in the U.K., this funding is now contingent on children meeting a "merit and means" test: legal aid will only be granted in cases where appellants are indigent and where the grounds of appeal reveal that the child would be entitled to protection under the Refugee Convention if the facts of his or her account were accepted by the immigration judge. The U.K. research also suggests that there is a much higher tendency for unrepresented children not to show up for their appeals. Sadly, similar constraints are placed on children's access to legal aid in Australia for assistance in the judicial review of adverse asylum claims.

Recommendations and Positive Practice

The report presents cogent evidence that the absence of representation is profoundly detrimental to children's best interests and urgently need to be rectified.

- Children seeking asylum in the U.K. are entitled to free legal representation during the initial screening interview, though this does not always happen in practice. This is an excellent policy which needs to be implemented in all three countries.

- The lack or shortage of adequately trained and publicly funded legal representation for separated and unaccompanied children at each stage of the

asylum process needs to be addressed and remedied. The adoption in the U.K. of a more favorable merits test when considering the grant of publicly funded legal representation is an example of positive practice. All children should be entitled to the assistance of a publicly funded legal representative.

The Asylum Process: Application for Asylum

As this report makes clear, the way in which an asylum claim is initially presented makes a critical difference to the progress of the application and to the wellbeing of the child applicant. Legal proceedings are always technical and threatening to non-specialists. *A fortiori* they are daunting experiences for unaccompanied and separated children, far from home and often contending with a foreign language, a new cultural environment, and the trauma of separation and loss resulting from the migration process itself. It is not just a question of navigating difficult legal procedures. Few legal decisions can have as dramatic an impact on someone's life as the outcome of an asylum application. Outcomes can mean the difference between life or death (the case of the Guatemalan street child Edgar Chocoy described in 3.2 is an example in point). Success or failure can also mean the difference between being granted a legal status and a route to citizenship and inclusion in the destination state, and becoming an undocumented, irregular migrant with minimal life prospects and prolonged uncertainty and insecurity.

■ Application Preparation

A critical issue in all three countries was the assistance given to children in lodging asylum claims (see above). In Australia's *mainland* system, migration agents provide government funded application assistance (some of whom are not legally trained). A defect of this otherwise positive scheme is that contracts are let after a tender process that does not guarantee that agents appointed to assist children possess appropriate skills and expertise. Particular problems were observed in the practice of processing applications in blocks or "task forces." Both migration agents and decision makers were found to be placed under time constraints that inevitably undermine the quality of the process. Intense periods of activity are frequently followed by long waiting periods.

■ Inadequate Training of Officials

Our research revealed that, more often than not, child-specific training of officials has been inadequate. This applies to those who administer asylum interviews, and to case workers assessing application forms or reviewing asylum cases. Having said this, attempts appear to have been made in the U.K. and the U.S. to train decision makers. Australian researchers could find no evidence of training during the period of 1999 to 2002, although the Department

of Immigration, Multicultural and Indigenous Affairs (DIMIA) asserts that programs have been instituted after that time.

In the U.K. children are not generally interviewed by decision makers. Rather their applications are assessed on the basis of the written material and questionnaire evidence submitted. Though effective training procedures exist for decision makers, those assessing written applications from unaccompanied or separated children need further training to identify persecution that is specific to children and to understand the particular evidentiary difficulties facing unaccompanied and separated children. A broader appreciation of the concept of child-specific persecution is one of the key goals of this report: see further below.

■ Interview

A common criticism of the interviews in both the U.S. and Australia is that officials have frequently failed to adopt techniques that are either child sensitive or culturally appropriate. Our research revealed a common perception among both child applicants and their advocates of aggression, disbelief, and suspicion on the part of decision makers. Such hostile behaviors exacerbate children's tendency to withdraw into themselves, and their reluctance to tell their story fully and trustingly. Poor interviewing techniques were found also to lead to misunderstandings and a simple failure on the part of officials to "get the story" of the children being interviewed.

■ Interpreters

In all three states, unaccompanied and separated children encounter not only legal but also language difficulties. These have an impact on the child's ability to articulate a case in the first place, to respond appropriately to interview or court questions, and to complete the forms, questionnaires, and other application requirements. The overwhelming majority of unaccompanied and separated children thus require an interpreter, a role that is critical to the proceedings. Not only is the interpreter the person to whom the child speaks and listens most directly, psychologically, the interpreter is often seen by the child as a mediator between the home and host societies. This represents a very complex set of dialogues and interactions. Well-trained and highly skilled interpreters are an invaluable resource in children's asylum proceedings, particularly if the same interpreter stays with a child's case through-out. However there are numerous reports of poor interpreting, and of bias or hostility on the part of interpreters, especially where the interpreter is drawn from a faction, clan, or group hostile to that of the child.

U.S. and Australian practice appears particularly problematic, although the findings were disputed by Australia's DIMA. Children typically encounter their interpreters just as their immigration hearings begin, so there is no opportunity for familiarity let alone for the establishment of trust. Moreover, it is common for courts and tribunals to use interpreters who translate over the phone or by video link when children give evidence and are cross-examined. Clearly this is not conducive to full disclosure of information, or comfort in the court or tribunal. Moreover there is concern that little attention is paid to dialect and accent variation in the assigning of interpreters, which hinders full comprehension and accurate translation. Small translation errors or incorrect nuances can dramatically prejudice pro-ceedings for an applicant, particularly a child, and thus can negatively affect the outcome of a case. In the U.K. similar criticism are raised. There is also concern that in some cases the unaccompanied or separated child will have lost all trust in adults from his or her own community. As a result the presence of interpreters from that community, far from encouraging, actually discourages the unac-

companied or separated child from making full disclosure about their previous persecution.

■ Slow Pace of Decision-Making Process

A common shortcoming is the slow pace of the administrative decision-making processes. As men-tioned in chapter 5, in the U.S. where asylum officers and supervisory asylum officers who review cases disagree, a national oversight process is instituted which further prolongs decision making. Policy about which types of unaccompanied or separated children's cases are to be reviewed has been unclear[10] and needs to be reviewed. Complaints about pro-cessing delays in Australia's asylum process were also common. In the U.K. there were target times for processing applications but on occasions these deadlines prevented the unaccompanied or sepa-rated child from having the time they needed to disclose the full extent of their persecution or the reasons for such persecution.

Recommendations and Positive Practice

The following examples of good practice in the U.K. asylum process should be adopted by the U.S. and Australia: allocating extra time for the submission of children's asylum applications; the creation of child-specific teams within the Immigration and

Nationality Directorate; the production of guidance for immigration judges; using an application form which is broken down into questions that signpost for both the children and their legal representatives the most important issues to be addressed.

▪ The Training of Officials

An example of excellent practice is the development, by the training arm of the Asylum Office in the U.S., of an entire "Lesson Plan" focused on the Guidelines for Children's Asylum Claims. This plan covers topics such as international guidance, child development, interview considerations, and the legal analysis of claims. The training program includes a documentary film related to refugee children, role-play, and instruction by officers who have conducted interviews with children themselves. Similar training programs should be instituted within other states.

▪ Interview Techniques

The UNHCR Handbook sets out three key provisions for deciding a child's legal status: expert advice on child development, a focus on objective country conditions, and a generous exercise of the benefit of the doubt in favor of children. All three provisions should be more widely implemented within the countries studied.

▪ There may be important information relevant to a child's asylum case that children either may not feel comfortable disclosing or whose significance they may be unaware of. At a minimum, decision makers have to be trained in and familiar with the specialist requirements of eliciting information from traumatized and frightened children.

▪ Advisers and representatives should have knowledge of the law so that they can help the child seeking asylum to recognize and disclose the material critical to the success of their claim.

▪ Interpretation

Interpreters need to be chosen carefully to ensure their linguistic and social compatibility with the child applicant. They need to be screened for competence and impartiality, and the same interpreter should be allocated to a case for its entirety. Interpreters should never be accessed over the telephone but should attend in person during asylum hearings, nor should children meet their interpreter for the first time immediately before being called to give evidence or answer questions in court.[11]

The Asylum Process: Appeals and Hearings

▪ Low Success Rates in Appeals

The rigidity of the time limits for appealing represents a particular problem for unaccompanied and separated children as many lose the right to appeal because of ignorance, disorganization, or lassitude induced by depression. In the U.S. many children abandon their appeals in favor of "voluntary departure" because the prospects of indefinite detention are too oppressive. In Australia, statistics supplied by IOM suggest that a high proportion of children detained on Nauru and Manus Island reacted in a similar manner, opting to return home. In the U.K., our research showed that a significant number of unaccompanied and separated children do not or are not entitled to appeal unsuccessful asylum applications.

More importantly, the research also suggested that fewer unaccompanied and separated children succeed in their appeals than do similarly placed adults. This worrying finding confirms our thesis that governments do not take seriously enough the importance of asylum as a suitable remedy for children. Qualitative analysis of a sample of three months worth of determinations of appeals by unaccompanied and separated children revealed that few children were relying on child-specific forms of persecution even where there appeared to be an evidential basis for doing so. This suggests that advocates and immigration judges may also be responsible for a failure to adequately present and argue cases.

■ Culture of Disbelief During the Appeal Process

In all three countries studied, we encountered a widespread and disturbing "culture of disbelief" directed at unaccompanied and separated children during the appeal process. Both case workers and immigration judges seem to find it hard to believe children who are seeking asylum alone and do not take their age and level of understanding into account. Where support and compassion need to complement official interactions, the research often revealed suspicion, hostility, and punitive attitudes instead. This official stance compounds the rights violations from which many of the child asylum applicants have fled.

■ Lack of Sensitivity During the Appeal Process

The failure to consider asylum as a serious remedy for children is reflected in a general tendency to make few concessions for children during appellate processes. The defensive asylum process in the U.S. system is more adversarial than the affirmative process, making it more intimidating and difficult for the client to talk. Yet, the need for sensitivity is just as great at the appeal level as at the stage of primary decision making. Researchers in the U.K. found that up until 2005, adjudicators who hear asylum appeals had not had any child-specific training for children's appeals. In Australia, training regimes for tribunal members and policies on the processing of children's claims are also recent. In the U.S. children's representatives reported intimidating and insensitive questioning of children by the trial attorneys who represent the government's interests in Immigration Court.[12] Similar shortcomings were reported of appellate processes in Australia.

Recommendations and Positive Practice

- In all three countries, better training of decision makers at every level is needed in basic child psychology and child-sensitive cross-cultural understanding. Decision makers hearing children's cases require specialist training if they are to perform this complex task satisfactorily. Even in the U.S., where training courses for adjudicators and judges already exist, current and former U.S. immigration judges interviewed for this study emphasized the need for additional training and/or specialization in children's issues.

- Judges should be trained to recognize that children, especially young children, usually will not be able to present testimony with the same degree of precision as adults. Judges should not assume that inconsistencies are proof of dishonesty. Rather they should recognize that a child's testimony may be limited not only by his or her ability to understand what happened, but also by his or her skill in describing the event in a way that is intelligible to adults. The official and pervasive "culture of disbelief" directed at unaccompanied and separated children urgently needs to be addressed and rectified.

- In the U.S., the more child-friendly procedures available through the affirmative asylum system stand out as a preferable alternative for those unaccompanied and separated children (the majority) who currently have no alternative but to initiate their asylum claims in an adversarial court environment. The more formal Immigration Court process should remain as the secondary procedure for children's cases, rather than as the primary adjudicatory context it currently serves.

Use of the Refugee Convention

It has been our argument that the grant of asylum or permanent protection under the Refugee Convention represents the most protective state response for many unaccompanied and separated children who have reason to fear return to their country of origin. In chapter 7 we explored ways in which the Refugee Convention has and has not been used in cases involving vulnerable children. The following section attempts to summarize some of this discussion.

It is our view that none of the three countries studied adequately applies to unaccompanied and separated children the obligations arising under the Refugee Convention, even though all three have signed and ratified the Convention, and incorporated its provisions, including its definition, into their domestic legislation. To some extent, this deficiency is a reflection of a broader retrenching of refugee protection, and of a political climate which is increasingly hostile to the humanitarian and pro-

tective obligations on which the Convention itself is founded. However, the deficiency goes beyond the generic antipathy and lack of generosity to asylum seekers evident in the refugee policies of all three states.

■ Establishing Well-Founded Fear

In general the applicant must both show a subjective fear of persecution upon return to his or her country of origin *and* demonstrate from an objective viewpoint that the fear is "well-founded." Unaccompanied and separated children may have greater difficulty than their adult counterparts satisfying both parts of this test. The child's capacity for subjective fear may be impacted by his or her developmental stage as well as particular experiences. In many of the cases reviewed for this study, the decision to flee was made by parents, guardians, or other adults conscious of a threat to the minor rather than by the child him or herself. Moreover the child's access to the resources necessary to corroborate the objective claim may be very limited; this reduces the child's chances of assembling the evidence required to make a compelling case.

■ Granting Asylum Under the Refugee Convention

It has been difficult to ensure the likelihood of a finding of persecution for unaccompanied and separated children both because of the absence of a rigorous or authoritative account of what constitutes persecution from a child's perspective and because of the difficulty in accessing the asylum determination system. As a result the grant of asylum under the Refugee Convention to separated or unaccompanied child applicants often represents the exception rather than the rule in all three countries studied, despite compelling and convincing evidence of persecution. In the U.K., in 2004, 98% of asylum applications by unaccompanied or separated children were refused. The success rate rose to 5% in 2005 and the first quarter of 2006 but was still a lower percentage than that of adults granted asylum.

■ Child-Specific Persecution

In chapter 7 we argued that consideration needs to be given to the particular way in which children can suffer persecution. Children can face harms that are indistinguishable from those facing adult asylum seekers. In all three countries it was found that decision makers seem to be most willing to recognize as refugees children in this category.

In addition, however, children can suffer persecutions that are particular to childhood. Examples in point are children conscripted as child soldiers, sold into slavery or oppressive marriages, and children suffering persistent discrimination as "black" (unauthorized) children. The recognition of this type of persecution as a basis for asylum is more uneven.

Finally, there are forms of persecution that involve harms that are only persecutory in nature because of the minority of the children. These are harms that might cause distress in adults but prove to be debilitating for children. It is in these cases that we argue that more consideration needs to be given to interpreting the Refugee Convention through the eyes of the child.

The failure to effectively articulate a doctrine of child-specific persecution to complement the generic concept of persecution is a reflection of a broader blindness to the needs and interests of children, particularly those who are unaccompanied and separated from their families. It is an instance of the widespread finding that children are practically invisible and inaudible in migration policy and in international law more generally.

This lacuna surrounding the needs and interests of children has several consequences common to the three countries studied. It results in a dearth of human rights reports which detail the persecu-

tion targeted at children. As a result, information gathering and substantiation of children's claims is problematic. It also leads to incredulity or skepticism about children's testimony, another problem in securing positive asylum outcomes. Finally, it produces a paradoxical set of obstacles for children. On the one hand, they encounter an attitude which discredits their particular suffering and needs and assimilates their situation to that of adults. On the other, they have to overcome discriminatory assumptions about their veracity, their vulnerability to attack, and their risk of persecution.

Neither the U.K.[13] nor Australia have promulgated specific guidelines concerning children's asylum applications. Although in the U.K. the Immigration and Nationality Directorate does produce an Asylum Policy Instructions on Children and also a chapter in its Operational Processes Manual on Applications from Children. The lack of guidance in Australia constitutes an impediment to the development of a body of case law which develops and explores child-specific persecution. It also allows decision makers and adjudicators to evade the importance of granting full asylum, as opposed to temporary forms of subsidiary protection, to children with well-founded fears of persecution. The precedent from and the relevance of the related field of women's asylum claims where guidelines were produced seems clear, but so far neither country has chosen to explore the relevance of this approach, or to follow the good example of the U.S., which has developed detailed and useful guidelines for judges and asylum officers concerning children's asylum applications. The U.S. judges' guidelines do fall short in certain ways: they focus on procedure rather than the substance of adjudicating claims, and are merely described as "suggestions." Nevertheless they represent an important and positive innovation.

Recommendations and Positive Practice

- In cases where the minority of an asylum applicant is a central factor in the harm inflicted or feared, an understanding of child-specific persecution, and an acknowledgment of its impact is critical to adjudication of the asylum claim. It is here that the expansive and evolving notion of what constitutes persecution must be applied to correct adult-centered and static conceptions of the role of asylum. The adoption of Guidelines on Children's Asylum Applications by the U.K. and Australia, following the good example of the U.S. government, would be a positive step forward.

- The development of a body of jurisprudence within the U.S. on the validity of asylum claims by Central American street children illustrates the proactive and child-centered use of refugee protection that we consider both appropriate within refugee law and necessary as a child protection measure. The refugee definition, and in particular the open-ended ground of "membership in a particular social group" could be applied much more widely and creatively to children's persecution cases than has been the case to date. Here the experience of advocates working on women's asylum cases

and developing jurisprudence on gender persecution is highly relevant. This expansive application of the Convention is a challenge for both advocates and decision makers to take on.

- In Australia, the recognition as refugees of children born in contravention of China's "One Child" policy is another example of good practice.[14] So too is the U.K. grant of asylum to trafficked children.

Protection Outcomes

Although the U.K. stands out for addressing the needs of vulnerable child migrants most comprehensively in the short term, this protection is generally confined to the child's minority or is of uncertain duration. Permanent refugee protection is rarely granted to unaccompanied and separated children in the U.K.

In Australia, the problem is more serious. No child who enters the country without a valid visa (the vast majority of unaccompanied and separated children fall into this category) can ever receive permanent refugee status at first instance. Instead, if he or she succeeds in obtaining temporary protection, that status will continue for three years, after which the whole asylum application process has to be undertaken once again. The introduction of the "seven day rule" in 2001 has had the potential of leaving some refugees on perpetual temporary protection visas (TPVs), requiring them to be re-processed every three or so years. For the unaccompanied and separated children, this process has presented many challenges. One critical drawback is that children holding TPVs are not eligible for family reunion. Nor can they access government funded education and training.

In the U.S., there are several statuses which can result in permanent protection. This is a positive feature of the U.S. system. The development of

Special Immigrant Juvenile Status (SIJS) for unaccompanied or separated children who are abandoned or abused is a unique aspect of the system. However, in addition to some procedural shortcomings including the delegation of a child welfare eligibility decision to an enforcement entity, a serious substantive defect is that a child recipient of SIJS is forever barred from submitting a family reunification petition. This permanent severance of the parent/child bond is unnecessary and unjust. Indeed it constitutes a violation of the right to respect for family life enshrined in international law.

In none of the countries studied is it common for victims of trafficking to be recognized as refugees. Many are simply not identified, and those that are frequently lack the specialist assistance needed to pursue an asylum claim or are hesitant about coming forward for fear of retaliation by their abusers. Despite the existence of specific visas for victims of trafficking in the U.S. and Australia, an astoundingly small number of children have received protection in this way. The amount of public attention to and outcry over this issue is not paralleled by effective intervention in practice.

Recommendations and Positive Practice

- Much greater consideration needs to be given to the categorization of vulnerable immigrant children as refugees. A more systematic consideration of child-specific needs and vulnerabilities is urgently required.

- An example of positive practice in the U.S. is the creation of a special permanent status to accommodate the needs of unaccompanied and separated children in need of protection. This Special Immigrant Juvenile Status, which caters to the needs of abused, abandoned, or neglected children without caregivers or legal immigration status, can lead to permanent settlement and eventually citizenship.

This model should be emulated by other countries and further improved by the U.S.

- Both the U.S. and Australia have instituted special visas to protect the interests of children trafficked into their jurisdictions. Though these visas have not been sufficiently utilized, their institution is a positive development. Child victims of trafficking should not be required to provide evidence against their abusers in order to be eligible for protective visas (as is the case in Australia). U.S. policy provides a good example by not requiring children to cooperate with the law enforcement process against their traffickers in order to avail themselves of the benefits of the visa, however advocates object that procedural requirements may violate this in practice. An approach without enforcement participation requirements should be adopted in the U.K., and re-examined in the U.S.

- Children granted special visas because of abandonment, abuse, or neglect should not be disqualified for life from exercising family reunion rights, if these become relevant.

- Children granted discretionary protection because it is in their best interests to be so treated, should not have this status automatically terminated when they turn 18; rather the presumption should be that the need for a permanent and legal immigration status continues in the absence of proof that home circumstances have changed fundamentally.

9.3 Conclusion

Our first argument is that the protection deficits highlighted above need to be recognized as a refusal to acknowledge and provide for the particular vulnerability of unaccompanied and separated children. To varying degrees, all three countries examined have persisted with policies that advance the immigration control agenda in the face of troubling and predictable human rights violations against children. We see it as an urgent responsibility to highlight this protection deficit, as a necessary prelude to policy reform and change. Child migration is not an exceptional or occasional occurrence, but a regular phenomenon, which needs to be recognized, acknowledged, and responded to appropriately. The research undertaken for this study demonstrates that each of the three countries studied falls short of desirable child protection practice, whether in respect of statistical data collection, government planning and legal structures, or in addressing the social needs of unaccompanied and separated children seeking asylum.

Our second argument is that many unaccompanied and separated child migrants have a stronger claim to asylum than is generally recognized or acknowledged. Here we seek to make two subsidiary points. One is that children with claims analogous to those of adults are being left out of the refugee protection system because asylum is implicitly assumed to be an adult remedy. Why else would children fleeing forced recruitment by government forces, or persecution by population control monitors in China, be excluded from protection? Why are fewer unaccompanied and separated child than adult asylum seekers in the U.K. initially recognized as refugees? The other point is that more attention needs to be paid to the interpretation of the Refugee Convention in the context of claims made by children.

Over the last 20 years or so, developments in refugee jurisprudence have expanded greatly the scope of the Refugee Convention for adults. Similar reasoning should now be adopted in cases involving children. This is not an argument for preferential treatment, but simply a claim for equal protection for children. Just as a broader range of adults have benefited from asylum than might have been expected half a century ago, in line with social and political developments, so the same dynamic and rights based approach should benefit children. Sexuality and other aspects of gender persecution, harms by non-state actors (including abusive parents), infliction of persecution without intent to harm (as with female circumcision) have all formed the basis of successful adult asylum claims. By contrast the approach to children has generally been conservative. Children's claims have been ignored because policy makers, administrators, and immigration judges have tended to operate with an adult-focused lens, missing the opportunity to listen to (and even to elicit) the factual basis for children's asylum claims. These missed claims include some of the stories we have described in the report. These are the cases of unaccompanied and separated children being trafficked into domestic slavery or facing fundamental discrimination at the hands of government by reason of their birth or social status or other actual or perceived disability. They should all be entitled to international protection under the terms of the Refugee Convention. We hope our report will stimulate advocates and decision makers to enter into these arguments and broaden their field of vision.

Our third and final claim is that the problems identified in this report can be solved relatively easily, without jeopardizing states' migration management programs. The solutions we propose do not involve open door immigration policies or reckless incentives to use children as migration anchors or investment commodities. Children need and deserve protection and where that is available in the home country, normally that is the best place for children to be. Accordingly, we believe that states do have a right to return children who are not entitled to protection in the destination state to family (though not institutional) care in the state of origin where there are no child protection concerns about doing so. In this sense, ours is not a call for a ban on return of all unaccompanied or separated children. Indeed, in many cases a more child-focused asylum system would allow from the speedier assessment of cases in which return is a viable option. In all cases, the views of the children in question need to be elicited with care. Trafficked children and children destined to bonded domestic service or other forms of forced labor should be entitled to effective state intervention, instead of the current vacuum of illegality or irregularity into which most unaccompanied and separated children slip.

However, where children clearly lack protection at home, they should be granted asylum or analogous and permanent protection in the destination state. This should be done in recognition of the primacy of their claim to protection as children. A protective status should be accompanied by law enforcement measures directed against those who would exploit and blackmail unaccompanied and separated child migrants. This approach would have several immediate and beneficial consequences. It would reinforce and render consistent fundamental ethical standards already accepted in principle in the three destination states. These are standards reflected in domestic child welfare laws and policies. It would uphold legal obligations derived from international human rights law regarding protection from persecution and torture, and promotion of the best interests of the child. And it would bolster new developments in international criminal law, by undercutting the incentives for traffickers and smugglers to use children as their most valuable commodities.

Once enslaved or bonded children are enfranchised as human beings with their own rights and entitlements, the stranglehold of criminal gangs would be undermined and the profitability of the enterprises compromised. Legalizing the status of trafficking victims thus helps to break the chain of blackmail and dependency that ties children to their exploiters.

Apart from legal consequences such as these, we suggest that a rights based approach to unaccompanied and separated children would have a broader social impact. It would place the state's role as *parens patriae* at center stage, privileging the health and welfare of children—all children. The questionable political benefits of stigmatizing and traumatizing a particularly vulnerable subset of immigrant children through interdiction, detention, interrogation, exclusion, abandonment, and fear would be exposed.

To be sure, a rights based approach might end up granting a secure immigration status to some children who could have remained in their home countries. However, it would also result in the protection of children who otherwise would have been returned to harm in their countries of origin. We suggest that this is a reasonable price to pay in the interests of the larger goal of child protection. Ultimately our calculation is a tradeoff. The immediate needs of vulnerable unaccompanied and separated children should be privileged over punitive and putatively deterrent measures. Since irregular migration is rarely the "fault" of the children themselves, punishing them is certainly unjust and most likely ineffective. The use of harsh immigration control measures which re-traumatize already damaged children harms the civility and ethical basis of the destination societies.

Endnotes

1   Bhabha, Jacqueline. "Demography and Rights: Women, Children and Access to Asylum." *International Journal of Refugee Law* 16 (2004): 227.

2   See Department of Homeland Security. "Implementation of the Agreement Between the Government of the United States of America and the Government of Canada Regarding Asylum Claims Made in Transit and at Land Border Ports-of-Entry." 45 *Federal Register* 69. 8 March 2004. 10623. Available at http://www.lexisnexis.com/practiceareas/immigration/pdfs/695137p74.pdf.

3   Interview with Shereen Faraj, Division of Unaccompanied Children's Services, Office of Refugee Resettlement, Administration for Children and Families, Department of Health and Human Services. 30 July 2004.

4   Migration Act 1958 (Australia), s91R.

5   UNHCR. *Policies and Procedures in Dealing with Unaccompanied Children Seeking Asylum.* UNHCR, February 1997. 8.

6   This approach is endorsed by the recent General Comment of the Committee on the Rights of the Child, see Committee on the Rights of the Child. General Comment No. 6: Treatment of separated and unaccompanied children outside their country of origin. UN, 2005. CRC/GC/2005/6.V(a)A.

7   For example, where the child's visa is found not to be valid.

8   Committee on the Rights of the Child, General Comment No. 6, V(b).

9   Amnesty International. *Unaccompanied Children in Immigration Detention.* New York: Amnesty International, 2003. 34–38.

10 Interview with Kathleen Wainio and Eudelia Talamantes, Quality Assurance and Training Officers, and Patricia Vasquez, Deputy Director, Miami Asylum Office. 14 July 2004.

11 This may be a particular problem in the U.K. where an unaccompanied or separated child will have been provided with an interpreter paid for by the Legal Services Commission and arranged by his or her own legal representative up until the hearing itself. The interpreter will then be a person employed and paid for by the Asylum and Immigration Tribunal, who will not use the same individuals as used by the unaccompanied or separated child's legal representatives. The interpreter booked by the legal representatives will merely be at court to interpret any conferences the unaccompanied or separated child may have with his or her legal representative before or after the hearing.

12 Asylum hearing transcript for respondent P.-N., held in Miami, Florida, dated 13 June 2003, documents attorney complaints to judge of trial attorney's intimidating questioning and badgering tone (full name of respondent withheld for confidentiality reasons). 109–110.

13 Although the Immigration Law Practitioners' Association has published *Working with children and young people subject to immigration control : Guidelines for best practice* November 2004, which was given to the Immigration and Nationality Directorate, circulated widely to immigration practitioners, and which is provided to each immigration judge by the Asylum and Immigration Tribunal.

14 *Chen Shi Hai v. MIMA* (2000) 201 CLR 293.

APPENDIX 1

Glossary of Terms

BIA	=	Board of Immigration Appeals (U.S.)
BID	=	Bail for Immigration Detainees (U.K.)
CAT	=	United Nations Convention Against Torture
CBP	=	Customs and Border Protection (U.S.)
CIPU	=	Country Information and Policy Unit (U.K.)
CIS	=	Citizen and Immigration Services (U.S.)
CRC	=	United Nations Convention on the Rights of the Child
DHS	=	Department of Homeland Security (U.S.)
DIMA	=	Department of Immigration, and Multicultural Affairs (Austl)
DIMIA	=	Department of Immigration, Multicultural and Indigenous Affairs (Austl)
DUCS	=	Division of Unaccompanied Children's Services (U.S.)
ECHR	=	European Convention on Human Rights
EOIR	=	Executive Office of Immigration Review (U.S.)
FIAC	=	Florida Immigrant Advocacy Center (U.S.)
HREOC	=	Human Rights and Equal Opportunity Commission (Austl)

IAS	=	Immigration Advisory Service (U.K.)
IAT	=	Immigration Appeal Tribunal (U.K.)
ICE	=	Immigration and Customs Enforcement (U.S.)
IDC's	=	Immigration Detention Centers (Austl)
IGOC Act	=	Immigration Guardianship of Children Act (Austl)
INA	=	Immigration and Nationality Act (U.S.)
IND	=	Immigration and Nationality Directorate (U.K.)
INS	=	Immigration and Naturalization Service (U.S.)
IOM	=	International Organization for Migration
MSI	=	Migration Series Instructions (Austl)
NASS	=	National Asylum Support Service (U.K.)
NGO	=	Non-Governmental Organization
OIG	=	Office of Inspector General (U.S.)
ORR	=	Office of Refugee Resettlement (U.S.)
PAM	=	Procedures Advice Manual (Austl)
RRT	=	Refugee Review Tribunal (Austl)

SEF	=	Statement of Evidence Form (U.K.)
SIJS	=	Special Immigrant Juvenile Status (U.S.)
TPS	=	Temporary Protected Status (U.S.)
TPV	=	Temporary Protection Visa (Austl)
UAM	=	Unaccompanied Minors
UNHCR	=	United Nations High Commissioner for Refugees
UNICEF	=	United Nations International Children's Emergency Fund
UNTOC	=	United Nations Convention on Transnational Organized Crime
VAWA	=	Violence Against Women Act (U.S.)
VWP	=	Visa Waiver Program (U.S.)

The Refugee Convention

United Nations Convention relating to the Status of Refugees

Smuggling Protocol

Protocol against the Smuggling of Migrants by Land, Sea and Air

Trafficking Protocol

Protocol to Prevent, Suppress and Punish Trafficking in Persons, Especially Women and Children

APPENDIX 2

Legislation, Cases and International Instruments

Legislation

Australia

Australia's Criminal Code Act 1995

Australian Citizenship Act 1948

Immigration (Guardianship of Children) Act 1946

Migration Act 1958

Migration Amendment (Detention Arrangements) Act 2005

Migration Regulations 1994

United Kingdom

Asylum and Immigration (Treatment of Claimants etc) Act 2004

Children Act 1989

Children Act 2004

Human Rights Act 1998

Immigration Act 1971

Immigration and Asylum Act 1999

Immigration Rules HC 395

Nationality, Immigration and Asylum Act 2002

United States

Child Status Protection Act 2002

Federal Rules of Procedure

Freedom of Information Act

Homeland Security Act 2002

Immigration and Nationality Act 2000

Refugee Act 1980

Unaccompanied Alien Child Protection Act (pending in the U.S. Congress)

Victims of Trafficking Protection Act 2000

Violence Against Women Act 1994

Cases

Australia

Applicant S v. MIMIA (2003) 217 CLR 387

Chen Shi Hai v. MIMA (2000) 201 CLR 293

Jaffari v. MIMA (2001) 113 FCR 10

Kuldip Ram v. MIEA and RRT (1995) 130 ALR 314

MIEA v. Teoh (1995) 183 CLR 273

MIMA v. Haji Ibrahim (2000) 204 CLR 1

MIMA v. Israelian (2001) 206 CLR 323

Odhiambo v. MIMA (2002) 122 FCR 29

Ozmanian v. MIMA (1996) 137 ALR 103

P1/2003 v. MIMIA [2003] FCA 1029 (26 September 2003)

SHBB v. MIMIA [2003] FMCA 82 (11 April 2003)

VFAY v. MIMIA (2004) 134 FCR 402

WACB v. MIMIA [2004] HCA 50 (7 October 2004)

WAJC v. MIMIA [2002] FCA 1631 (23 December 2002)

X v. MIMA (1999) 92 FCR 524

Canada

Bian v. Canada (Minister of Citizenship and Immigration) Federal Court of Canada, Trial Division, Givson J, 11 December 2000, IMM 1640–00, IMM 932–00

Canada (Attorney General) v. Ward [1993] 2 SCR 689

United Kingdom/Europe

ID & Others v. Home Office [2005] EWCA Civ 38

Islam v. Secretary of State for the Home Department (House of Lords) [1999] 2 AC 629

Selmouni v. France 25803/94 [1999] ECHR 66

T v. United Kingdom (2000) 30 EHRR 121

The Queen on the Application of Behre & Others v. the London Borough of Hillingdon [2003] EWHC 2075

The Queen on the Application of C v. London Borough of Enfield [2004] EWHC 2297

The Queen on the Application of I & Another v the London Borough of Enfield [2005] EWHC 1025 (Admin)

United States

American Baptist Churches v. Thornburg 760 F. Supp ND Cal (1991)

Bucur v. INS 109 F.3d 399 (7th Cir. 1997)

Eldin Jacobo Escobar v. Ashcroft 3rd Cir. No. 04–2999 (2003)

Elian v. Reno 212 F.3d 1338 (11th Cir. 2000), cert. denied. 530 U.S. 1270 (2000)

Lucienne Yvette Civil v. INS 140 F.3d 52 (1st Cir. 1998)

Mei Dan Liu v. Ashcroft 380 F.3d 307 (7th Cir. 2004)

Tchoukhrova v. Gonzales 404 F.3d 1181 (9th Cir. 2005)

Xue Yun Zhang v. Gonzales 9th Cir. No. 01–71623 (26 May 2005)

International Instruments

Declaration of the Rights of the Child

European Convention on Human Rights

Protocol Against the Smuggling of Migrants by Land, Sea and Air

Protocol to Prevent, Suppress, and Punish Trafficking in Persons, Especially Women and Children

United Nations Convention against Torture

United Nations Convention Against Transnational Organized Crime

United Nations Convention on the Rights of the Child

United Nations Convention relating to the Status of Refugees and Protocol on the Status of Refugees

Universal Declaration of Human Rights

Vienna Convention on the Law of Treaties

Bibliography

"Adrift in the Pacific: The Implications of Australia's Pacific Refugee Solution." Oxfam, March 2002. http://www.caa.org.au/campaigns/submissions/pacificsolution.

"No Place for a Child—Children in U.K. Immigration Detention—Impacts, alternatives and safeguards." Save the Children, 2005.

Admission Impossible. Film Australia, aired by Australian Broadcasting Corporation, *True Stories*. 31 March 1992.

Amnesty International. Public statement, "Italy: Government must ensure access to asylum for those in need of protection." http://web.amnesty.org/library/Index/ENGEUR300012004?open&of=ENG-ITA.

Amnesty International. *Unaccompanied Children in Immigration Detention*. New York: Amnesty International, 2003.

Anker, Deborah E. *The Law of Asylum in the United States*. 3rd ed. Boston: Refugee Law Center, 1999.

Ayotte, Wendy. *Separated Children Coming to Western Europe: Why They Travel and How They Arrive*. London: Save the Children, 2000.

BBC Television, *The Leaving of Liverpool*. 1993.

Bell, Adrian. *Only For Three Months: The Basque Children in Exile*. Norwich: Mousehould Press, 1996.

Bhabha, Jacqueline and Schmidt, Susan. *Seeking Asylum Alone, United States: Unaccompanied and Separated Children and Refugee Protection in the U.S.* Cambridge, MA: Bhabha and Schmidt, 2006. (U.S. Report.)

Bhabha, Jacqueline and Finch, Nadine. *Seeking Asylum Alone, United Kingdom: Unaccompanied and Separated Children and Refugee Protection in the U.K.* Cambridge, MA: Bhabha and Finch, 2006. (U.K. Report.)

Bhabha, Jacqueline. "Demography and Rights: Women, Children and Access to Asylum." *International Journal of Refugee Law* 16, April 2004.

Bhabha, Jacqueline. "Inconsistent State Intervention and Separated Child Asylum-Seekers." *European Journal of Migration and Law* 3, 2001.

Bucci, Maria. "Young, Alone and Fleeing Terror: The Human Rights Emergency of Unaccompanied Immigrant Children Seeking Asylum in the United States." *New England Journal on Criminal and Civil Confinement* 30, 2004.

Charlesworth, Hilary, Chiam, Madelaine, Hovell, Devika and Williams, George. "Deep Anxieties: Australia and the International Legal Order." *Sydney Law Review* 25, 2004.

Coldrey, Barry. *Good British Stock: Child and Youth Migration to Australia, 1901–83. Research Guide No. 11.* Canberra: National Archives of Australia, 1999.

Committee on the Rights of the Child. General Comment No. 6: Treatment of separated and unaccompanied children outside their country of origin. UN, 2005. CRC/GC/2005/6.

Crawley, Heaven. *Refugees and gender: Law and process*. Bristol: Jordan, 2001.

Crock, Mary. "Echoes of the Old Countries or Brave New Worlds: Legal Responses to Refugees and Asylum Seekers in Australia and New Zealand." *Revue Québécoise de Droit International* 14, no. 1, 2001.

Crock, Mary. "Lonely Refuge: Judicial Responses to Separated Children Seeking Refugee Protection in Australia." *Law in Context* 22, no. 2, 2005.

Crock, Mary. *Immigration and Refugee Law in Australia.* Sydney: Federation Press, 1998.

Crock, Mary. *Seeking Asylum Alone, Australia: A Study of Australian Law, Policy and Practice Regarding Unaccompanied and Separated Children.* Sydney: Themis Press, 2006. (Australian Report.)

Dauvergne, Catherine. "The dilemma of rights discourses for refugees." *University of New South Wales Law Journal* 23, no. 3, 2000.

Department of Education and Youth Affairs. *Immigrant and Refugee Youth in the Transition from School to Work or Further Study.* Canberra: Australian Government Publishing Service, 1983.

Department of Immigration and Multicultural Affairs (Australia). "Border Control." 2005. http://www.immi .gov.au/illegals/border.htm.

Department of Immigration and Multicultural Affairs (Australia). "Fact Sheet 75: Processing Unlawful Boat Arrivals." http://www.immi.gov.au/facts/75processing.htm.

Department of Immigration and Multicultural Affairs (Australia). "Fact Sheet 77: The Movement Alert List." 2005. http//www.immi.gov.au/facts/77mal.htm.

Department of Immigration and Multicultural Affairs (Australia). "Fact Sheet 86: Overstayers and People in Breach of Visa Conditions." http://www.immi.gov.au/facts/86overstayers_1.htm.

Department of Immigration, Multicultural and Indigenous Affairs (Australia). *Immigration Detention Contract.* http://www.dimia.gov.au/detention/group4/index.htm.

Department of Immigration, Multicultural and Indigenous Affairs (Australia). *Procedures Advice Manual.* 2003.

Fantz, Ashley and Wee, Gillian. "Chinese Teen Can Leave World of Abuse." *The Miami Herald.* 12 August 2004. http://www.miami.com/mld/miamiherald/news/breaking_news/9377253.htm.

Faulstich Orellana, Thorne, Barrie, Chee, Anna, and Wan Shun Eva Lam. "Transnational Childhoods:

The Participation of Children in Processes of Family Migration." *Social Problems* 48, November 2001.

Ford, Richard. "Second Asylum Plan Scrapped." *The Times.* 17 June 2005. http://www.timesonline.co.uk/article/0,,2-1657794,00.html.

Freiman, Jonathan M. "Migrant Interdiction: Law and Practice." Allard K. Lowenstein International Human Rights Clinic, Yale Law School, undated. Unpublished paper on file with the author.

Global Commission on International Migration. *Migration in an interconnected world: New directions for action.* http://www.gcim.org/en/finalreport.html.

Gordon, Michael. *Freeing Ali: The Human Face of the Pacific Solution.* Sydney: University of New South Wales Press, 2005.

Hathaway, James. *The Law of Refugee Status.* Toronto: Butterworths, 1991.

Her Majesty's Government. Education and Skills Committee's Inquiry. *Every Child Matters.* Cm 5860, September 2003.

Her Majesty's Government. White Paper, *Secure Borders, Safe Haven: Integration with Diversity in Modern Britain.* CM 5387, February 2002.

Holden, Robert. *Orphans of history: the forgotten children of the First Fleet.* Melbourne: Text Publishing, 2000.

Human Rights and Equal Opportunity Commission (Australia). *A Last Resort? National Inquiry into Children in Immigration Detention.* Canberra: Australian Government Publishing Service, 2004. http://www.hreoc.gov.au/human_rights/children_detention_report/report/pdf.htm.

Human Smuggling and Trafficking Center, U.S. Department of State. *Fact Sheet: The Distinctions Between Human Smuggling and Human Trafficking.* 1 January 2005. http://www.state.gov/g/tip/rls/fs/2005/57345.htm.

Humphreys, Margaret. *Empty Cradles: One Woman's Fight to Uncover Britain's Most Shameful Secret.* London: Doubleday, 1994.

Immigration and Naturalization Service, U.S. Department of Justice. "Guidelines for Children's Asylum Claims." 10 December 1998. http://uscis.gove/graphics/lawsregs/handbook/10a_ChldrnGdlns.pdf.

Immigration Law Practitioners Association (ILPA). *Working with Children and Young People Subject to Immigration Control: Guidelines for Best Practice.* London: ILPA, 2004.

Immigration Officer Academy (U.S.). "Asylum Officer Basic Training Course, Participant Workbook." Draft, 31 August 2001.

International Organization for Migration. *Journeys of Jeopardy: A Review of Research on Trafficking in Women and Children in Europe.* IOM Migration Research Series No 11, 2002.

International Programme on the Elimination of Child Labour. *Unbearable to the Human Heart: Child Trafficking and Action to Eliminate it.* International Labour Organization, 2002. http://www.ilo.org/public/english/standards/ipec/publ/childtraf/unbearable.pdf.

Kevin, Tony. *A certain maritime incident: the sinking of SIEV X.* Melbourne: Scribe Publications, 2004.

Kidane, Selam. *I did not choose to come here: Listening to Refugee Children.* London: British Association for Adoption and Fostering, 2001.

Manderson, Lenore, Kelaher, Margaret, Markovic, Milica and McManus, Kerrie. "A Woman without a Man is a Woman at Risk: Women at Risk in Australian Humanitarian Programs." *Journal of Refugee Studies* 11, 1998.

Marr, David and Wilkinson, Marianne. *Dark Victory.* Sydney: Allen & Unwin, 2003.

McGann, Chris. "U.S. Gives Harsh Welcome to Children Seeking Asylum." *Seattle Post-Intelligencer.* 19 June 2003.

O'Brien, Natalie. "The U.S. Government for the first time has named Australia as a 'destination' country for sex slaves." *The Australian.* 16 June 2004. http://www.theaustralian.news.com.au.

Office of International Affairs, Asylum Division, USCIS/DHS. "Affirmative Asylum Procedures Manual." February 2003. http://uscis.gov/graphics/lawsregs/handbook/AffrmAsyManFNL.pdf.

Office of the Chief Immigration Judge, Executive Office for Immigration Review, U.S. Department of Justice. "Interim Operating Policies and Procedures Memorandum 04–07: Guidelines for Immigration Court Cases Involving Unaccompanied Alien Children." 16 September 2004. http://www.usdoj.gov/eoir/efoia/ocij/oppm04/04-07.pdf.

Ortiz Miranda, Carlos, Associate General Counsel of the U.S. Conference of Catholic Bishops. "Open Letter to Customs and Border Protection." 12 October 2004. http://www.usccb.org/mrs/usccbexpedremcom.shtml.

Paladin Child: The Safeguarding Children Strand of Maxim funded by Reflex : A Partnership Study of Child Migration to the U.K. via London Heathrow. Reflex, Metropolitan Police, the U.K. Immigration Service, Association of Directors of Social Services, NSPCC, London Borough of Hillingdon, 2004.

Physicians for Human Rights and the Bellevue/NYU Program for Survivors of Torture. *From Persecution to Prison: The Health Consequences of Detention for Asylum Seekers.* Boston and New York City, June 2003.

Refugee Review Tribunal (Australia). "Guidelines on Children Giving Evidence." 2002. http://www.rrt.gov.au/publications/RRT%20Guidelines%20on%20Children%20Giving%20Evidence.pdf.

Renland, Astrid. *Trafficking of Children and Minors to Norway for Sexual Exploitation.* ECPAT Norway/Save the Children Norway, 2001.

Royal College of Pediatricians and Child Health (U.K.). *The Health of Refugee Children: Guidelines for Paediatricians.* November 1999.

Sarah McDonald. "Australia's Pacific Solution." Aired 29 September 2002, BBC. http://news.bbc.co.uk/hi/english/static/audio_video/programmes/correspondent/transcripts/2279330.txt.

Senate Community Affairs References Committee (Australia). *Lost Innocents: Righting the Record—Report on child migration.* 30 August 2001.

Senate Legal and Constitutional References Committee (Australia). *A Sanctuary Under Review: An Examination of Australia's Refugee and Humanitarian Processes.* Canberra: Australian Government Publishing Service, June 2000. http://www.aph.gov.au/SENATE/committee/legcon_ctte/completed_inquiries/1999-02/refugees/report/contents.htm.

Spijkerboer, Thomas. *Gender and refugee status.* Aldershot: Ashgate, 2000.

Steinbock, Daniel J. "The Admission of Unaccompanied

Children into the United States." *Yale Law and Policy Review* 7, 1989.

Steinbock, Daniel, Ressler, Everett and Boothby, Neil. *Unaccompanied Children: Care and Protection in Wars, Natural Disasters and Refugee Movements.* Oxford: Oxford University Press, 1988.

Swarns, Rachel L. "U.S. to Give Border Patrol Agents the Power to Deport Illegal Aliens." *The New York Times.* 11 August 2004.

Teichroeb, Ruth. "Jail Alternative Safeguards Teen Aliens: 3,000-Mile Trip from El Salvador Ends in Fife Facility." *Seattle Post-Intelligencer.* 2 December 2004.

Thronson, David B. "Kids Will Be Kids? Reconsidering Conceptions of Children's Rights Underlying Immigration Law." *Ohio State Law Journal* 63, no. 3, 2002.

U. K. Immigration Service. *Best Practice: Unaccompanied Minors.* January 2004.

U.K. Home Office. *The role of early legal advice in asylum applications: Home Office Immigration Research and Statistics Service Online Report.* June 2005.

U.S. Department of Homeland Security, Office of Inspector General. "A Review of DHS' Responsibilities for Juvenile Aliens." OIG–05–45, September 2005.

U.S. Department of Homeland Security. "Implementation of the Agreement Between the Government of the United States of America and the Government of Canada Regarding Asylum Claims Made in Transit and at Land Border Ports-of-Entry." *Federal Register* 69, Number 45, 8 March 2004. http://www.lexisnexis.com/practiceareas/immigration/pdfs/695137p74.pdf.

U.S. Department of Homeland Security. *2002 Yearbook of Immigration Statistics* (formerly the *Statistical Yearbook of the Immigration and Naturalization Service* prior to the 2002 edition). http://uscis.gov/graphics/shared/aboutus/statistics/IMM02yrbk/IMM2002.pdf.

U.S. Department of Justice, Office of Justice Programs, Office of Juvenile Justice and Delinquency Prevention. "National Report Series Bulletin: Juveniles in Court." June 2003. http://www.ncjrs.org/html/ojjdp/195420/contents.html.

U.S. Department of Justice. "Guidelines for Children's Asylum Claims." 10 December 1998.

U.S. Department of Justice/Office of the Inspector General. "Juvenile Repatriation Practices at Border Patrol Sectors on the Southwest Border." Report Number I–2001–010, September 2001.

U.S. Coast Guard. "Alien Migrant Interdiction, Overview." http://www.uscg.mil/hq/g-o/g-opl/AMIO/AMIO.htm.

United Nations High Commissioner for Refugees Population Data Unit. *Trends in Unaccompanied and Separated Children Seeking Asylum in Industrialized Countries, 2001–2003.* Geneva: UNHCR, July 2004.

United Nations High Commissioner for Refugees, Refugee Children Coordination Unit. Summary Update of Machel Study Follow-up Activities in 2001–2002.

United Nations High Commissioner for Refugees. *2003 Global Refugee Trends.* Geneva: UNHCR Population Data Unit/PDGS, Division of Operational Support, 15 June 2004. http://www.unhcr.ch/cgi-bin/texis/vtx/home/opendoc.pdf?tbl=STATISTICS&id=40d015fb4&page=statistics.

United Nations High Commissioner for Refugees. *Handbook on Procedures and Criteria for Determining Refugee Status.* Geneva: UNHCR, 1979, 1992.

United Nations High Commissioner for Refugees. *Policies and Procedures in Dealing with Unaccompanied Children Seeking Asylum.* Geneva: UNHCR, February 1997.

United Nations. *Impact of Armed Conflict on Children.* Report of Graca Machel, Expert of the Secretary-General of the United Nations. UN, 1996. http://www.unicef.org/graca/.

United Nations. *World Economic and Social Survey 2004: International Migration.* Department of Economic and Social Affairs.

FOR MORE INFORMATION

Harvard University
Committee on Human Rights Studies
79 JFK Street, David Rubenstein Building 112
Cambridge, Massachusetts 02138

E-mail us at: humanrights@harvard.edu

Sydney Centre for International and Global Law
Faculty of Law, The University of Sydney
173–175 Phillip Street
Sydney NSW 2000
Australia

E-mail us at: scigl@law.usyd.edu.au

The University of Sydney

Please visit our Web site at:
http://www.humanrights.harvard.edu

This report is available on-line at:
http://www.humanrights.harvard.edu, and also

http://www.law.usyd.edu.au/scigl/publication.htm
and click on "Other Monographs, Submissions and
Research Reports"

DESIGN

Winge Design Studio
Chicago, Illinois
studio@wingedesign.com

Editorial assistance provided
by Four Eyes Editing
www.4eyes.com.au